CRITICAL EDUCATION PRACTICE
VOL. 3

OCCUPIED
READING

GARLAND REFERENCE LIBRARY
OF SOCIAL SCIENCE
VOL. 860

CRITICAL EDUCATION PRACTICE

SHIRLEY R. STEINBERG
JOE L. KINCHELOE
Series Editors

OCCUPIED READING

Critical
Foundations for an
Ecological Theory

Alan A. Block

GARLAND PUBLISHING, Inc.
New York & London / 1995

Library of Congress Cataloging-in-Publication Data

Block, Alan A.
    Occupied reading : critical foundations for an eco-
logical theory / Alan A. Block.
        p.   cm. — (Garland reference library of social
science ; vol. 860. Critical education practice ; vol. 3)
    Includes bibliographical references (p.   ) and
index.
    ISBN 0-8153-0932-5 (hardcover). —
    ISBN 0-8153-1925-8 (pbk.)
    1. Reading—Social aspects.   2. Reading—Language
experience approach.   3. Critical pedagogy.   4. Cognition and culture.   I. Title.   II. Series: Garland reference library of social science ; v. 860.   III. Series:
Garland reference library of social science. Critical
education practice ; vol. 3.
LB1050.2.B56   1995
372.41—dc20   94-22358
                                                      CIP

Printed on acid-free, 250-year-life paper
Manufactured in the United States of America

To Emma and Anna Rose, whom I love

Contents

Acknowledgments

Books are collaborative efforts on which sometimes some of us are fortunate enough to affix our own names. I am one of those fortunates in this fortuitous circumstance. But I would like to thank some people whose marks are indelibly inscribed on this manuscript.

First, I would like to thank Joe Kincheloe and Shirley Steinberg for having such faith in me that I had the opportunity to work on this book. Without their support I would never have begun this project.

I would like to thank my friends and colleagues who, too, offered support for my efforts. Not a few times they took their own valuable time to permit me to sit in their offices to discuss my ideas, my frustrations, and complaints. These people are numerous, but specifically I would like to mention Bill Pinar, Gayle Squires, Amy Gillett, and Mary Hopkins-Best.

Several people read portions of this book in its development and provided critical comment. The completed form of this book owes much to their readings. Mary Ann Doyle, Lynn LaVenture, Jim Byrd, Tom Franklin, Joan Potter-Tomforh, and Ron Potter-Efron gave of their own time to read portions of the manuscript. Tim Shiel read the entire manuscript, and over a series of lunches discussed his thoughts with me. I am ever grateful to their kindness and their critiques.

Finally, I thank my wife, Beth Peck, who had the patience to put up with my own working processes amidst her own. Without her support, this project would have remained incomplete.

Introduction

Joe L. Kincheloe
Shirley R. Steinberg

Something very provocative is happening in this text. Alan Block
is, of course, writing a book on reading instruction, but beneath
the surface an earthquake is rumbling. Unlike many books in
this field, Block transcends both the reduction of reading to mere
method and the isolation of that method from the social and
political currents of our time. *Occupied Reading* is a prototype for
critical analysis in education, and, as such, it serves appropriately as one of the first volumes in Garland Publishing's series
Critical Educational Practice.

Critical pedagogy analyzes schooling in historical context
and in light of the social and political dynamics that shape the
dominant culture. Ever concerned with power and politics,
critical teaching has challenged the decontextualized and
depoliticized approaches to education that dominate both the
public schools and teacher education. Led by scholars such as
Peter McLaren, William Pinar, Maxine Greene, Joanne Pagano,
Janet Miller, Henry Giroux, and Michael Apple, the critical
perspective on teaching has provided an alternative to the stale
perspectives of the educational status quo. No "orthodox"
version of critical teaching exists—there is no party line. Still,
common theoretical threads run through most critical work:
critical theory, postmodern/poststructural analysis, feminist
theory, and Deweyan progressivism.

In our own critical work and certainly in Block's *Occupied
Reading*, there exists an attempt to balance the progressive and

democratic aspects of modernism with critical postmodern insights concerning the failure of reason, the tyranny of Western grand narratives (for example, the story of progress, the logic of capital, patriarchy), and the limitations of empirical science. In light of the confusion produced by such cultural/political conflict, we have attempted to find meaning in the fray, insight in the ruins. In various venues we have tried to construct a critical system of meaning grounded on feminist notions of passionate knowing, African-American epistemologies, subjugated knowledges (ways of knowing that have been traditionally excluded from the discourse of mainstream educators), liberation-theological ethics, and progressive modernist concerns with justice, liberty, and equality. *Occupied Reading* can be generally situated within this philosophical, political, social, and educational frame of reference.

Block is explicit in his effort to expose the sociopolitical baggage of dominant forms of reading pedagogy. Emerging from scientistic modernism—which held that the world can be completely understood, measured, and controlled by empirical science—reading education has played a supporting role in the establishment of an expert-guided, patriarchal social order. As in other spheres of the science-driven society, reading experts sought the one best way, the empirically validated way, of teaching individuals to read. This "gospel" of technique was thus taught to techno-disciples who employed only authorized reading strategies in their everyday practice. In such a setting, individuals and their idiosyncrasies were virtually irrelevant. The reading act was consequently reduced to a series of subskills that negated any need for individuals to construct meaning in the context created by the collision of the written text with the reader's personal experience. As a series of authoritarian procedures, reading instruction subverts learner creativity and self-direction. The possibility of deeper levels of understanding gives way to linear rule following.

The key to the political and historical significance of *Occupied Reading* involves its position in the larger debate between critical advocates of new ways of interpreting the world and the proponents of traditional, empirically grounded frames of reference. While the differences between these two "ways of seeing" signify different epistemologies and different pedagogies of reading, they also represent antagonistic ways of life, conflicting ways of defining human beings. The critically grounded ecological theory of reading proposed by Block, drawing upon the previous work of John Dewey, Frank Smith, and Patrick Shannon, to name only a few, confronts the dominant ideology on its home turf. Rejecting the parts-over-the-whole empirical tradition, Block aims his arrows at a compartmentalized reading pedagogy that fails to see reading as an emancipatory act. He refuses to allow scientifically anointed power wielders to continue to "adjust" young people to the realities of the workplace without a challenge.

In the role of the challenger, Block exposes how power shapes the rules of the game without anyone knowing it. Reflecting the power of the dominant culture, reading experts not only dictated teaching methods but also what could and could not be read. With his solid background in curriculum theory, Block recognizes this for what it is—an expression of the power of the dominant culture to determine what and whose knowledge is of most worth. Dangerous ideas, experts assert, must be extracted from the reading list; more importantly, however, young readers must derive "correct meanings" from texts, for students have an "unfortunate" tendency to construct their own interpretations if they are not "properly" guided.

Basal readers have long attempted to control the perception of students, basing their activities on the assumption that learning is not a self-directed process but one determined by experts. Reflecting Patrick Shannon's notion that a scientifically managed reading pedagogy undermines literacy as self-understanding, as a method of uncovering the relationship between the reader and the social structure, or as a form of social action, Block maintains that dominant reading methodologies promote a passive, nonreflective form of thinking. This mode of cognition renders the learner much more vulnerable to the manipulative messages of advertisers and postmodern politicians.

Using the critical frames previously described, Block draws upon Ken and Yetta Goodman's whole language and Gregory Bateson's ecological theory to produce a neo-progressive reading pedagogy. Situated in the tradition of Deweyan pragmatism, whole language argues that language is understood and learned as a whole rather than in the analysis of its separate parts. Language is learned through its use in the lived world; thus, it is best learned in a context that gives it meaning. The linguistic fragmentation of the traditional scientistic approaches undermines meaning in a way that destroys a student's perception of the need for literacy. It is not surprising, therefore, that while many American students learn to read using the scientistic approaches, they refuse to do much reading outside of reading class.

Block articulates the notion that this neo-progressive pedagogy attempts to make sense of the world, discerning patterns within it, and developing new cognitive processes that might provide insights necessary in the attempt to change the world. Indeed, Block asserts that removed from its political roots, his neo-progressive pedagogy loses its meaning, its ability to subvert the technocratic culture of twentieth-century America. Critical reading can only be appreciated and deployed within its social context, its sociopolitical ecology. Reading comprehension is always a situated act, a dynamic dance between reader and text.

Because social context is so important in the reading act, Block argues that educators must attend to a student's linguistic background. The language experience derived from the student's home, peer relations, and popular culture dramatically affect his or her academic success and vocational orientation. Having ignored such experiences, traditional scientistic reading methodologies fail to gain a cogent picture of the students being taught. Insights into which particular students might have trouble with particular methods or particular texts are lost. Traditional empirically grounded perspectives are both unwilling and unable to connect patterns of language use in the community to the reading performance of students. Is there any wonder why students from socially and economically marginalized groups continue to be labeled as "problem readers"?

Block's neo-progressive ecological theory does not lend itself to commercial packaging; it will not be hawked by John

Ritter on cable TV; and unlike phonetic approaches to reading, no one will get hooked on it. More than simply a compilation of classroom practices and methods, the theory is in essence a way of life. Reading is an act of creation, a social activity that involves the production of self. In this context, we begin to understand that what Block has presented is a constructivist theory of reading. In the reading process, we discover both the construction of the reader and the text he or she reads. In the construction of self and text, meaning is also produced.

Occupied Reading sets the stage for other conversations about critical educational practice. Not only do we appreciate Alan Block's important contribution in this book, we also appreciate Marie Ellen Larcada for her courage and vision in making Critical Educational Practice a reality. Her insight and expertise have made this series a major force in the academic and public discussion of education.

Occupied
Reading

CHAPTER 1

Occupied Reading

What Is the Debate?

Addressing the question of literacy, Jeanne Chall and John Carroll have written: "The last thing an Establishment would do to consolidate its position would be to promote literacy unless it were in order to dictate what should and should not be read"(in Kozol, 1985, 125). I find this an interesting statement for two central reasons. First, because in their assertion the authors explicitly address the problem of curriculum with which as an educator I, too, am fundamentally concerned. Mandates of what one should and should not read determine the nature of curriculum; indeed, as I will argue later, they often are curriculum. What one should and should not read are questions of what and whose knowledge is of most worth, and this is the arena within which the struggle for the American curriculum has been waged in the twentieth century. Herbert Kleibard (1987, 29) has noted that, "The twentieth century became the arena where . . . four versions of what knowledge is of most worth and of the central functions of schooling were presented and argued." As Kleibard portrays curriculum theorizing, four groups—the humanists, the developmentalists, the social efficiency educators, and the social meliorists—engaged in the struggle for the American curriculum during the twentieth century with no one group ever gaining control over it but rather, settling for a "loose, largely unarticulated, and not very tidy compromise"(Kleibard, 1987, 29). The most recent and often vituperative debate over the canon and multicultural education is our contemporary version of this dispute.

3

Of course, this issue is not one particular to the twentieth century, but has, during this present century, been explicitly *named* curricular struggle because it is only within the last one hundred years that curriculum has been a field that may be studied.[1] Nor is this struggle—and its not so tidy compromise—particular to the curriculum field. But as Carroll and Chall note, issues of reading are tied intimately to questions of literacy, to issues regarding the quality of education. The inquiry into reading is and has always been central to matters of curriculum. But like curriculum, reading is a relatively new field of *study*, though reading pedagogies may be found since at least the time of the Greeks. "As soon as there existed among the Greeks a body of written material, reading became both possible and desirable. Boys could now be set to learn to read and write" (Mathews, 1966, 4). Controlling the pedagogy controlled what was and could be read, determined the education of those placed under such pedagogical direction, often, it will be argued, at the expense of reading itself. Before the book revolution, this control may have been easier: The dearth of books constrained reading to be "intensive" rather than "extensive." Kaestle (1991) notes in his historiography of reading and literacy that intensive reading meant that the few books available were read over and over, and reading proved to be more devotional and ritualistic than informational. "Such intensive reading could be revolutionary if the text was revolutionary, but given the preponderance of Bibles and books about mainstream religion, traditional literacy tended to be conservative"(Kaestle, 53). I will discuss later how this intensive reading was also hermeneutical, and how this tradition of reading maintained conventionally defined literacy and influenced reading instruction even when books became plentiful and more evidently politically and socially radical in theme and content. But in both instances, intensive and extensive reading, what could be read determined the pedagogy, and the pedagogy determined what would be read. American school and social authorities have consistently argued for a "channeled literacy," which could deny access to certain books considered trash. Reading and its pedagogy have always been premised on an idea of reading that understood the activity as potentially seditious. The control of the process necessitated the control of the pedagogy.

For the most part, reading instruction throughout history has been a disputatious and painful process; methods have been imposed more to regulate the learner, or to regulate what may be read, or indeed to regulate both, than to offer a pedagogy of reading. If society means to control what is to be read, then it must first control the process of reading instruction. Hence arises the argument over reading pedagogies and methodologies, which occupy the twentieth-century debate over reading and of education. "Hundreds of methods of teaching reading exist," says Frank Smith (1985, 5), "mostly minor variations on a few traditional themes, and literally tens of thousands of research studies have been done comparing one method or procedure or set of materials with another." Mitford Mathews (1966) claims that there are basically three reading pedagogies and assorted variations on the themes. But these pedagogies and method-ologies can be understood as more than procedure: reading instruction becomes curriculum. The way one is taught to read becomes the purpose and manner of reading: the technique becomes the thing. And the pedagogy makes possible what is readable, and what may happen when reading is practiced. "In schools and other formal instructional situations," Frank Smith complains, "reading may be regarded as only those activities, often ritualistic, that are engaged in in the name of reading. Children, parents, and teachers come to believe that drills and exercises constitute important reading" (Smith in Goelman et al., 1984). In most pedagogies, reading is not an activity engaged in for itself but is, rather, a means to another end. Reading is not a fundamental process of thought itself but rather, a means to thought. "Reading," says Ron Carver, in a recent issue of the *Journal of Reading* (1992), "is to look at words and determine meaning"(84). In this formulation, the reified text and the objectified reader remain separate. And what is taught in the drills, activities, and formal exercises, which for the most part are reading instruction, becomes the rationale by and for which people learn to read. Without the worksheets, book reports, and pseudo-Socratic questioning that always accompany school reading, in concert with accepted behaviorist theory, the purpose and design of reading ceases to operate. Thus it is that the tragedy of American education is not that people really do not learn to read (research suggests that any method, even no method, will result in a reader), but that after school few people read books because they have never learned the purpose of reading. Kaestle (1991) reports that only 20–25 percent of the population reads regularly—a book every two weeks (189).

I will argue in a later chapter that reading *is* curriculum and that to discuss one apart from the other is to falsify both. And I will argue now that reading and its pedagogy, though a subject that has been discussed for centuries, is an intrinsic part of what must be understood as the struggle over and for the American curriculum during the twentieth century. For this great debate in which the reading field engages, a debate that Chall (1967) claims involves issues of methodology of teaching reading, also concerns issues that extend far beyond just reading pedagogy. This debate concerns not merely whose and what knowledge is of greatest worth, but also how that knowledge may be known. Dorothy Strickland, in a recent article in *Education Week* (in Rothman, 1990), says of the issues: "What happens is, people start with the view they are dealing with opinions about reading. But as things get played out, people want power over the reading program. It goes beyond what is good for kids. It's a power struggle that has very little to do with kids [and more to do with] control over what happens in schools" (10). Situating the political in literacy education is an acknowledgment that far more is at stake than learning to read and write.

The issue of literacy as discussed in the twentieth century, indeed, throughout American history, has concerned the ability to read what the Establishment has deemed readable, an overtly ideological issue. In *Anonymous Toil* (1992), I described under what conditions a specific body of literature had been eliminated and/or marginalized by forces whose vested interests were called into question by such writings. In that book, I tied that marginalization to a pedagogy of reading. I argued (117) that in American schools today, "reading instruction . . . dehistoricizes and posits reading as the accumulation of various competencies which may be tested on standardized skill-oriented tests and which denies the historical nature of the text itself as the sense, feeling, truth, and attention of an author through the words he uses or she uses in [the] text." Nor, I argued, does reading instruction today account for the production of the self in the very act of reading: To "search for the main idea," I argued (117), "leads not to the production of knowledge but to its discovery. And for this search there are guides, rules and hierarchies which lead the reader to knowledge." This body of proper materials is known as the canon, and it includes the works of Homer, Shakespeare, and Mark Twain, even as it includes the collected works of Silver Burdett and Ginn, Macmillan, Harcourt Brace Jovanovich, and other publishing companies responsible for the plethora of basal readers by which 85 percent of American schoolchildren still receive their reading instruction. The reification of reading and the text which is read is the result of this pedagogy and prescribes interactions between the self and the text as operations of interpretation. Reading is either an escape from meaning, as in the phrase, "getting lost in a book," in which case the self is allowed to disappear as the creator of the text and the text is rendered autonomous; or reading is the search for the correct meaning, in which case, too, both reader and text are objectified. Pedagogies are then organized to ensure correct representation of meaning. In this manner, meaning is not only controlled by the explicit presentation of certain curricular materials but is ensured by the specific pedagogy that organizes those materials to be read so that reading will be learned.

What knowledge may be known may be also understood as a matter of a pedagogy of perception, what may be empirically perceived and, therefore, read. John Carroll, in "The Nature of the Reading Process" (1970), writes that "The essential skill in reading is getting meaning from a printed or written message" (296). For such intellectual mining, there are requisite skills that can be discovered and for which pedagogies may be organized and taught. Carroll defines eight such skills and suggests that the conflict in reading pedagogies concerns merely the order in which those skills ought to be taught. Carroll identifies the first skill as the ability to recognize the words. In Carroll's formulation, the text has knowledge contained first in words; one reads by locating words, and knowledge is then extracted by a skilled reader from the found words. Here, the pedagogy of reading determines what is to be read by determining the process identified as reading. Seeing words is the essential character of reading, knowing words is the prerequisite for reading, one reads that for which one knows the words. Edward Thorndike, in 1921, published a *Teacher's Word Book* containing the 10,000 most common words. "This word book," writes Thorndike, "helps the teacher to decide quickly which treatment (of pedagogy) is appropriate by telling her just how important any word is"(iv). The importance of a word is determined by its frequency. Later Thorndike expanded that base list to 30,000 words. Ernest Hilgard, in his mammoth *Psychology in America: A Historical Survey*, describes Thorndike's rationale, which still determines the construction of most reading instruction in the United States today:

> After all, language is composed of words, and if the child does not understand the words, such thought processes as may be involved in reading will be nonfunctional. . . . [Thorndike] sought to eliminate the useless words and to see that textbooks (the favorite American vehicle for guiding learning) would be limited to the words that were most needed because they were most frequently met. (Hilgard, 1987, 675)

Reading pedagogy determined reading material. Controlled vocabularies, an intrinsic part of basal readers, is a direct result of Thorndike's work, and determines the actual material which may be read during reading instruction. Ken Goodman (1988) writes that publishing a basal series text requires two types of revision. The first "is intended to make the literature fit the readability, vocabulary, and skill criteria of the publisher. . . . The second kind of revision is to make sure the stories fit the publisher's standards of acceptability for content, language, and values"(33). How one learns to read determines what one reads.

  In contrast to Carroll's skills approach, which in part derives from Thorndike but whose history extends to at least the Greeks, theorists such as Ken Goodman have referred to reading as a psycholinguistic guessing game (1970) in which not greater precision but improved guessing facilitates reading. The fluent reader is she who can get the most cues from the least amount of visual information. And information is whatever reduces alternatives in the process of prediction. That reduction is a product of what the reader already knows. Goodman's approach posits the reader as an active constructor of meaning, Carroll's as the processor of information and the text as embodied information. But the difference involves more than identifying the locus of meaning: it identifies the possibility and agency of the reader. Jane Tompkins writes that "once the literary work has been defined as an object of knowledge, as meaning not doing, interpretation becomes the supreme critical act" (1980, 222). In Tompkins' frame, both the world and the self already exist; the objective reader must learn only to read the objective text rightly. First, however, that text must be precisely perceived. Traditional reading pedagogy organizes the possibilities of perception and therefore organizes what may be seen. Reading instruction in this regard might be understood as a technique in which certain responses are valorized based on controlled contexts of learning that may be endlessly repeated—the control of perception. This is the program of the basal readers and literature-based programs of schools.

This instructional model is also what Gregory Bateson might refer to as deutero-learning (1972, 167), or learning to learn, a subject much discussed in contemporary pedagogical circles and often referred to as meta-cognition or even critical thinking. Bateson says that deutero-learning is ". . . a synonym for the acquisition of that class of abstract habits of thought . . . the states of mind which we call 'free will,' instrumental thinking, dominance, passivity [and which] are acquired by a process which we may equate with 'learning to learn'"(166). Deutero-learning is, in fact, learning how to see, to discover information. He argues that a subject's learning in experimental situations is learning to look for contexts and sequences of one type rather than another, a habit of "punctuating the stream of events to give repetitions of a certain type of meaningful sequence"(166). Needless to say, in experimental situations, of which schooling and laboratory work are two sides of the same coin, the subject finds that for which it has been taught to look. Dominant reading pedagogies for the past two thousand years have organized those experimental situations in order to organize what may be seen. "The view that learning must be controlled, which is built into the basal, takes meta-cognition, a property of the learner, and makes it the property of the program"(Goodman, K. et al., 1988, 100). In so doing, reading pedagogies determine the possibility of meaning production, and determine of what reading may consist and what may be, therefore, read. Learning is not what a person does for himself, but what may be given to him/her. The teaching of reading may then be best organized by those with the necessary expertise, and what one will learn is dictated by the pedagogy to which one has been exposed. The hierarchy has not only been maintained, but justified as well in the sacred name of literacy. Of course, says Bateson, "To suggest that the only method of acquiring one of these habits is through repeated experience of learning contexts of a given kind would be logically analogous to saying that the only way to roast pig is by burning the house down" (1972, 170). Yet in classrooms all over the United States, learning to read is methodically and methodologically prescribed, suggesting, indeed, that burning down the house is the only way to roast a pig. Hence, the conclusion of Marilyn Adams' *Beginning to Read* (1990) suggests that though reading is primarily dependent on background knowledge and language facility, students can only read broadly once they have mastered the necessary basic skills. This seems, as Bernice Cullinan and Dorothy Strickland argue in an afterword to the book, to ignore the body of research on emerging literacy which suggests that there is no such thing as a pre-reader, no such thing as someone who has not yet received formal instruction. In fact, they write, "Children's uses, motives, and functions associated with reading and writing in authentic situations, their knowledge about reading and writing and their psycholinguistic processes are, to a surprising degree, similar to those of adults and older children"(Cullinan and Strickland in Adams, 1990, 427). The work of Jerome Harste, Virginia Woodward, and Carolyn Burke (1984), as does the pioneering work of Emilia Ferreiro and Ana Teberosky (1982) and Yetta Goodman, attests to the emergence of literacy in children even in the absence of any and all formal instruction. This work contrasts not only with that of Marilyn Adams, but also with a pedagogy epitomized by Mitford Mathews (1966, 190), who says of reading that it is "one of the most unnatural activities in which man has ever engaged. Nature has never taught anyone to read and never will." Opposing this position are emergent-literacy researchers who view reading as a natural activity that must be supported but cannot be taught. Adams' book, *Beginning to Read*, and the study which led to Adams' commission to write, *Becoming a Nation of Readers* (Anderson, 1985), however, only seem to maintain a perspective which eschews formal skill-based instruction; both texts, in fact, argue for just such an approach and for the separation of the reading self from the read text, the reification of the latter and the passivity of the former.

Thus, I return circuitously to the second reason for my interest in the Carroll and Chall statement: the silence it speaks. Chall and Carroll are clearly concerned with what is read and the power of the Establishment to control that material. But the authors do not voice any concern about the relationship between reading pedagogies and what is sub-sequently read; Carroll and Chall assume that once a person has learned to read, everything may be read. But I want to examine the notion that how we are taught to read already determines what is to be read. And how we are taught to read too often reifies the knowledge of a text by situating that knowledge there. According to this pedagogy, ideas in books may be considered dangerous because they are deemed autonomous. In the perspective to be offered in *Occupied Reading*, however, the practice of reading books ought to be considered dangerous not because such works may contain dangerous ideas as the New Right agenda would propose, but because pedagogies of reading do not offer strategies for accounting for the construction of those ideas by the reader, who herself must be simultaneously constructed. Ideas become dangerous because they are objects over which the reader presumably has no control, save in ignoring them.

This belief ought to be understood as a result of a type of reading pedagogy. How we are taught to read is a result of our beliefs about what constitutes reading and language. As long as reading is considered a skill—or a compilation of subskills, as long as language is considered a logical system whose study can explain its orderly acquisition—then a pedagogy of reading cannot ecologically account for the appearance of the text and the self, but rather, must merely be concerned with the development of specific subskills. Patrick Shannon, in *The Struggle to Continue*, (1990) argues that, "When literacy programs are organized according to the principles of scientific management, virtually no one, including the teacher, is asked to use literacy to understand themselves, to make connections between their lives and the operations of the social structure, or to use literacy as a form of social action" (156–7). Research in the field of reading must then be concerned with models of information-processing which act on already precoded messages. But, Jerome Bruner argues (1990, 4), theories of information-processing systems cannot account for the working of the mind because "information-processing inscribes messages at or fetches them from an address in memory on instruction from a central control unit, or it holds them temporarily in a buffer store, and then manipulates them in prescribed ways: it lists, orders, combines, compares precoded information." Noam Chomsky (1975) notes that the mind is not cognitive structures but the capacity to develop those structures. Yet, if by experiment—the preferred methodology of quantitative reading researchers—we wish to test behavior for which no cognitive capacity exists, as we might argue do many cognitive psychologists and reading specialists steeped in cognitive psychology,[2] then we will have to invent experiments using nonsense syllables, verbal associations, and such, because only in this way will we get regular, smooth curves showing regular increments and extinctions. But we will never be able to account for the meaning construction of the individual reader in the process of reading. Rather, like Martin Dysart, the frustrated psychiatrist in Peter Shaffer's *Equus* (1979), the reading specialist can trace Alan Strang's system out but can never understand why the particular attraction to the horses occurred in the first place, may understand what a reader comprehends but not the whole system from which the meaning derives and on which it has effect.

> A child is born into a world of phenomena all equal in their power to enslave. It sniffs—it sucks—it strokes it(s) eyes over the whole uncomfortable range. Suddenly one strikes. Why? Moments snap together like magnets,

forging a chain of shackles. Why? I can trace them. I can even, with time, pull them apart. But why at the start they were ever magnetized at all—just those particular moments of experience and no others—I don't know. *And nor does anyone else.* (76)

Why the brain forms certain images and systems which then comprise "reality" and which are powerful is beyond the scope of cognitive psychologists. These systems and images are the basis of reading, yet are not considered by the work of cognitive psychologists who desire merely to understand the mechanisms by which those images function and comprise systems. Rather, cognitive psychology is concerned with the processing of information, assuming that information is a preexisting entity and not a production of the knower.

In the current promotion of universal literacy, then, the Establishment argues its position in order to determine what is to be read; but it also determines what is reading and its consequent pedagogy, though it does this surreptitiously without acknowledging the effect of the latter on the former. In other words, how we teach reading will determine what reading is and what is to be—what will be—read. And conversely, how we teach reading is a product of what reading is considered to be. Therefore, it is important to situate historically the development of reading pedagogy and its psychology in the present century. And it is equally important to historicize the presence, marginalization, and suppression of an alternative perspective to the practice and pedagogy of reading, a look at reading which posits it as a perfectly natural activity as complex and as spontaneous as speaking and listening. This latter approach posits the reader as an active constructor of meaning and of self. Yet as I have said, this view of reading has not predominated, and though it now goes under the name whole language, and though Ken Goodman attests to its growing power (1992), it still figures minimally in education today. So, for a brief time, I would like to explore the development of dominant reading pedagogies, address their rationale, and explore the marginalization by, among others, the behaviorist and cognitive psychologists/scientists in the twentieth century of an alternative idea of reading. This alternative view of reading may be understood as an affective approach to reading, and its marginalization has had serious effects on reading and its pedagogy.

Reading and Education: The Puritans and Plato

Of course, from its very inception, the origin and nature of public schooling in the United States has prescribed the proper reading materials useful not only for schooling but for the non-school-age population as well. The directive for public schooling passed in 1647, and known as the Olde Deluder Satan Law, mandated that children be taught to read so that they could read the Bible.

> It being one chief point of that old deluder, Satan, to keep men from the knowledge of the Scriptures, as in former times, by keeping them in an unknown tongue, so in these latter times, by persuading from the use of tongues, that so at last the true sense and meaning of the original might be clouded by false glosses of saint-seeming deceivers, that learning might not be buried in the grave of our fathers in church and commonwealth, the lord assisting our endeavors.—It is therefore ordered that every township in this jurisdiction, after the Lord had increased them to the number of fifty householders, shall then forthwith appoint one within their town to teach all such children as shall resort to him to write and read. (Smith, 1986, 13)

First, we must understand that by this law education was considered to be reading, and reading was characterized as an engagement with a reified object and as a way to thought. Meaning lay beyond the words and existed prior to them. Reading was learning the true meaning of the words. Not only is what is to be read mandated—the Bible—but the method of reading instruction is also prescribed: The law demands that every student know "the true sense and meaning of the original." The pedagogy is based upon the idea that there must be an authority from whom the true sense and meaning may be derived, whose abilities are algorithmic and incontrovertible, and by whose instruction the skill of reading may be acquired.

Of course, the essential contradiction between this mandate and the Puritan ideal that each person must communicate with God in his/her own manner is one that pervades American history. But for our purposes here, we must note that pedagogies of reading—and of course, psychologies of it—are prescribed and, therefore, necessarily proscribed as well. Learning to read is learning the definitions of words—learning what meaning is possible. And because very few responses were valorized (note the fates of Ann Hutchinson and Roger Williams), education and reading were forms of indoctrination, ideologies that were designed to create, announce, and strengthen Puritan purpose. Alternative readings were not tolerated, and the only recourse to silence was self-exile. For the Puritans, reading instruction was mandated as a means to ensure the religiosity of the populace, and reading instruction defined the act of meaning that reading would be.

Nila Banton Smith (1986) argues that reading instruction in the pre-Revolutionary years was a pedagogy that was designed to inculcate religious values. Reading instruction was identified with religious instruction. Smith claims the primer—the reading textbook—was so named because it contained the "minimum essentials deemed necessary for one's spiritual existence." Mitford Mathews (1966) suggests that there is another tradition which associates the name for these first reading books, "primer," with the *Prime*, the first canonical hour of the day in the divine office. In either case, the primer was a pedagogical text meant to teach children to read and to indoctrinate them into and with religious values. Learning to read was learning religious values. Originally, the primer contained the Lord's Prayer, a few essential psalms, the Creed, and the Ten Commandments. Later, to these essentials were added the alphabet and lists of syllables and words. With these additions, the primer became the standardized book of reading instruction.

In other words, learning to read was originally learning to read the Bible and its ecclesiastical formulas and dictates. The methodologies worked out seemed tied to traditional beliefs regarding language. The first principle upon which reading pedagogy was founded argued that the ability to read was intimately tied to the sound of the language.[3] Reading was a

correlate of the oral tradition. Hence, knowledge of the alphabet
and the lengthening syllables would provide practice in the
phonetic aspects of language and reading. Reading was oral
reading. Noah Webster's spelling book admonished that

> Among the defects and absurdities found in [reading]
> books hitherto published, we may rank the want of a
> thorough investigation of the sounds in the English
> language, and the powers of the several letters—the
> promiscuous arrangement of words in the same
> table. . . . In attempting to correct these faults it was
> necessary to begin with the elements of the language and
> explain the powers of the letters. (in Smith, 1986, 69)

Nila Banton Smith notes the influence of this belief concerning
the relation between the sound of the language and the meaning
of it in the pedagogy of reading, but perhaps the words of Caleb
Bingham, an author of an early primer, best expresses this
dominant belief: "The first object of a reader or speaker is to be
clearly understood by his hearers. In order for this to be possible,
it is necessary that he should pronounce his words distinctly and
definitely; and that he should carefully avoid the two extremes
of uttering either too fast or too slow. . . . Perhaps nothing is of
more importance to a reader or speaker than a proper attention
to accent, emphasis, and cadence . . . the word should be
pronounced by the reader or speaker in the same manner as he
would pronounce it in ordinary conversation" (in Smith, 71). The
relationship between reading and orality was principal.

   Originally, reading may have been considered an oral
activity because it derived directly from the oral tradition of
story telling. In the early years of the colony, reading was
confined to a small segment of the population. Later, though a
major expansion of the reading public seemingly took place, "the
newspaper-reading public was far from universal . . . and the
book-reading public had expanded only from a tiny minority to
a more substantial minority of all adults"(Kaestle, 1991, 54). It
could be argued that for much of the population, access to
reading remained in the oral tradition, in listening to people read
aloud. Hence, pedagogies of reading, as for Caleb Bingham,
were tied to the oral tradition. Furthermore, the Platonic doctrine
that oral language could argue for itself, and could therefore

assert its truth compared to written language, may have also led to the dominance of the oral tradition in reading instruction. In an age when news was carried mostly by word of mouth and mass communication was minimally available, the oral tradition remained the source of information and truth. Walter Ong (1982, 96), in his study of the technologizing of the word, claims that, "Long after a culture has begun to use writing, it may still not give writing high ratings. A present-day literate usually assumes that written records have more force than spoken words as evidence of a long-past state of affairs, especially in court. Earlier cultures that knew literacy but had not so fully interiorized it, have often assumed quite the opposite." Thus, it would seem that the oral tradition which was deemed valid had influence on writing which, as in the Platonic tradition, had to rely on the oral tradition for its credibility.

Indeed, it may be asserted that the success of the system of writing based on the alphabet, a system upon which the Western world has built, owes its own success to its ties to the oral tradition. "Alphabetic writing," says Mathews, "won its victory over picture writing just because it preserved sounds and enabled the reader to repeat the author's words. To get the full benefit of what he read it was necessary for him to read aloud" (1966, 12). Of course, the assumption of this pedagogy assumed that repeating what the author said was equivalent to meaning what the author meant. The relationship between the spoken and written word was evident in the earliest forms of print; even as speech seemed seamless, so early writing was constructed in one continuous stream without breaks, "written in a crabbed hand, full of contractions . . . with no space between paragraphs or chapters, no headings or page layout" (Febvre and Martin, 1990, 87). It was not until the sixteenth century that the book achieved its contemporary appearance with regard to spacing and page layout. The link between the oral tradition and print is also evident in the irregular spellings which occur in printed material and which can be traced to the printers' understanding of the sound of the language.[4]

Ties between reading and its pedagogy and the oral tradition are clear, and though we ought to recognize the confusion between reading and writing that this pedagogy assumes, nonetheless, we might acknowledge its base in a Platonic conception of language whose link to an oral tradition determines a specific pedagogy. In writing, each individual letter must be drawn in a linear regular pattern. Each letter must be separately delineated. The same is not true of reading. Cattell (1886) showed in the nineteenth century that the perception of a whole word occurs as quickly as perception of individual letters. Yet, early reading pedagogy insists on letter learning. This emphasis on letters derives, in large part I believe, from early Platonic philosophy. Plato says in *The Republic* that ". . . we must know the letters themselves before we can recognize images of them, reflected [say] in water or in a mirror. The same skill and practice are needed in either case" (in Mathews, 1966, 4). And though Cattell's research (in Huey, 1908) showed that we do not even have to see letters to recognize a word, that the ability to read does not necessarily require knowledge of the alphabet, nor is such knowledge an indication of the sound of the word, nonetheless, reading instruction was originally tied to the learning of the alphabet, indeed, remains tied to letters in the predominance today of phonics instruction. Marilyn Adams' book, *Beginning to Read* (1990), was produced as a result of a congressional mandate to authenticate phonics as the official government ideology. Phonics is a set of rules that ties orthography to sound and posits reading as the decoding of the written text first into sound. That Adams' book is widely touted by the conservative agenda is indication of the politics of reading pedagogy.

This persevering relationship between the spoken and the written word and subsequent reading practice is derived in part from the syllabic origins of the English language in Greek, a source responsible for the dominant theories of language and reading pedagogies in practice in the United States historically and in the present. The Greek conception of language has dominated Western linguistic development and theorizing and has been the basis for reading pedagogy in the United States formally at least since the Olde Deluder Law of 1647. As Julia Kristeva (1989) has noted, ". . . if each period and tendency has deciphered in its own way the models bequeathed to it by the Greeks, the fundamental conceptualization of language, as well as the basic classifications of it, have remained constant" (104). The Greeks, borrowing the Phoenician alphabet and accommodating it to their own language (whose radicals are not consonantal like those of Semitic languages), were forced to introduce marks for vowels. Each letter received a name (alpha, beta, gamma), and the letter marked the initial phoneme of its name: β = βετα. Kristeva analyzes the results of the Greek movement into phoneticism. She traces the Greek philosophy—and the traditional Western philosophical base—to the Platonic belief that language was separate from nature[5] but could be employed to describe it. Kristeva writes that ". . . the very type of phonetic writing, as well as, no doubt, the economic and ideological needs of Greek society, kept suggesting and finally did impose a conception of language as an ideality that reflected an outside, one whose only link with that outside was conceptual"(106). Language was therefore understood not as creative of the world, but as distinct from it. Language could describe a world, but could not of itself constitute it. A separate entity, language could be a specific subject of study separate from the world which it purported to describe.

Language, Socrates argues in the *Cratylus* (Jowett, 1937), was a human invention whose function is to image the Ideal. Reading pedagogy as an aspect of language study—hence its centrality in the language arts curriculum—is the direct result of this belief. The implication of Plato's philosophical position is that language could no longer be understood as capable of creating the world by organizing it as it had been in earlier civilization; rather, language was now an autonomous entity and the Greeks autonomous subjects.

> Plato opted for the (natural) character of language . . . postulating that language was indeed a human *creation* (and in this sense, conventional), which resulted, nevertheless, from the essence of the things it represented (and in this sense, this creation was natural); because of this, language became an obligation. . . . Language had therefore a *didactic* function, it was an instrument of *knowledge*. The name itself was already knowledge of the thing. . . . The name revealed the essence of things. (Kristeva, 108)

We may trace traditional reading pedagogies in the United States to this adherence to the Platonic belief in the reality of words and the autonomous subject who could, with skill, learn to understand the meaning contained in the word. The role of authority in knowing and communicating meaning was central, it will be recalled, to the early colonial Puritan ideology, despite constant contention in the colonies against that authority. And that power extended, as I will show, into the twentieth century through the authority of science.

To Plato, names were images of the thing named and were intimately tied to the material world. "The business of a name," Socrates asserts in the *Cratylus*, "is to express the nature" of the thing named (Jowett, 1937, 186). And the assignment of a name was a matter designated to those social groups whose skills made the naming possible. Since a name is an instrument, for teaching, giving information, and distinguishing objects according to their natures, then only the skilled can be teachers. The teacher teaches the name that has been given by the legislator. Legislators were considered those social members who were sufficiently skilled to give names, dialecticians those with the authority to question the legislator whether the form given [the word] was the correct form to express the thing; and the teacher he who was so skilled as to use the instrument—the word—to approach the nature of things of which words were representatives. We may see here the basis of the traditional school hierarchy and of teacher-directed pedagogies. In Plato, we may discover the foundation upon which education seems to have been traditionally organized. Platonic authority is embedded in the notion of the Ideal, and for Puritan ideology that authority rests in the Bible and its true meaning. For both Plato and the Puritans, there are those who are skilled to know and to teach that meaning. Linguistic philosophy was based on these concepts, and reading instruction was founded on this premise.

Thus, we may also begin to understand how at the end of the nineteenth century, as the hold of religion further weakened under the influences of Darwin, Freud, and Marx, science, as I will show, assumed the position of the new authority, and its path to meaning was taken as true. For Plato, only the skilled can be teachers because words are instruments for giving information about things and distinguishing them according to their nature. Only those who are skilled in the use of these instruments ought to teach them since ". . . things have names by nature, and that not every man is an artificer of names, but he only who looks to the name which each thing by nature has, and is able to express the true forms of things in letters and syllables" (180).

In part, the *Cratylus* is an exploration of how language developed and how it must be studied to enable its use as the instrument for teaching. What Socrates is interested in is the capacity of language to express Essence: Language is an instrument which may represent Essence, the Ideal; how language may so function is the subject of the Dialogue. Since all of language develops from the imitation of Essence, then breaking it down into its component parts is the only way to arrive at the comprehension of Essence.

> Imitation of the essence is made by syllables and letters; ought we not, therefore, first to separate the letters, just as those who are beginning rhythm first distinguish the powers of elementary, and then of compound sounds, and when they have done so, but not before, they proceed to the consideration of rhythm. (213)

Then, having separated the letters individually, ". . . we shall apply letters to the expression of objects, either single letters when required, or several letters; and so we shall form syllables . . . and from syllables make nouns and verbs; and thus, at last, from the combinations of nouns and verbs arrive at language, large and fair and whole"(214). The whole is formed from the compilation of the parts; hence, we have the basis of the subskill approach to reading. If we would know the whole, then we must begin with the parts: the letters and the syllables. Indeed, in the early primers the first dozens of pages are filled with lists of syllables the student must learn before passing on to the study of words and then sentences. Reading instruction is solidly based in the Platonic conception of language as the representation of the thing. The related belief, by which early reading instruction in America was and still is organized, concerns what reading may actually be as an activity. If, as Plato asserts, names—words—are imitations of the things named, then education is learning how to recognize in the word the thing named. Hence derive the requirements accruing to the learning of the alphabet, spelling, and handwriting. We have not yet gone much beyond Socrates' dictum. In the *Cratylus*, he asserts that "A name rightly imposed ought to have the proper letters. . . . And the proper letters are those which are like the things" (Jowett, 1937, 222). If words were an imitation of the thing, then learning to read was learning how to discover the thing in the word. The process was a matter of breaking the whole into its parts, of analysis, and then of synthesis.

Reading and the New Nation: Nineteenth-Century Developments

To the Puritans, reading was learning the correct meaning of the Bible, an early hermeneutic orientation which has not ceased to influence American pedagogy and which derived, we have seen, from Platonic philosophy. In the post-Revolutionary United States, the nationalistic values sometimes complemented and sometimes competed with religious ones as organizing ideologies. But whatever the prevailing belief system, reading was getting the meaning that the author originally intended; reading was not an activity which in itself was identical to thought but was, rather, the means to thought itself. In the early years of the nation, reading instruction was designed to inculcate a patriotic fervor by establishing and promoting a system of prescribed values. Noah Webster, whose reader sold more than 24,000,000 copies by 1833 and may have reached a hundred million copies by the end of the nineteenth century when it was still in use, simply adopted the form of the catechism in one section of the book to teach a more secular morality (Smith, 1986; Mathews, 1966). Moral instruction viewed through a nationalistic lens, as compared with an ecclesiastical one, was Noah Webster's purpose in organizing both his early readers and his dictionary, the latter an attempt to create an authentic American language. David Simpson (1985, 55) argues that

Webster's nationalistic motives determined his pedagogy: those prioritized values must be instilled in the process of reading.

> American manners must be influenced by persuasion, by convincing every citizen to behave in one way rather than another. The medium of persuasion for Webster's generation was the printed word: hence the urgency of providing cheap, American books for American readers. This would not only stimulate a native book trade, but would embody a native morality, politics, culture, and fashion. (55)

In order to read these books, a pedagogy needed to be employed: Since the correct meaning was sought, a pedagogy which would ensure that end was utilized. That pedagogy had already been established by the Platonic tradition. Reading was knowing the proper meaning of the right word—and its pronunciation. A pedagogy of reading focused on words.

These early traditions seem basic to an understanding of the pedagogy of reading today. Early reading pedagogy was predominantly alphabet oriented, was focused on subskills, and tended to view reading as an hermeneutic process. Of course, that this pedagogy failed from the beginning is indicated by the suffering students experienced in learning to read. Learning the alphabet and syllables was so painful that various methods needed to be employed to sweeten the task, including baking the letters in gingerbread form so that they might be eaten by the fortunate child when they were correctly named. Reading instruction from its inception must have been tedious to all but the most inured learners. The subtitle of an early popular speller, *The Child's New Plaything*, announced its purpose as "Intended to make the learning to read a diversion instead of a task" (Smith, 1986, 29). As this text was meant to replace the tedium of reading instruction with distraction, the subtitle declares clearly the popular view of reading as a task. These early primers, consisting mostly of the alphabet, syllabariums, tedious word lists, and moralistic stories from the Bible, identified and taught reading as the result of an ordered development beginning with the isolated parts: learning the alphabet which led to learning syllables which led to the pronunciation of short words. In what must be seen as a predecessor to the ubiquitous phonics instruction which has consumed the twentieth century, this early reading instruction practiced only oral reading and correct pronunciation as reading. All that seems to have changed over the next fifty years, until about 1870, was the material used to teach reading: Religious materials were replaced with nation-alistic materials, and the early alphabet and syllabariums were replaced with more elaborate phonics-oriented instruction.

Of course, this pedagogy may be tied to the early associations of reading with the oral tradition and with what will be called hermeneutics, a view which suggests that reading is the discovery of an author's intention. As Robert Scholes (1982, 9) cogently notes, however, the strength of the appeal of hermeneutics rests in the "sense that students are in fact not adequate readers, and hence are in need of a rigorous discipline in which there must be a standard for 'right' and 'wrong' readings."[6] For hermeneutics, the roots of which grow deep in biblical exegesis, the author is identified with God. What we must note, however, is the idea that in hermeneutics, though reading is always associated with thought, it is never identified as thought. Hence, in the early reading instruction, the function of reading was to get the thought of the author, and pedagogies were organized to facilitate that process. If reading was getting the thought, then issues of what was the largest grouping in which a thought was contained could become topics of discussion. Issues in psychology, a discipline that developed formally during the nineteenth century with experimental science as a model, began to have influence on issues of reading. Pedagogies of the mid to late 1800s, derived from Germany where psychology was a rapidly developing field, would emphasize whole words as the basic unit of thought, and from this emphasis, the word method evolved. Samuel Worcester averred in his primer that, "It is not, perhaps, very important that a child should know the letters before he begins to read. It may learn first to read words by seeing them, hearing them pronounced, and having their meanings illustrated, and afterwards it may learn to analyze them or name the letters of which they are composed" (in Smith, 1986, 86). The word method eschewed early learning of the alphabet and syllables and opted for whole words as the smallest unit for pedagogy.

> In teaching reading, the general practice has been to begin
> with the alphabet, and drill the child upon the letters,
> month after month, until he is supposed to have acquired
> them. This method, so irksome and vexatious to both
> teacher and scholar, is now giving place to another, which
> experience has proved to be more philosophical,
> intelligent, pleasant, and rapid. It is that of beginning with
> familiar and easy *words*, instead of *letters.* (in Smith, 1986,
> 87)

Interestingly enough, however, the word method was often just
a means to approach the alphabet: After learning the words by
sight, students were often led to analyze the words into their
parts. And of course, as we have already said, the word method
assumed that the thought consisted of the right meaning of the
word.

Two operating philosophies may have driven entry into
the word method: first, the meaning of the words was assumed
known so that reading became a practice of concatenating
known words together to arrive at a expected meaning which
would steep the word method in the Platonic tradition; or
second, words were learned for their phonic value and served as
a means to the alphabet and syllables, which would place
reading in direct relationship to the oral tradition. Horace Mann
wrote that "After children have learned to read words, the
twenty-six letters as they stand marshalled in the alphabet, will
be learned in a few hours" (in Mathews, 1966, 81). We may see in
this rationale an attempt to assert the notion that reading ought
to be meaningful, that thought is meaningful, and that the
smallest unit in which thought is contained must be the
pedagogical instrument for such development. Reading is the
perception of thought contained now in the word; hence, we
have arrived back at the Platonic conception of the word as the
image of reality. The word is approached here as the minimal
unit of thought, a development seemingly away from the Greek
conception but one actually steeped in it, as it conceived of sense
as a development of small units associated in the mind. Word
meanings were already prescribed; in what context they were
achieved became the issue of reading pedagogy.

Later opposition to the word method recognized that
words consisted of more than connected letters. Edmund Burke

Huey (1908) reported that the word "worm," though held together by dominant letters, is not linked by the letters but is welded together by sense. In other words, perception in reading of the word is mediated by sense. In isolation, perhaps, words may be recognized as wholes, but this would occur only in artificial conditions, in testing or experimental situations, for example, but not in sustained reading. The word method seems to be an attempt to retain the Platonic tradition without abandoning the alphabet or syllables, and by acknowledging that, as meaning is the goal of reading, the smallest unit of meaning is the word.

Reading was still conceived as the path to the correct thought, to the correct interpretation, and this powerful belief is tied to the strength of authority—to hermeneutics. Reading has traditionally been understood as the acquisition of meaning from a text, as if texts had meaning that could be discovered, and the word method simply identifies meaning with the word rather than with the letters. This tradition remains unabated into the twentieth century. Dr. William Gray, who wrote one of the first doctoral dissertations in reading (Smith, 1986, 187), said in 1935, "If reading is to serve its largest function in social life, teachers face real problems and responsibilities; they must promote clear understanding and discriminating insight into each of the broader phases of contemporary life; [teachers must] develop habits of accurate, precise comprehension and interpretation, including critical evaluation" (1937, 13). Arthur Gates (1935, 285), another early reading specialist, said that "The specific skills and abilities of reading are conceived as a means for getting thought and for putting the results of reading to some constructive use." And E.D. Hirsch, one of America's foremost hermeneuticists and equally renowned for his series on cultural literacy or what every literate person ought to know, holds, as Terry Eagleton avers, that meaning is "something which the author *wills*: it is a ghostly, wordless mental act which is then 'fixed' for all time in a particular set of material signs. It is an affair of consciousness, rather than of words" (Eagleton, 1983, 67). One may hear in Eagleton's characterization of Hirsch's hermeneutics the claim of the basal readers which remain still predominantly word centered. As Goodman et al. document in their extensive study,

Report Card on Basal Readers (1987), "A major organizing principle of basal readers is that learning to read is more than anything else, learning words and skills for identifying words. Though there is considerable focus on phonics in all of the basals, even when a series is labeled as a phonics program the emphasis is on words, with phonics as a means of 'decoding' or identifying the words" (66).

Alternative ways of looking at reading, as I will show, were marginalized as soon as they appeared; first, because they threatened the hegemony of those in power; and second, and of equal and related importance, because the tradition of reading placed its pedagogy in hermeneutics and the requisite skills for learning which hermeneutics demanded. Alternative methods of reading and its pedagogy denied the very idea of knowledge held in the dominant ideologies of the United States. Hierarchies of power were evidence of the fact that the foundation upon which hermeneutics seemed to rest was the governing principle for the development of hierarchies of organization, progress, and, therefore, of reading pedagogy. What one thought reading was determined how it was to be taught; how it was taught determined what reading became and what one read. Reading's ties to ideology and its bastard child, tradition, reified reading and determined its definitions.

As the nineteenth century progressed, reading instruction moved away from the alphabet and towards larger and larger units; first by the word method, advocated prominently by Horace Mann from his studies of Jacotot in Germany,[7] and then progressively to the sentence method, as advocated by George Farnham (1891/1895). For Farnham, thought was contained in the sentence.

> The first principle to be observed in teaching reading is that things are recognized as wholes. Language follows this law. . . . The question arises, "What is the whole? or what is the unit of expression?" It is now quite generally conceded that we have no ideas not logically associated with others. In other words, thoughts, complete in their relations, are the materials in the mind out of which the complex relations are constructed. . . . It being admitted that the thought is the unit of thinking, it necessarily follows that *the sentence is the unit of expression.* . . . The

> sentence, if properly taught, will in like manner be
> understood as a whole, better than if presented in detail.
> The order indicated is, first the sentence, then the words,
> and then the letters. The sentence being first presented as a
> whole, the words are discovered, and after that the letters
> composing the word. (17)

I think what is significant here are two related ideas. First,
Farnham situates reading as a psychological activity which
identifies ideas with thoughts and thoughts with complex
relations.[8] It becomes necessary to think, then, of the expression
of thought as necessitating a complex structure. Hence, the
sentence becomes for Farnham the unit of expression. It is an
associationist perspective on reading that continues to situate
meaning in the text and that is, therefore, knowable if the proper
unit—in this case, the sentence—is addressed. "Reading
consists," says Farnham, "in gaining the thoughts of an author
from written or printed language" (11). Second, Farnham also
focused attention on reading as an activity that can only be
taught by acknowledging this psychological basis and
accounting for it in the pedagogy. These were not issues
addressed directly by previous pedagogues who tended to view
reading as an exercise of mind which did not think to read but
rather, read to find thought. Farnham was interested in the
psychology of reading, but he seems to have situated it not in the
original creative activity of a reader but in the information-
processing schemas that left meaning situated in the text and
identified comprehension as the movement of that thought
through the mind's structures.

> In our educational processes we have but to ascertain the
> manner and order in the use of intellectual faculties and
> power in performing real life work, and then guide and
> direct the study of the youth, that they may acquire the
> use of the powers in the same manner and order. (vi)

Reading was filling the mind with the best, the most beautiful,
and the brightest. One had only to learn how the brain processed
information in which these qualities were represented to
discover them in the books that were to be read. It is on this basis
and for these purposes that the authorities were prepared to
instruct and for which reading pedagogy was designed. It never

ceased to identify meaning and quality in the text and reading as the ability to discover it. This pedagogy, as I will show, fit perfectly with the study of cognitive science of information processing.

What Farnham does not seem to address, and what I would argue accounts for the disparate strains of reading pedagogy in the twentieth century, is in what sense the sentence contains the whole if it is not merely the concatenation of the words, themselves the sum of the letters. In other words, what is a thought that it might be contained in a sentence but not in the separate words within that sentence. How is it that thought may be apperceived by a reader correctly as a product of words? And why does Farnham limit the thought to the sentence: Would not several sentences make a greater whole even as several separate words form the greater sentence?

On the one hand, we may identify in Farnham's method the old word method: All he meant to do was to put the word in a meaningful context that it might be learned. The pedagogy he proposes is ultimately recognition of new words in whole sentences. "The pupil should not be allowed to guess [at unrecognizable words], but when he hesitates, the teacher should point out the sentence for him" (31). Thought becomes the conceptual recognition of a word as a representation of a specific thing.

On the other hand, Farnham's ideas seem to hold with hermeneuticists that thought is contained in the text and that it simply requires identifying the proper unit to discover it. This continues the Platonic tradition of separating the reader from the text, of declaring that the written word, as Socrates says, "if it is ill-treated or unfairly abused [by unsuitable readers] always needs its parent to come to its rescue; it is quite incapable of defending or helping itself" (*Phaedrus*, 1986, 97). This pedagogy separates the text from the reader in ways no different from that of Plato two thousand years before. And it continues to see pedagogy as the transfer of thought from one source into another. The debate over the relationship between reading and thought, where thought may be contained and how it may be mined, discovered, or created seems to determine the larger debate in the United States over reading pedagogy for the next century. It also seems to underlie the often hostile debate between skills-oriented pedagogy and whole-language philosophy. I will suggest that the ruling hegemony may account for the dominance of skills-based approaches to reading as opposed to whole-language approaches.

Alternative Traditions

For such whole-language approaches did exist and have an antiquity equal to that of Platonic doctrine. Ultimately these approaches viewed reading as a natural activity and which is an original act of thought. Cratylus (Jowett, 1937) asserts at the end of the dialogue that his view of language still inclines toward that of Heracleitus, whose position was that language was always in flux. This protean nature of language denies the identity of the word as the image of the thing named. If the word is not the image of the thing, then how the word functions is called into question by returning identity to the encounter with the word by a reader/listener. This places autonomous agency in the reader and situates reading as the primary and original act of thought. Edmund Burke Huey will say (1908/1968) that

> To know how reading occurs would be to know how almost any abstract representation of information—a traffic sign, a meter reading in the laboratory, or spoken words themselves—are evaluated and understood. It would be to know how people make sense of the welter of information from the environment and themselves with which they are constantly bombarded . . . to completely analyze what we do when we read would almost be the acme of a psychologist's achievements, for it would be to describe the very many of the most intricate workings of the human mind, as well as to unravel the tangled story of the most remarkable specific performance that civilization has learned in all its history. (6)

It is often said that in this statement Huey prepares for the takeover of reading by cognitive psychologists with his apparent formulation that reading seems to be a matter of simple processing: that thought is the processing of information.

However, this belief seems to ignore Huey's later statement that "The simple fact is that the words and all the other objects that we ever see are thus thrown outward projected upon a page in the case of reading, somewhat as a lantern might throw them outward upon a screen" (106). Ultimately, Huey's conclusions will suggest that what we perceive is a result of our prior knowledge and cannot be determined by the markings on the page. "Perception is always a projection or localization outward of a consciousness which is aroused or suggested by the stimulations that have come inward, but which is conditioned strongly, also from within" (105). In other words, what we perceive is also a product of our consciousness. Reading is identified as a function of consciousness and not a path to it. Hence, situating meaning in the text would have to be construed as a denial of the agency of the reader. Such denial, according to progressive educators, denied agency to the self in the direction of his/her education. "It seems to me," said Francis Parker (1894/1969, 97), "an indisputable fact that the human organism, or the brute organism for that matter, determines absolutely the creative influence of externality; that the organism of the brain itself, with its convolutions and fibres, and sub-organs, determines that which shall enter it and vivify it." Parker says that the original act of attending to print is the first creative act and that it is "indisputable" then that no two people can see the same thing. Furthermore, the traditional reading pedagogy steeped in hermeneutics, in placing meaning in the text, denied whatever knowledge the learner/reader always already maintained for the authority of the text.

The influence of hermeneutics on reading pedagogy had, it was averred by some, to have frustrated education. John Locke complained that "orthodox methods of education [charged] children's memories with rules and principles"(in Avrich, 1980, 10). Rousseau had held that "No creature in human form will be expected to learn anything but because he desires it and has some conception of its utility and value" (Avrich, 10). Peter Kropotkin described modern education as "producing superficiality, parrot-like repetition, slavishness, and inertia of mind" (Avrich, 11). William Godwin wrote that in the ideal school "no such characters are left upon the scene as either preceptor or pupil. The boy, like the man, studies because he desires it. He proceeds upon a plan of his own invention, or which, by adopting, he has made his own. Everything bespeaks independence and equality" (Avrich, 13). Indeed, libertarians and anarchists advocated an education that placed autonomy in the child, that treated children not as inferior or undeveloped adults but rather as "creators," not "creatures." "All education," Parker says, "is by self-activity, and, at the same time, it may be said that self-activity is an evidence of human growth beyond the threshold of the educative stage; that the basis of human development, that is, heredity, the physical organism of the body, and the spontaneous action of external attributes, form the foundation or present the conditions absolutely necessary for self-activity" (Parker, 1894/1969, 119–20). Reading pedagogy did not exist for such theorists; rather, reading was an activity that was made possible by the desire to read. Indeed, teaching reading as a means to learning was to deny the nature of reading and creativity in the child. Parker (202) would say learning to read ought to occur as a natural correlate of other self-directed activity: *"That which is best is education, that which is best for the body and mind and soul, is unconsciously acquired."* Martha Fleming (1904, 545), an advocate of a free education, would write that

> To know the words that meet the eye and to be able to speak them is neither reading nor reading aloud. It is to have a valuable tool of whose true use the possessor may know nothing . . . we center all the children's attention on the word, instead of letting it come naturally out of the work with real things and real experiences, out of the stories and poetry, and out of the demands made by the community life of the school. . . . Necessity awakens the desire to know words, and the child's will is then enlisted in mastering the difficulties. The symbol becomes a living thing, and the book, when its hour come, does not mean a struggle with dry, meaningless signs, but another source of knowledge.

These advocates of education denied that a hierarchy of skills was necessary for the practice of reading, but believed that the natural inclination and experiences of the child would make reading not only possible and practical but unavoidable and alluring. Meaning was not to be found in the word nor in the sentence; rather, it was embodied in the reader and could be created in an interaction with the whole text itself. Who the reader was would then determine how reading functioned; reading made possible the developing self. Any pedagogy of reading was useless unless it addressed the specific students and the specific world from which they came and in which they lived. Bayard Boyeson, writing a prospectus for the Ferrer School, the first regular institution of the Modern School Movement, and in a language that John Dewey would adopt in *The School and Society* (1902/1956), said that

> education is a process of drawing out, not of driving in;
> that the child must be left free to develop spontaneously,
> directing his own efforts and choosing the branches of
> knowledge which he desires to study; that, therefore, the
> teacher, instead of imposing or presenting as authoritative
> his own opinions, predilections, or beliefs, should be a
> sensitive instrument responding to the needs of the child
> as they are at any time manifested—a channel through
> which the child may obtain so much of the ordered
> knowledge of the world as he shows himself ready to
> receive or assimilate ... We take the centre of gravity,
> which has lain hitherto in the teacher, and put it firmly in
> the child itself. (in Avrich, 1980, 73, 75)

One could understand this statement, and others like it, as anticipatory of the development of reading readiness concepts. But to me, to understand it as such, one would have to pervert the sense of freedom explicit in Boyeson's belief that children will learn when learning is a natural part of their activity and not one arbitrarily imposed by the artificiality of the contemporary school system. The idea of reading readiness in the development of reading pedagogies in the twentieth century is lauded by Nila Banton Smith (1934/1986, 260), who attributes to none other than John Dewey the solidification of the notion of reading readiness. Smith claims that Dewey's notion that children should not be taught to read until the age of eight is evidence of his advocacy of reading readiness concepts. But I believe that Smith reads Dewey to further her purposes of tracing what she believes are important, linear, and progressive developments in the understanding of reading and its pedagogies in the United States. Smith reads Dewey out of context and misrepresents his position on reading. In fact, Dewey (1898), in his discussion of reading, was responding to the relationship between the contemporary emphasis placed on reading in elementary education and to the drastic historical change which had taken place in a child's life during the modern era. For Dewey, the mushrooming development of urban and suburban life had denied to children the opportunity for participating in the practical life which had been intrinsic to their education as participants in family life in rural settings. What had previously been learned in the organic functioning of community life, Dewey said, was now relegated to the sterility of the classroom and to the isolated activity that now comprised reading. What modern education failed to develop was ". . . the development of hand and eye, . . . the acquisition of skill and deftness . . . [or an] initiation into self-reliance, independence of judgment and action, [which] was the best stimulus to habits of regular and continuous work" (Dewey, 1898, 319). Reading had now become necessary for acquiring that knowledge and those characteristics that life had once offered to children. But, though historical conditions had changed, Dewey claimed, reading pedagogy had not. This focus had made reading an academic exercise in isolation from purposeful activity.

> Reading is made an isolated accomplishment. There are no aims in the child's mind which he feels he can serve by reading; there is no mental hunger to be satisfied; there are no conscious problems with reference to which he uses books. The book is a reading lesson. He learns to read not for the sake of what he reads, but for the mere sake of reading. When the bare process of reading is thus made an end in itself, it is a psychological impossibility for reading to be other than lifeless. (322)

Dewey's argument with reading was that it had *become* a pedagogy and been divorced from the mental and emotional needs of the child. Reading was no longer organic to functioning; one read to discover purpose.

> The material of the reading lesson is thus found wholly in the region of familiar words and ideas. It is out of the

> question for the child to find anything in the ideas
> themselves to arouse and hold attention. His mind is fixed
> upon the mere recognition and utterance of the forms.
> Thus begins that fatal divorce between the substance and
> the form of expression, which, fatal to reading as an art,
> reduces it to a mechanical action. (322)

For Dewey, as for others, reading ought to be an original act of thinking, not a mere exercise in reading. Dewey did not propose the concept of reading readiness, but advocated the postponement of reading pedagogy until the child had been given cause to read and was engaged in activities that reading would enhance. In this way, reading would be organic to activity and not separate from it.

Reading in the schools constrained children and denied them the freedom of their own imaginations. In this way, reading pedagogy falsified the very nature of reading. Francis Parker, who was to Dewey the father of progressive education, said that

> . . . a reader does not think the thought of an author, he
> simply thinks his own thought. By the action of words
> upon the mind ideas arise above the plane of
> consciousness; individual concepts and judgments that
> have formerly been in consciousness reappear, and are
> recombined and associated; new units are formed and
> fresh judgements suggested; but the mental results of
> written or printed words upon the mind are
> predetermined by the mind itself. (Parker, 1894/1969, 189)

For Parker, each individual is naturally capable of independent thought stimulated by the material object of the text, which consists of words, sentences, and paragraphs. That independent thought is a product of an always ready consciousness, and what we perceive is a product of what consciousness expects and/or desires to see. All understanding arises from this original creativity.

> The common saying that reading is getting the thought of
> an author is [wrong]. Strictly, no one can ever have any
> thought but his own. The mental value of reading (the
> study of text) depends entirely upon the ideas which lie
> below the plane of consciousness; upon the individual

> concepts that have formerly been in consciousness, and
> upon personal experience, inferences, comparisons and
> generalizations. Upon the richness, fullness, and quality of
> one's own mind depends the action of printed words.
> Sentences recall concepts, unite new ones, and arouse the
> power to understand or to draw original inferences. (162)[9]

For Parker, all reading is the activity of a reader, and in the act of
reading, the reader comes into existence.

Parker's approach suggests that reading might be viewed
not as a matter of exercising greater precision to get meaning, as
skills-oriented theorists proposed, because, in Parker's view,
there was no meaning to be gotten. Rather, reading ought to be
understood as an act of original thought itself. Thus, pedagogy
that focused on the teaching of skills falsified not only the very
nature of reading but pedagogy itself. Flora Cooke, a teacher in
Parker's Cook County Normal School, in an article entitled
"Reading in the Primary Grades" (1900), wrote "The Present
Working Hypothesis is that children may learn to read as
naturally as they learn to talk and for exactly the same reason,
i.e., from the desire to find out something or to tell
something. . . . They must first desire to read; after the desire is
awakened the child will learn by any method, with or without
school. *He will find a teacher* [emphasis added]"(1). Reading need
not be taught in order for it to be learned any more than speech
must be taught. The child's natural curiosity and desire to belong
to community will impel him/her to reading. In his article "The
Primary Education Fetich" (1898), John Dewey notes that in
schools

> . . . the significant thing is that it is possible for the child at
> an early day to become acquainted with, and to use, in a
> personal and yet relatively controlled fashion, the methods
> by which truth is discovered and communicated, and to
> make his own speech a channel for the expression and
> communication of truth; thus putting the linguistic side
> where it belongs—subordinate to the appropriation and
> conveyance of what is genuinely and personally
> experienced. (318)

Decrying skills-oriented education, of which the reading fetish
represented a primary example, Dewey advocates what will later

be referred to as "whole-language instruction." The tragedy of modern education, said Dewey, was that though the means of progressive education existed, they were denied for the traditional pedagogies.

> The conception that the mind consists of what has been taught, and that the importance of what has been taught consists in its availability for further teaching, reflects the pedagogues's view of life. The philosophy is eloquent about the duty of the teacher in instructing pupils; it is almost silent regarding the privilege of learning. It emphasizes the influence of intellectual environment upon the mind; it slurs over the fact that the environment involves a personal sharing in common experiences. It exaggerates beyond reason the possibilities of consciously formulated and used methods, and underestimates the rôle of vital, unconscious, attitudes. It insists upon the old, the past and passes lightly over the operation of the genuinely novel and unforeseeable. It takes, in brief, everything educational into account save its essence,— vital energy seeking opportunity for effective exercise. (1916/1966, 71–72)

Despite Dewey's contention that he never read Marx, it is difficult to imagine that he did not have that famous chapter in mind when he called reading the primary education fetish.[10] You will recall that in this section of the first chapter of *Capital*, Marx refers to the "Fetish of the Commodity" as the attribution of the power, which actually resides in human beings, to the products of human labor. Reading as the primary education fetish creates reading as an activity independent of learning and makes it learning's tool. Reading is conceptualized as an independent activity that then can be used for learning and has power in and of itself that can be appropriated by the individual for varied purposes.

This is the direction reading pedagogy will take in the twentieth century under the hegemony of the dominant culture. In this vein, Arthur Gates (1935) will argue in a language that could not respond more clearly or oppositionally to Dewey's that "Reading is both the most important and the most troublesome subject in the elementary school curriculum . . . it is most troublesome since pupils fail in reading far more frequently than many other elementary skills." For Gates, "failure in the primary grades is almost wholly due to deficiencies in reading" (1935, 2). Reading seems postulated here as a skill apart from knowledge of the world but which, if properly taught and practiced, could lead to such knowledge. Similarly, in the *Thirty-Sixth Yearbook of the National Society for the Study of Education*, William Gray[11] writes

> With increasing frequency the fact has been emphasized that reading must provide more largely in the future than in the past for promoting clear understanding, developing habits of good thinking, stimulating broad interests, cultivating appreciations and establishing stable personalities. (1937, 5)

These views of reading, which situate knowledge in the text, continue the mind-body split characteristic of Western philosophical traditions and pedagogies and continue to dominate reading instruction in the United States today.

Gray's view, and those of others like him, represent one diametrically opposed to that of Dewey, Parker, and Cooke, extending right up to Goodman, Smith, and the whole-language advocacy, which holds that reading is a model of thinking. For the latter group of educators, reading is not the path to thought: it is thought, and a pedagogy of reading is the process of cultivating thinking. This alternative tradition to that of mainstream theory highlights the confluence of reading pedagogies with the available materials that could be read, the issue addressed earlier by Chall and Carroll. This alternative tradition recognizes the political nature of pedagogies. Huey (1908/1968) had theorized earlier that the reverence given books stemmed from the mystery of the written symbols accessible only to and therefore jealously protected by the clergy who could then reify and control knowledge. And, of course, access to the written word was believed to provide access to knowledge—to the possibility of its production. Restriction of the populace from the reading process restricted the possibility of knowledge and kept the church—and others—in control. This is a paradigm of pedagogy we have seen dating back to the Platonic era. Reading pedagogy has consistently premised meaning as residing in the text and situated the reader as the discoverer and interpreter of that meaning. Walter Ong (1982) argues that Plato rejected poets from his Republic because studying them was learning to "react with 'soul,' to feel oneself identified with Achilles or Odysseus," (46) and therefore to be incapable of analytic thought. The whole-language movement, however, argues for reading as a natural activity of thought which need be taught only by its use, even as oral language is learned in its use.[12] It is an education for democracy. Patrick Shannon (1990, 112–113) notes that at the Highlander School "Staff members were to teach by demonstrating their capacity to learn . . . literacy was at the center of many of the Highlander projects." As Myles Horton (1990, 101), founder of the Highlander School, would say regarding the campaign to establish Citizenship Schools throughout the South to develop literacy and enroll voters, "Certainly the first people you want to avoid are certified teachers, because people with teaching experience would likely impose their schooling methodology on the students and be judgmental. . . ." Reading in this alternative tradition, however, need not be taught, indeed, could not be taught but only learned. In this pedagogy, reading was understood as a natural activity. Martha Fleming (1904), writing in the *Elementary School Teacher* noted that

> Reading is imaging, thinking, in response to the stimulus of the written or printed word; it presupposes a mass of experiences on a subject or on related subjects. It focuses all these, and in each person arouses emotions corresponding to the depth and wealth of his emotional nature, his humanity, and his sympathy for all living things; his perception of beauty, and his richness in that power of remaking all thought, imagery, and emotion into a new and marvelous world of his own—which passeth beyond experience—his real world, one that endureth forever. (541)

More recently, Frank Smith (1988) in *Understanding Reading* has argued that "Reading is thinking . . . the thinking we do when we read, in order to read, is no different from the thinking we do on other occasions. . . . Reading is thinking that is partly focused on visual information of print; it is thinking that is stimulated and directed by written language" (177). But these views have not been mainstream ones; they have, indeed, been effectively marginalized. The marginal-ization of John Dewey has been described most recently by Robert Westbrook (1991) and Cornel West (1989). And promulgators of this Deweyan perspective have been rapidly dismissed by the mainstream theorists of reading. Note the fates of such educators as Francis Wayland Parker, the theorists of the Modern School Movement, and most recently the advocates of whole language. Jeanne Chall (in Rothman, 1990) dismisses the work of whole-language advocates: "It's not that whole language does not have research—and it does not—but that they are deliberately turning their backs on the existing solid research that exists for the opposite . . ." (189). Yet, just the year before, Ken and Yetta Goodman had published in the *Elementary School Journal* (1989) an article addressing the research foundations of whole language. In his article Ken Goodman declared that "the practice of whole language is solidly rooted in scientific research and theory" (205).

The Inventions of Science: Two Traditions

I have tried to show that this division of traditions in reading pedagogy occurs in part as a product of a dispute between ideologies that argue for different definitions of knowledge and contradictory models of knowledge construction. The dominant tradition, which has organized society according to hierarchies employing knowledge as the tool of social control, argued that knowledge existed in the world and that it could be discovered by students if instructed by the proper teachers and if they used the correct tools. Reading pedagogies were developed premised upon these beliefs. Knowledge was equated with power, and reading became the quintessential tool of prerogative. The argument over literacy that rages in the United States today concerns the very definitions of literacy, with the dominant ideologies situating it in the ability to read and write. This equating of knowledge with power has been a program from which Michel Foucault (1978) has explored the development of the hegemony of a particular social order and its institutions.

Reading and its pedagogy have played important roles in the establishment of that social order, which has been able to define knowledge by controlling the means of access to it. What one ought to know and how it might be known were organized by those dominant powers whose authority resided historically in God or Country or both. But during the twentieth century, as the strength of either God or Country waned, the powers have maintained their hegemony in part as a result of the developing authority of science, which the reading specialists have adopted. Science, which appeared to demystify existence and made material what was once spiritual, became the new religion, the new patriotism. Coincident with the teachings of science, dominant cultural forces advocated for the establishment and efficacy of hierarchical structures to ensure the continuance of a stable social structure and continual progress. In part, these structures produced schools and the curricula that they maintained. They also produced conditions that led to the dominance of one tradition of reading and its pedagogy over another.

In this chapter, I would like to link the hegemony of science with the rise of experimental psychology and to explore the latter's developments in the twentieth century and its contiguity with and influence upon pedagogy in general and reading theory and research specifically. I intend to show how reading has been occupied by those whose research designs and results perpetuate the mind-body split central to reading theory in the United States and thereby determine not only what reading is but what may be read. In the next chapter, I would like to portray the development and marginalization of an alternative reading tradition as situated in a partisan arena and to trace the fate of this reading pedagogy to political fortunes. Though I must arbitrarily split these two tracks into categories of science and politics, they are nevertheless interrelated, a point I hope will become evident in the discussion.

Science gave credence to phenomena that loss of faith could no longer explain. The ability to quantify experience made experience knowable. Edward Thorndike, whose course in educational measurement entitled "Application of Psychological and Statistical Methods to Educational Theory and Practice"

would have so much influence on curricula and methods during
the twentieth century, set the tone for research saying:

> Whatever exists, exists in some amount. To measure it is to
> know its varying amounts. Man sees no less beauty in
> flowers now than before the day of quantitative botany. It
> does not reduce courage or endurance to measure them
> and trace their relations to the autonomic system, the flow
> of the adrenal glands, and the production of sugar in the
> blood. If any virtue is worth seeking, we shall seek it more
> eagerly the more we know and measure it. (in Jonçich,
> 1968, 282).

A knowable experience was consistent with the dominant
ideology that experience was monolithic and the path to its
meaning constrained and defined. That the world was infinite
and infinitely knowable was the dominant belief of the
nineteenth century. Important, as well, and as the developing
science seemed to promise, a knowable experience could be
ultimately controlled. Reading as an activity of experience and in
experience could be ultimately known and regulated.

The faith in the authority of science replaced the
perennially waning faith in the authority of religion, and the
energy of faith would ultimately bolster a rabid nationalism that
would permit all kinds of imperialistic activities during the
twentieth century. Writing in 1907, William James (1907/1970)
notes that "Never were as many men of a decidedly empiricist
proclivity in existence as there are at the present day . . . our
esteem for facts has not neutralized in us all religiousness. It is
itself almost religious. Our scientific temper is devout" (23). This
ideology, which derived from a belief in science, contrasts with
the traditional Christian millenarian teleology, but as I have said,
science replaced religion as a foundation of belief structures.
Christopher Lasch (1991) argues that our idea of progress in the
twentieth century owes its definition not to the teachings of the
Bible but to the developments in science. In the latter, there is no
end to history, only continuous linear movement.

> The idea of progress never rested mainly on the progress
> of an ideal society—not at least in its Anglo-American
> version. . . . The modern conception of history is utopian
> only in its assumption that modern history has no

> foreseeable conclusion. We take our cue from science, at once the source of our material achievements and the mode of cumulative, self-perpetuating inquiry, which guarantees its continuation precisely by its willingness to submit every advance to the risk of supersession. (48)

The authority of science coincided with the program of the Platonists who, as I have shown, advocated the bottom-up approach to reading instruction. Science was deployed to confirm Platonic doctrine, giving it the empirical authority it apparently lacked, even though that science itself had evolved from within that tradition. Strict observation became the hallmark of science, with the assumption that what was observed existed apart from the observer, continuing the separation of the human organism from nature. Reading, as a human activity imposed on nature in order to know it, posited a separate subject and object and supported a pedagogy that could enable the decoding of that object by a subject. Science, nevertheless, monolithically set the course of reading instruction during the twentieth century. "The dramatic period beginning within the year of 1910 ushered in the first truly great breakthough in American reading instruction . . . with the advent of instruments of measurement it was possible for the first time to obtain scientific information about the effectiveness of reading methods and materials and of administrative arrangements for teaching reading in the classroom" (Smith, 1986, 157). Linked to psychology by Farnham and others, reading now required, and had available, a scientific pedagogy to validate it as a science. A developing experimental psychology that posited mind as material, quantifiable, and hence knowable and steeped in scientific method, coincided with American pedagogical needs. But it was, perhaps, a misrepresentation of experimental psychology that permitted its development as a tool for fixing reading instruction in the bottom-up, skills-oriented approach.

Experimental Psychology and Reading

Experimental psychology developed during the last half of the nineteenth century and ripened in the schism between Kantian idealist and Millian materialist philosophies. On the one hand, Kant argued from the position of a rational psychology that was incompatible with an experimental quantified psychology. Kant believed that nothing about mind could be quantified. On the other hand, working in the Lockean tradition, radical materialists like John Stuart Mill argued that mind was wholly material and that there was nothing in consciousness but the products of sensations, which were eminently measurable. Wilhelm Wundt, a German philosopher/psychologist steeped in the Kantian tradition, attempted to create a synthesis by which rational and experimental psychology could be fused. Of his efforts Wundt would say that

> We mean only to denote the maximum scope of one single complex whole . . . [in measuring] our scope of consciousness in one diameter of surface, and not the whole extent of it . . . there may at the same time be other elements of consciousness scattered about beside the ones we are just measuring. They can, however, be left out of account, since in a case such as ours consciousness will be directed to the content that is measured, and the elements outside of this will be unclear, fluctuating, isolated. (1897/1969, 9)

Though he would conceptualize what he was measuring as a whole (hence his identification with Gestalt psychology), Wundt would not measure consciousness itself as a whole. Furthermore, Wundt was suggesting that consciousness would be defined by measurable contents but that it could not be contained in that measurement. In the attempt at separation, Wundt would make possible the future separation by behaviorists of figure and ground and the ignoring of the necessary relationship of the one on the other. The effect of this split on future reading research was powerful; it meant that the processes of reading might be conceptually defined apart from the actual contents. From this situation, both behaviorism and cognitive psychology would eventually develop. Neither would attempt to consider reading from a gestaltist perspective.

This separation was not Wundt's intent. Searching for an understanding of behavior, Wundt proposed that an event could be conceptualized as deriving from two points of view: that of natural science, which was a mediated perspective, and that of psychology, which was an immediate one. From this Wundt developed the doctrine of *psychophysical parallelism,* which hypothesized that each experience had two causes, one physical and one psychological. What Wundt would call "centres of the brain" were those areas where a complexity of physical connections were evident, and their presence supported his conceptualization of the two parallel processes. "The expression 'centre' in all these cases is, of course, employed in the sense that is justified by the general relation of psychical to physical functions, that is, in the sense of a parallelism between the two classes of elementary processes, the one regarded from the point of view of the natural sciences, the other from that of psychology" (1897/1969, 206). Wundt's project was to show the connection between these two causes, the one physical and the other psychological, and he found that connection in what he called *apperception.* Thus, Wundt would argue that memorizing a passage without comprehension involves physical causes and responses, and that though individually the words may have meaning in associative connection, it is only as a result of apperception that the unity of the whole can be realized. "The activity of apperception," Wundt declared, "is the essential factor, which makes a difference in the formation of such a combination from that of a mere association row" (1912/1973, 129). Apperception was intentionality and preceded physical perception.

Wundt argued that apperception constituted the basic form of all mental activity and, in so doing, advocated a position in the Leibnizian and Kantian tradition, which posited a volitional self. Opposed to this tradition was that of Locke and Herbart, whose theories argued for a more mechanistic and associationist view of behavior, which minimized volition and voluntary acts, and declared the contents of consciousness to be the product of associations and/or habitual patterns of action. Lockean psychology focused on the mental contents, Leibnizian psychology on mental acts. The former would be consistent with a traditional pedagogy of reading that would posit reading as linking certain stimuli with specific responses. It has been argued (Blumenthal, 1980) that Wundt, whose influence on experimental psychology is uncontested, advocated a psychology of mental acts but was misinterpreted and over-simplified by British and American psychologists more comfortable with the Lockean empiricist tradition. Blumenthal argues that ". . . in Titchener's [Wundt's student] hands, Wundt's principles of apperception, his voluntarism, his purposivism, and his dominant interests in history were extremely muted or even fundamentally changed" (128). What is important for our purposes here is to note that Wundt is often described as the innovator of experimental psychology and that experimental psychology became the model for reading research and instruction based upon that research.

> Many researchers . . . accepted the premises of the technology and designed research to fine tune it; Which skills should be taught first, what was the best way to teach a skill, how could we eliminate teacher difference as a factor in school success? This consistency between research, text, and tests created an illusion of science . . . summaries of research have claimed to show the soundness of the technology. (Goodman, 1992, 191)

But we must also understand that Wundt's work is misrepresented and that his psychological principles and methodology, as applied by experimental psychologists and reading researchers, may have been, at best, misapplied and/or misrepresented. Thus, the importance to reading instruction of the evolving experimental psychology, which itself will evolve into educational psychology, derives from this misleading, if not outrightly specious because partial, appropriation of Wundt's work.

The overriding question in nineteenth century psychology concerned the extent to which behavior is voluntary, willed, and volitional. Reading, of course, is a behavior. Empiricist psycho-logists would argue in an associationist vein that behavior is the result of associative connections. This is the philosophical thrust of Adams' (1990) description of learning to read. William James (1907/1970) describes these positivist, empiricist scientists: "Man is no lawgiver to nature, he is an absorber" (24). The German philosophical rationalist tradition, to which Wundt subscribed, argued differently, positing mind as an active participant in knowledge construction and not a passive spectator of it. Wundt (1912/1973) declared that ". . . in all psychical combinations the product is not a mere sum of the separate elements that compose such combinations, but that it represents a new creation" (165). The whole is greater than *and different* from the sum of its parts. Wundt theorized mind as a creator, an active participant in the formation of reality.

> In place of the older theory's reliance on the formation of mental pictures or copies of the external world, Wundt substituted *process*. In place of the percipient as a passive screen upon which the world of fact projected itself, Wundt installed an active, inwardly directed mind whose entire history participated in each of its acts; a mind so constituted as to impose logical coherence on all its intellectual operations and furnished by associations only in its nonconceptual operations. (Robinson, 1982, 166)

For Wundt, apperception was not merely a matter of clear and distinct perception, but rather, the influence of the organized mind upon the separate sensations that reach it, producing and resulting in structure and order. These sensations could include motor sensations as well, and could, of course, be measured. Apperception

> is a central process that operates in two directions. On the one hand, it operates on sensory content producing the complex forms of perception and ultimately of ideation . . . [and] apperception also operated on the motor apparatus. . . . Just as the contents of the cognitive field were structured in terms of focus and periphery, so the field of skeletal movements involved some that were apperceived and others that were peripheral at any particular time. (Danziger, 1980, 104)

What this would mean is that "to appear clearly in consciousness, a mental content must be apperceived, and this means that we are never aware of simple sense elements but only of compounds. Similarly, the role of apperception on the motor side means that actual movements, even impulsive movements, are not motor elements but are generally compound patterns" (Danziger, 105). Hence, the explanation of learning language, for example, could not be adequately described in bottom-up terms as had been promulgated since Plato, because awareness is not of elements but of compounds. It is only in artificial experimental conditions that the compound may be broken up into its separate elements, even though, as Wundt would admit, consciousness recognizes wholes rather than separate elements. Indeed, Wundt would argue that the experimental method is useful only for the investigation of a limited set of problems in psychology. One can, Wundt said, measure how large a whole one can grasp in consciousness, for example, the number of beats of a metronome, but the experiment could not account for the total workings of the mind.[13] Beyond these ultimately limited problems accessible to experimental methods, historical methods must take over.

> There are, indeed, certain facts at the disposal of psychology, which although they are not real objects, still have the character of psychical objects inasmuch as they possess these attributes of relative permanence, and independence of the observer. Connected with these characterisitics is the further fact that they are unapproachable by means of experiment in the common acceptance of the term. These facts are the *mental products* that have been developed in the course of history, such as language, mythological ideas, and customs. (Wundt, 1897/1969, 22)

One could, Wundt explained, infer the origin and development of these resultant processes, but experimental methods would be ineffective. "It soon became clear that for Wundt, social psychology was a source of data and of principles that had to be taken into account by general psychology, whereas for the Herbartians, social psychology had been simply an application of the principles of individual psychology" (Danziger, 1980b, 83). I will discuss later how it is these unclear, fluctuating, and isolated elements that make reading possible.

For Wundt, experiment could introduce a psychological orientation to what was previously a purely physiological problem. And since our awareness and our movements consist of an awareness of compounds, it could be possible to separate and then measure the elements of which those compounds are comprised. But, Wundt acknowledged, the elements separated and added would never be mistaken for the compound, the parts totaled did not equal the whole. In his laboratory Wundt measured reaction times and the time necessary to make decisions, employing his theory of volition—willed behavior— and was able then to throw light on issues that seemed psychological rather than physiological.

> The experiments which serve this purpose are the so-called *reaction experiments*. They may be described in their essentials as follows. A simple or complex volitional process is incited by an external sense-stimulus and then after the occurrence of certain psychical processes which serve in part as motives, the volition is brought to an end by a motor reaction. (Wundt, 1897/1969, 197)

In this way, Wundt attempted to follow "with exactness the succession of psychical processes in such a volition, and at the same time, by the deliberate variation of the conditions, to influence this succession in a systematic manner" (197). These studies constitute the first historical example of a coherent research program, explicitly directed towards psychological issues (Danziger, 1980, 106).

Wundt's work, and his influence through his students and their subsequent work, was in large part responsible for the establishment of experimental psychology laboratories throughout the United States, but it was the misrepresentation of his work by that same genealogic strata that led to the direction experimental psychology was to take in America and Great Britain in the twentieth century and which determined the scientific study of reading. "Indeed, for all the American students who went abroad to attend Wundt's lectures, very little of Wundt's psychological system survived the return passage" (Blumenthal, 1980, 130). This may have occurred for several reasons. First, Wundt's students did not speak German very well. "G. Stanley Hall dropped out of Wundt's lectures after one semester to turn to more understandable lectures that concerned physiology," and William James was appalled at the "intricacies and subtleties of [the German] language" (Blumenthal, 1980, 130). As an epigraph to his article, Blumenthal quotes what must be noted as a sarcastic James: "I must confess that to my mind there is something hideous in the glib Herbartian jargon about *Vorstellungsmassen* and their *Hemmungen* and *Hemmungssummen*, and *sinken* and *erheben* and *schweben*, and *Verschemelzungen* and *Complexionen"* (117). Second, Wundt's Kantian tradition, situated as it was in metaphysics, was rejected in favor of the more Spencerian and Millian physiological and materialist orientation of psychology. As G. Stanley Hall said of American psychology: "We need a psychology that is usable, efficient for thinking, living and working, and although Wundtian thoughts are now so successfully cultivated in academic gardens, they can never be acclimated here, as they are antipathetic to the American spirit and temper" (Blumenthal, 1980, 117).

Interestingly enough for our purposes, an alternative psychology existed that did understand and incorporate German philosophical tradition, and it was headed by John Dewey: "John Dewey was rather the exception among the early American psychologists for being thoroughly at home in German idealist philosophy" (Danziger, 1980b, 85). Later we will pursue the importance of Dewey's ideas to the tradition of reading and its pedagogy in American education. Dewey notwithstanding, though a significant number of Americans studied with Wundt, when they returned to America they did so with the laboratory equipment but not the same philosophical foundation with which to operate them as Wundt had developed. Nevertheless, his students, including the influential Titchener and Cattell, opened experimental laboratories in the United States and established this practice as psychology. Acknowledging the philosophical disparity between Wundt's views and those of his students, Hilgard (1987) notes that, "Rightly or wrongly, American psychologists sought to learn, from their empirical work, types of relationships that could be incorporated into existing American conceptions of psychological science, without adopting or even giving serious attention to the philosophical views behind the new psychology" (95). Titchener, a student of Wundt, would argue that sensation was the content of consciousness from which other aspects of experience could be derived. Titchener's textbook was organized by an incremental discussion of the qualities of the more elementary processes towards the development of our more complex thoughts, representing a bottom-up portrait of human psychology. And eschewing introspection altogether as overly subjective and not quantifiable, behaviorists looked for methods of psychological investigation that did not rely at all on introspection, which they felt to be an inexact method at best. John Watson, rejecting reflective contemplation, required a unit other than sensations, images and simple feelings to explain habits. His idea of the conditioned reflex derives from this program. Wundt's principle of apperception had disappeared from experimental psychology to be replaced by the reflex arc.

Wundt's detractors, such as Watson, explored an even more drastic experimental psychology that denied consciousness altogether. Empirical science became the hallmark of science, and reading as a form of psychology fell within the purview of experimental psychology from which it has not yet freed itself. Extremely influential reading specialists, such as Arthur Gates, were trained in experimental psychology labs dominated by Thorndike's systems of measurement and statistical analysis. Gates received his Ph.D. from Columbia with Robert Woodworth, a friend and colleague of E. L. Thorndike, whose own work in reading was to have great effect on reading pedagogy in the United States.

Wundt himself had argued that the experimental method was useful only for the investigation of a limited set of problems and that beyond these problems the historical and social methods must take over explanation. The experimental method was limited by its very nature. It was valuable, said Wundt, for studying the properties of a mind already developed, but it could not tell how this development occurred or how a particular individual mind actually functions in culturally significant settings.

> Wundt's conception of psychology was of an historical unfolding of human potential, a process based upon universal human characteristics but directed by extra-personal forces; forces that can only be understood at the level of *culture* and that can only be identified through the study of language and custom . . . it was not psychology's mission to establish the truth or falsity of the claims of other sciences, but to help come to understand and explain the stages reached by these other disciplines in the various epochs, and the factors governing their evolution within definable human aggregates. (Robinson, 1982, 150)

Yet, despite the self-imposed limitations of Wundt's psychology, which Wundt perhaps never fully acknowledged, American and British students of Wundt followed a different practice. Twentieth-century reading pedagogy adopted the developments of nineteenth-century science without question as the model for not only the reading process itself but for its study as well.

Nineteenth-Century Science and Reading Pedagogies

What did nineteenth-century science offer reading instruction in general, and why did America adopt a materialist behaviorism so readily and wholeheartedly? These are complex questions, and only partial and tentative answers may be offered here. First, behaviorism suggested that all reference to consciousness was mistaken and that all psychologists could expect to accomplish was to observe, as objectively as possible, the connection between stimuli (perceptions) and responses. Of course, in a country that continually reinvented itself and justified all activity on that reinvention, behaviorism proved a valuable resource in avoiding guilt and responsibility. The massacre of Native Americans, the rabid xenophobia that derived from the Puritan heritage, and the entire history of slavery in the United States could be discounted by doubting, as did behaviorism, the possibility and power of consciousness and the unconscious. The effects of history could be minimized by denying the power of the past to influence the present and by looking instead at acontextualized bonds between isolated stimulus and response. If human behavior could be comprised of innate or acquired (learned) habits, then the interest in psychology was in the connection and not the contents of the connection. Thorndike's psychology was "of the empirical kind, looking for explanation in physiological correlates, and [was] intentionally non-mentalistic" (Jonçich, 1968, 336). Thorndike will say that "History records no career, war, or revolution that can compare in significance with the fact that the correlation between intellect and morality is approximately .3, a fact to which perhaps a fourth of the world's progress is due" (in Jonçich, 310). There was, of course, much in American history that was better left unreflected upon. Events of the twentieth century offered little succor, and soldiers returning from war would prefer never to remember the actual experiences of what they had seen and done (Hemingway, 1921/1954). Thus, behaviorism would grow in a fertile, inviting bed in the United States.

Developments in nineteenth-century science made conditions for this growth viable. First, experimental science provided a framework by which staid beliefs were given new authority by scientific invention. Plato had suggested that the Ideal was represented in words that were the images of the things, that one needed to learn from authority the proper meaning of words, and that the whole was comprised of the sum of its parts. Thus, learning must proceed, under the direction of the one who knows, from the parts to the whole, starting with the letters. The Puritans had adopted Platonic linguistic theory as consistent with their experience of the world and as necessary for the continuation of reliance on hierarchical authority organized around orthodox beliefs. Phonic instruction, a practice institutionalized in the late nineteenth century but whose history coincides with public education in the United States, was founded upon the established belief that reading was intimately connected to the sound of the language. I have explored this association above and traced that association back to Platonic linguistic theory. The pervasiveness of this philosophy permeates reading instruction, as the literature will show. Frank Smith (1973) argues that "the belief that reading involves decoding, or transforming, or reconverting written symbols into spoken language . . . underlies practically all approaches to reading instruction . . ." (70). Charles Fries (1963) notes that the first stage in reading is the transfer stage, when auditory signs for language are transferred into a set of visual signs for the same signals. Jeanne Chall (1983) identifies the first stage of reading as the "Decoding State," when the learner must learn the arbitrary set of letters and associate these with corresponding parts of spoken words. And most recently, Marilyn Adams (1990) has argued that "programs explicitly designed to develop sounding and blending skills produce better word readers than those that do not." "I have even argued," she adds, "that synthetic phonics is of special value for young readers" (293).

Nineteenth-century science lent credence to this aspect of Platonic philosophy without requiring, indeed, by perhaps itself replacing, the spiritual component that had been so central to Puritan ideology. Focus on the parts supplanted emphasis on the whole as experience was reduced to its components by nineteenth-century science. Wundt had searched for ways to explain subjective experiences so that the events could be described without altering them. He had held that experimental introspection could only study sensation and perception, "where conditions could be repeated and the demands of the observer were so limited that they could be essentially automatized and could then approach the accuracy of [those of] external perceptions" (Hilgard, 1987, 44). These experiments would lead to valuable reading research (Cattell, 1886) in perception and tended to establish a reliance exclusively on experimental methods.

> The exact observation of volitional processes is . . . impossible in the case of volitional acts that come naturally in the course of life; the only way in which a thorough psychological investigation can be made, is, therefore, that of *experimental* observation. To be sure, we can not produce volitional acts of every kind at will, but we must limit ourselves to the observation of certain processes which can be easily influenced through external means and which terminate in external acts. (Wundt, 1897/1969, 197).

Those reading processes that could be measured became reading, and a science of reading arose based on the dubious assumptions of theorists who took their theories as reality. But reading as a natural ecological activity was not accessible to empirical scientific experimentation and therefore was denied identity as reading. As Ken Goodman notes, "The researchers became the test and the textbook authors . . . this consistency between research, text, and tests created an illusion of science" (1992, 191). Reading as a natural volitional activity could not be scientifically quantified for the motives and the conditions in which this reading are undertaken are never simple and are not always empirically evident.

Wundt's procedures and that of those who purported to follow him and adopt his practice, however, assumed a purity of perception and attention in experimental situations that were not conceivable in the world of daily life. Wundt seemed to know this; his followers ignored this realization. Reading as an activity engaged in with self-directed purpose in a particular ecology could not be experimentally recreated in the psychology laboratory. If reading was to be studied at all, and to be a science it had to be available to study by empirical methodology, it had first to be made quantifiable. Experiments, tests, and instruments were subsequently devised from a theoretical framework that presumed certain skills that could be subsumed under the rubric 'reading' and whose developmental acquisition made reading possible. Usually, the whole—reading—was defined in these tests by the sum of the parts—the series of subskills. For example, Arthur Gates, whose doctoral degree was earned in educational psychology under Edward Thorndike at Columbia University and who worked to a great extent in the area of reading, would note that when students were given the Gates Pronunciation Test,[14] which requires the reading aloud of 100 words ranging in length from short to long, those who were taught to read by a systematic approach [phonics] scored five and a half times better than those students who learned to read "opportunistically" (Gates, 1926, 686). However, what Gates does not address is the idea that students who have learned to read opportunistically could not be expected to read words out of context as well as students who have learned to do so: for the former, the very process of reading includes a context and occurs as a result of one. But Gates' work, and other experimental and educational psychologists who applied their work to the area of reading, was able, through the authority of science, to define reading and its pedagogy.

Experimental psychology itself, to which contemporary skills-based reading pedagogy is thoroughly wedded, was a product of the wedding of developing science to psychology in the nineteenth century. Helmholz's principle of conservation had suggested that all energy transformations result in energy at the end equal to that at the beginning. This principle suggested that mind, previously understood in rationalist philosophy as immaterial, might not in fact be so, and made way for a materialistic and deterministic psychology. Edward Thorndike, a psychology professor and researcher at Columbia University in New York in the late nineteenth and early twentieth century, was enormously influential in defining learning and pedagogies for the twentieth century. His laws of learning proceeded in part from his belief that mind and its matters were material and might be empirically measured and controlled. "No response of any human being occurs without some possibly discoverable cause and no situation exists whose effect could not with sufficient knowledge be predicted . . . the same situation acting on the same individual will produce always and inevitably the same response" (in Courtis, 1926, 559). The effect of this statement on reading instruction in the development at least of basal readers is beyond question.[15] Reading theory steeped in a materialistic and deterministic psychology would demand a firm pedagogy. In his work Thorndike established the methodology which persists today:

> 1. Consider the situation the pupil faces. 2. Consider the response you wish to connect with it. 3. Form the bond; do not expect it to come by a miracle. 4. Other things being equal, form no bond that will have to be broken. 5. Other things being equal, do not form two or three bonds when one will serve. 6. Form bonds in the way that they are required later to act. (in Gates, 1926, 550).

Here are described forms of reading pedagogy practiced in classrooms throughout the United States today. It is whence derives the entire notion of scope and sequence upon which not only basal readers but much of traditional curricula is built. From Thorndike's postulates will derive the mystique of "reading between the lines" or "finding the hidden meaning." Pedagogies built on such espoused beliefs fetishize reading, making it into the obsession Dewey earlier decried, requiring an authority to validate the process of reading, thereby ensuring its definitions.

But nineteenth-century science offered other buttresses to developing experimental psychology and, therefore, to reading pedagogies. Reinforcing associationist learning theory, developing atomic theory suggested that the whole could be broken up for analysis into smaller and smaller units as a procedure for scientific theory. Associationist theory declared that learning was a product of the concatenating of perceptions in consciousness and that concepts could be analyzed by reducing them to their separate parts. Resulting from these beliefs would be scientific support for a subskill approach to reading and language study. Other developments and characteristics of nineteenth-century science influenced psychological development in this direction in the twentieth century and had a powerful effect on reading pedagogy. Hilgard (1987) notes the tremendous influence of reductionism/elementarism in chemistry and physics on the developing experimental psychology. These principles argued for reducing the complex to the simple and focused emphasis on the elementary as a means of identifying the whole. Reductionism and elementarism argued that the whole was comprised of the sum of its parts and was no more than them. As I have said, science offered principles and techniques by which psychological phenomena might be quantified. Furthermore, developments in the study of electricity led to the production of instruments of measurement that would facilitate the discovery and/or invention of skills. The tachistoscope is one such instrument, and it has dominated reading research and instruction for the century since its development.

Not coincidentally, a divergent and hence only marginally influential development, also a product of nineteenth-century science but more the misbegotten than legitimate offspring, was represented in the notion of developing field theories and holism. These latter two developments, whose influence has been minimalized, were offered as a corrective to the reductionism and elementarism that dominated nineteenth-century science. And it may be that it is in this last influence that we will later trace in part some origins for the ideas of whole language espoused today. Field theories and holism derived in part from the work of physicist James Clerk Maxwell, who said that the idea of a magnetic field did not depend upon elementary particles. Rather, magnetic fields consisted of more than the sum

of the elementary particles. However, this holistic view, as with
the fate of Gestalt psychology, was marginalized over the next
century by the dominant powers, and subskill approaches to
reading prevailed. Subskill approaches to reading today still
predominate, now linked to cognitive psychology and science.
Crowder and Wagner state in their text *The Psychology of Reading*
(1992) that

> ... most experimental psychologists prefer to believe that
> the rules don't change radically as processing moves from
> simple to complex but instead the rules begin to interact
> and are more concealed than in the simple tasks. (56)

Cognitive Psychology

Experimental psychologists require a foundation that posits the
whole as the sum of its observable—and quantifiable—parts, and
Crowder and Wagner approach reading from the point of view
of cognitive psychology, a development of experimental
psychology during the latter part of the twentieth century.
During the first half of the twentieth century, the importance of
thinking to psychology was not clear, and as I have shown, there
was also not a satisfactory theory (of mind) leading to useful
experiments until the second half of the twentieth century. Prior
to the "cognitive revolution," Jerome Bruner (1983) tells us, "In
experimental psychology, 'thinking' was not a 'mainstream'
topic in psychology. Too mentalistic, too subjective, too shifty"
(105). Cognitive psychology, a strong and extremely influential
reaction against the positivistic and reductionist methodologies
of the first half of the century, offered an alternative view to
thought and a new area of research into mind. George Miller had
joked about psychology at the moment of the cognitive
revolution, "You're supposed to get at the mind through the eye,
ear, nose and throat if you're a real psychologist" (in Bruner,
105), and the developing cognitive psychology attempted to
recover mind from its material basis. Howard Gardner (1983)
traces the rapid development of cognitive science in the latter
half of the twentieth century. He suggests that it was Karl Lashly

who, in 1948, struck the first decisive blow against behaviorism and for cognitive science by arguing that in language production first comes meaning in the hierarchy of skills, with movement proceeding "down to syntax and choice of sounds" (9). Lashly's would seem to contrast with the dominant view of language, which derived from Platonic doctrine, and would offer an alternative to the dominant subskills approach to reading pedagogy. But it is also true that this early identification of a hierarchy verified so closely by cognitive science would soon permit discussion of a bottom-up view of thinking and reading as well. Cognitive science, or at least its dominant branch, would become merely another hermeneutical explanation of reading, and the various cognitive processes would be viewed as subskills that together comprised thinking. The alternative view, one we will suggest here and take up later, the top-down approach or an ecological approach to reading, has, Gardner admits, "rarely been followed up" (126). Later we will explore reasons for this rejection, but for now we must explore the development of the dominant branch of cognitive psychology and its influence on reading.

Gardner suggests that cognitive psychology grew as a product of nineteenth-century scientific efforts, when scientists' knowledge of physical matter and the nature of living matter had been so carefully explored that it seemed that questions concerning the matter of mind might be available to solution as well. It grew as well when aspects of the dominant psychological orientation proved ineffective for answering questions of mind. For example, behaviorism did not offer a satisfactory answer to cognitive scientists exploring aspects of learning; questions of the efficacy of the Stimulus-Response (S-R) psychology continued to be addressed in the literature. William James had criticized this reflex arc, and Dewey addressed the matter as early as 1896 in his criticism of the reflex arc. There Dewey argued that experience was not broken up into stimuli and consequent responses but rather, ought to be understood as a "continuous circuit" by means of which learning may be achieved. Each moment along the circuit was conceptualized not as an isolated instance of existence, stimulus, and response, rather, said Dewey, these successive moments are ". . . teleological distinc-

tions, that is, distinctions of function, or parts played with
reference to reaching or maintaining an end"(in Westbrook,
1991, 69). Experience could not be dichotomized into the
dualisms of sensation and idea posited by the classical S-R
response. Rather, one must see experience as a whole and each
moment must be understood functionally based on a specific
end and not on an identified connection. This clearly was
antithetical to the dominant learning theory being developed by
Thorndike and promulgated by reading theorists, such as Gates
and Gray. Later, Lewis Tolman (Gardner, 1983) would argue that
stimulus-response theory left out the principle of the Law of
Emphasis, by which certain "stimuli" in the environment were
highlighted for relevant cues.

    As the critiques of behaviorism and positivism grew and
alternative psychological explanations developed, and in an
attempt to gain acceptance, practioners and theorists attempted
to minimize the differences between the dominant ideologies
and the newer developing cognitive science. At first, Bruner
says, the whole notion of mind as a topic seemed to become
legitimate only by "clever ruses, procedural conventions for
making mental processes look more 'objective.' The basic trick
was to state your findings in centimeters, grams and seconds—
c.g.s." (1983, 107). The tools invented by nineteenth-century
science proved valuable in this effort, and the tachistoscope and
its variants have so thoroughly dominated reading research in
this present century that one does not have to look far to
discover a study based upon these mechanisms. But the direction
of the discourse systems in cognitive psychology developed and
offered new areas for study— cognition, the processes of thought
replacing learning, the products of that thought. In such a
manner, cognitive psychology assumed, says Bruner, an early
disguise for espousing mentalism "in an age of behaviorism,"
and information theory replaced learning theory as the focus of
experimentation. Now psychologists began to discuss processes
rather than outcomes and to focus on the activity of mind rather
than its contents. The importance of this shift for understanding
reading and reading research is immense.

    Information processing suggests that information is
managed in an ordered sequence of stages, in which at each

stage information is acted upon before passing on to the next stage. As one textbook on cognition describes the process: "Our sensory receptors receive information, which is changed during one stage and passed on through a sequence of stages until we either respond or store the information in memory" (Maitlin, 1983, 4). In this schema, activity of mind could now be defined and studied as the concatenation of separate mental processes identified as perception, attention, recall, and conceptualization of experience, and the unification of those processes to create concepts. Reading could now be viewed as the product of the coordination of varying processes into a combined whole. Of course, though that whole could be viewed as greater than and different from the sum of its parts, the identification of separate processes and the still strong influence of behaviorism and hermenuetics seemed to lead in just the opposite direction. As a recent book concerning the psychology of reading states: "A theory of reading must explain how and when different parts are interrelated as a reader progresses through a text . . . a theory of reading must describe how the different component processes are coordinated" (Just & Carpenter, 1987, 16). Again, meaning was already defined, and reading could be understood as the procedural coordination of cognitive processes that could discover that meaning. In discussing processes—acts of the mind—cognitivists, of whom Just and Carpenter identify themselves as two, were able to ignore the actual contents of the mind, thereby continuing the split with which psychology had wrestled since its consolidation into a formal discipline. As Wittgenstein would say:

> The confusion and barrenness of psychology is not to be explained by calling it a "young science"; its state is not comparable with that of physics, for instance in its beginnings. . . .
>
> For in psychology, there are experimental methods and *conceptual confusion*. . . .
>
> The existence of experimental methods makes us think we have the means of solving the problems which trouble us, though problems and methods pass one another by. (in Bruner, 1983, 129)

Hence, in attempting to establish psychology as a science, cognitivists eshewed philosophy, thereby ignoring aspects of the larger concerns regarding mind and its nature. This was the earlier justification for the rejection of Freud and Wundt, whose insistence on the relevance of philosophy—what Bruner will call later "folk psychology"—to human mind was central. "For there are no causes to be grasped with certainty where the act of creating meaning is concerned, only acts, expressions, and contexts to be interpreted" (Bruner, 1990, 118). But the direction cognitive psychology took made it possible to quantify experience based on particular processes studied and to ignore the enormous influence of culture and environment on thinking and reading.

Reading and Information Theory

Equally important to reading research and pedagogy was the work on information theory, an enormous influence on the theory and practice of the gestating cognitive psychology. By reconceptualizing the nature of information, information theory made it possible to think of information apart from its particular content. Information theory suggested that information could be thought of as a matter of a "single decision between two equally plausible alternatives." Hence, for information theory the process took precedence over the content. The basic unit of information was defined as the *bit* (short for binary digit); that is, "the amount of information that was required to select one message from two equally probable alternatives" (Gardner, 1983, 21). Clearly, however, information theory accepted the idea that alternative choices could be preestablished and based on known grammars and syntaxes and that, therefore, it was unnecessary to explore the meaning-making capacities of individuals. Meaning was the result of the processing of information, an already defined category. Meaning making could only function within well-defined categories of possibility. "Information processing needs advance planning and precise rules" in order to recognize possibilities, argues Bruner (1990, 5), though, of course, the world of actual experience is hardly so definable.

Such precise rules restrict meaning making rather than enhance it, can define meaning making in only a limited sense, but cannot account for aspects of experience such as doubt, polysemy, and metaphor. Information theory cannot answer how children conceive of the notion of reading, but it can address issues of what is the most efficient way of teaching them to perceive specific text. However, as I have argued, how we teach students to perceive text will determine how texts will be defined. In Italo Calvino's *Invisible Cities* (1972), Marco Polo describes the city of Tamara, where everything is known by its sign:

> Your gaze scans the streets as if they were written pages: the city says everything you must think, makes you repeat her discourse, and while you believe you are visiting Tamara you are only recording the names with which she defines herself and all her parts. (14)

Of course, having learned how to read in Tamara, "you leave Tamara without having discovered it. Outside, the land stretches, empty, to the horizon; the sky opens, with speeding clouds. In the shape that chance and wind give the clouds, you are already intent on recognizing figures: a sailing ship, a hand, an elephant" (14). Having learned to read signs, one looks for signs and not meaning. Tamara has been read but not comprehended. So too with reading pedagogies and information theory: The latter may throw light on how readers perceive words—an already defined category, but cannot explain how Moby Dick may be understood by a particular individual as a symbol of *either* God or the Devil or both or neither. Nor could information theory account for the particular world view of a machinist in the latter part of the twentieth century with regard to robotics as compared with the world view of the engineer who devises the robot. Information theory, valuable as it was as an alternative to behaviorist orientations toward stimuli, could not account for the meaning making that comprises thinking and reading. And though depth processing has replaced linear sequential processing as a model of information systems, both are still premised on known entities which are information.

Information theory made possible the consideration of information apart from the particular transmission device, for whatever was information preexisted and could be processed along certain channels that could be mapped and explained. How to account for the meaning of the word STOP on a traffic sign as compared to its appearance in the Supremes' song, "Stop, In the Name of Love," were not issues immediately addressable by information theory. Based in part on the work of Claude Shannon at Bell Laboratories, information theory posited information as already existent in the text and which must then be processed by the brain. With the advent of cognitive psychological approaches, researchers could now focus on the effectiveness of a communication via any mechanism and could consider cognitive processes apart from the particular embodiment of the message. And scientific experiments could be devised to characterize processing in the human mind; indeed, this accounts for the plethora of experiments using nonsense syllables. Also, with the computer as exemplar, programs were written to simulate actual activity of mind.

> The theory that we have developed to describe skilled reading has been expressed as a computer-simulation model. . . . The simulation, called READER, provides a single, integrated model of the various processes of skilled reading. The model ensures that individual processes and structures function properly together. . . . READER was designed to simulate how human readers comprehend a technical passage, and, in particular, to account for the time they take to read successive words and phrases in the passage. (Just & Carpenter, 1987, 19)

In other words, cognitive scientists attempted to describe the mechanisms underlying the processing of thought without regard to the content of that thought. Here seemed to be a structuralism that denied agency but that could be employed to explain the production of meaning, an issue behaviorist S-R theory would not address. Language was viewed as a mechanism for producing meaning and could, therefore, be studied as a mechanism. In this structure, the meaning of a speech act is the intention of the speaker to communicate certain things. The meaning of a sentence is a set of possible speech acts/intentions that it can be used to exhibit. The meaning of a word is the use to which it can be put. This can be explored in either a paradigmatic or syntagmatic strategy and could lead to interesting studies in various disciplines (see Pettit, 1975; Fries, 1963). But in either case, language is understood as a system of contrasts that operates according to laws that can be discovered. Reading theory and its pedagogy proceeded from such ideas. As Crowder and Wagner (1992) argue in the introduction of their study and which, of course, indicates the rationale for their selection of reported studies, ". . . this particular book . . . does not take comprehension as a primary responsibility or even as a coequal responsibility next to the process of coping with print"(5). Of course, as Derrida and others have noted, these and all other contrasts are arbitrary. For Derrida, there is nothing wrong with writing or reading a text against a background of unconventional contrasts and giving it quite an unconventional meaning. Reading for structuralists was the study of language as a mechanism for meaning production, but they denied agency to the reader and seemed to maintain the old split which had begun with Plato. Cognitive psychologists, working in the area of reading, also underestimated the importance of meaning in the process of reading.

Gardner (1983) suggests that cognitive science claimed to have dissolved the mind-body problem that had plagued earlier psychology. Using the electronic computer as a model central to understanding mind, cognitive science now had a vocabulary and a model for describing the software, the program itself, in computer language apart from the physical hardware of brain/mind. Shannon had mapped paths of communication which have since been revised. Now the structure of problem solving could be described regardless of the equipment. Of course, this only seemed to resolve the mind/body problem in the direction of mind, a typical Cartesian solution to a much more complex problem, as Parker had noted in the century earlier. But cognitive science, says Gardner, made a deliberate decision to de-emphasize certain factors that may be important for cognitive functioning, but whose inclusion would only complicate unnecessarily the cognitive-scientific enterprise. These factors included affective factors or emotions, contributions of historical and cultural factors, and the role of background context in which particular thoughts and actions occur. Cognitive scientists believed that they could discuss the manipulations of symbols without having to talk about the content of those symbols. Mind was now not the physical brain itself, but was, rather, the software program, which could be identified, explored, and mapped by what had become classic reductionist theory, breaking the whole into its parts. Hence, a psychology of reading could begin with perception: as if perception itself is not willed. In this approach to cognitive psychology, the agency of self was ultimately denied. In "depth of processing" schools of cognitive psychology, "the nature of incoming information is determined by the operations performed during its input, which include analysis not only of sensory aspects but of semantic aspects as well" (Gardner, 1983, 127). But this direction of psychology, as Gardner suggests, though it might attempt to explain what structures one brings to experience, may be traced back to Wundt's ideas and is hardly revolutionary, indeed, may no longer be psychology but cognitive science. But, as we shall see, this approach to psychology had existed early in the twentieth century but for various reasons was discounted and marginalized by other more powerful ideologies that served other interests.

Jerome Bruner acknowledges that this perspective flawed cognitive psychology from its beginning. Claiming that cognitive science/psychology has shifted from studying the construction of meaning to the processing of information, Bruner attributes this direction taken to the computer model.

> Very soon, computing became the model of the mind, and in place of the concept of meaning there emerged the concept of computability. Cognitive processes were equated with the programs that could be run on a computational device, and the success of one's efforts to "understand," say, memory or concept attainment, was one's ability realistically to simulate such human conceptualizing or human memorizing with a computer program. . . . This new reductionism provided an astonishingly libertarian program for the new cognitive science that was being born. It was so permissive, indeed, that even the old S-R learning theorist and associationist student of memory could come right back into the fold of the cognitive revolution so long as they wrapped their old

concepts in the new terms of information processing.
(Bruner, 1990, 7)

Hence, even with the advent of cognitive psychology and evolving science, reading instruction could and did remain embedded in older, traditional pedagogies. In their mainstream text, *The Psychology of Reading and Language Comprehension* (1987), Just and Carpenter identify a theory of reading with a cognitive approach. This approach focuses on the processes underlying an identified cognitive skill. The first such process identified by Just and Carpenter includes "what information in the text starts the process [of reading]" (4). What is immediately evident is that this cognitive approach situates information in the text and identifies reading as the operation of processing this information through various psychological loops. It does not account for perception as itself a willed activity. The role of the reader in constructing meaning is minimized, reduced to the manipulation of information through a network.

Not that there were not alternatives to the cognitive psychology tradition; there were and they were quickly marginalized. They are epitomized in Gardner's distinction between the Establishment and Gibsonian perspectives on perception. Briefly, it is an argument over intentionality, with the Establishment eschewing belief in the natural basis of perception and the Gibsonians espousing the ecological perspectives for it. Gibsonians find the relevant information for understanding perception and cognition within the environment and the organism's relationship to it, whereas Establishment psychologists/scientists "pay attention instead to the presuppositions and biases built into the organisms and to the way information in the world becomes transformed or reconstructed upon its apprehension by the organisms" (Gardner, 1983, 317). I will deal in a future chapter with a more detailed exploration of this distinction, but we may see here the embedding of traditional reading pedagogy in the ideology of the latter, who argue that reality must conform to conceptual images, and the former, who argue that there are natural laws governing the organism's relationship to the environment. Gibsonians search for natural laws governing the organism's relation to the environment, and cognitive scientists look for cognitive laws that carry out operations on mental representations. Research and pedagogy into reading are quite different based upon which psychological school one follows. Cognitive scientists retain the mind-body split explicit in Platonic philosophy, and the Gibsonians attempt to dissolve that split.

This is the traditional polemic concerning reality and learning that has consumed philosophy and reading pedagogy for two thousand years. Complains Gardner,

> Here we are, two thousands after the first discussions about perception, several hundred years after the philosophical debates between the empiricists and the rationalists raged, and leading scientists are still disagreeing about fundamentals. (Gardner, 1983, 317)

And it is the polemic that organizes differing philosophies of reading and its pedagogy today. Clearly, the debate is heavily weighted on the side of the cognitivists. This occurs as the hegemonic group continually strives to discover methods that leave traditional authority embedded in hierarchies in power. Deborah Meier says in *The Nation* of September 21, 1992, that "By 1950, Dewey's progressive vision of schools for democracy had lost out and efficiency-driven, rigidly tracked schools won the day" (272). That efficiency is today linked by Frank Smith to computers and can be traced back to the powerful influence of cognitive psychology and its models. But I am convinced that the marginalization of alternative views of reading was also accomplished by a concerted effort to discount those views by the hegemony of science, itself serving the interests of dominant powers and cultures. At least in large part, alternative views of reading can be found embedded in Deweyan pragmatism, which I will show later to be connected to ecological perspectives of perception. But it is in the travails of pragmatism that we may discover, in part, the processes by which reading instruction has been marginalized in the twentieth century, allowing the occupation of reading by cognitive psychologists/scientists. This is always a matter of ideology and so we must again look to history to understand our position in the present. Dewey's pragmatism would offer philosophical support for a whole-language reading program. That is to say that pragmatism, in which whole language is deeply embedded, is a philosophy organized around the primacy of practice and defines action as the production of knowledge. Whole language argues that reading is a natural activity learned as unaffectedly as speech. Reading and learning are equivalent activities and are not hierarchically related, with the former making possible the latter. But the destruction of this hierachy by pragmatism and whole language threatened the entire educational system, itself a buttress of the political system. The fate of pragmatism and whole language is directly linked to the prevailing ideologies in which they developed and which they demanded be changed. I would like in the next chapter to discuss the relationship between pragmatism and whole language and to address the political world in which both grew and were hostilely received.

NOTES

1.   See William Schubert's discussion of curriculum history in his *Curriculum; Perspective, Paradigm, Possibility* (1986).

2.   For an excellent discussion of the relation of the oral tradition to literacy see Walter Ong (1982).

3.   Strains of this tradition remain in the emphasis on phonics given in contemporary reading pedagogies. It assumes that saying the word ensures knowing the word. Of course, this is so only if the word is part of the oral vocabulary of the reader.

4.   We know that spelling was regularized, in part, by the demands of printers who needed to stock their print trays with letters and who required a standardized orthogrpahy to enable the extended marketing of their product throughout an area.

5.   We may here note the echo of Mitford Mathews' (1966) belief that reading is unnatural and has nothing to do with nature.

6.   Of course, the notion of children as helpless and in need of protection that could only be afforded by an educational system is addressed in Philip Aries (1965) and Alan Block (forthcoming).

7.   It is interesting how influential Germany has been on pedagogy in the United States. Most recently, the former superintendent

of the Department of Public Instruction in Wisconsin, Herbert Grover, returned from visits to Germany and Japan advocating the instant infusion of what has come to be known as Tech Prep into curricular construction.

8.   Farnham's philosophical base in psychology is, of course, consistent with the contemporary rise of psychology as a formal discipline of consciousness and learning, with which he must have been familiar.

9.   It is interesting to compare this view of the sentence with that of George Farnham who suggested that thought was bound in the sentence.

10.   Cornel West, in *The American Evasion of Philosophy: A Genealogy of Pragmatism* (1989), says that though Dewey claims never to have read Marx, he finds Dewey's statement hard to accept: ". . . Dewey confessed in 1930—at the age of seventy-one—that he did not know enough about Marx to discuss his philosophy. This seems not to have deterred him from listing *Capital* as the most influential book in the past twenty-five years" (102).

11.   William Gray seems to have written the first doctoral dissertaion on reading, a quantitative study entitled "Studies of Elementary School Reading Through Standardized Tests" (in Smith, 1986).

12.   For a discussion of language learning as the development of learning functionings of language see Michael Halliday, *Learning How to Mean* (1975).

13.   For contemporary illustrations of Wundt's methods, see the moving window experiments reported in Rayner and Pollatsek (1987).

14.   This test is still administered today under the name Gates-Macgintie.

15.   For a more complete analysis of the influence of Thorndike's laws of learning on the construction of basal readers, see Goodman et al., *Report Card on Basal Readers* (1987).

CHAPTER 2

Pragmatism, Populism, and Whole Language

Whole Language and Pragmatism: Roots

Whole language is an umbrella term that refers to a plethora of pedagogical practices that are developed from the assumption that language is known and learned as a whole, functional entity in the process of use rather than through the concatenation of its separate and isolable parts which are learned for future use. In light of this construction, whole language can be situated within American pragmatism, itself to be situated within the development of populism in the latter decades of the twentieth century. To historicize whole language in this manner will be to explore the particular set of practices that were responsible for the marginalization of this alternative theory by the practices of the dominant ideologies and which led to the rise of subskill approaches to reading and learning in the twentieth century.

Whole language asserts that language is acquired only in a functional and meaningful manner and context. Whole language asserts that language is not learned to be used; rather, language is learned in the exercise of its use (Halliday, 1975). And whole language means that, just as language cannot be acquired except in a functional and meaningful ecology, neither, says pragmatist philosopher[1] Richard Rorty (1991, xix) in a related context, can language be understood separate from its users. Language is not an extrinsic tool to be acquired for the pursuit of truth; rather, language is a resource for making truth. There is no truth outside of language. Rorty asserts that there is no way to "break out of language in order to compare it with something else" that might better serve human purposes. Whole language means that language is central to human communication and thought and that knowledge comes into existence within a specific ecology that includes language and that can only be understood within that ecology. As whole-language theorists aver, "A reality that exists within the limits of language may not be reality in some absolute sense, but it is as much a reality as the individual and the language community will ever know" (Goodman, Smith, Meredith & Goodman, 1987, 20).

Whole language, like pragmatism, is a method, says William James (1907/1970, 42) "of settling metaphysical disputes that otherwise might be interminable . . . to try to interpret each notion by tracing its respective practical consequences." Whole language, like pragmatism, is a perspective on the self, on learning and community; it is a mode of learning and relationship. "American pragmatism," says Cornel West (1989, 5) "is a diverse and heterogeneous tradition. But its common denonominator consists of a future-oriented instrumentalism that tries to deploy thought as a weapon to enable more effective action." As I will show in Chapters 3 and 4, reading occurs, as does all thinking and learning, based on the anticipation of the future. This anticipation is not a simple algorithmic procedure but is situated in the entire social context of the individual and may only be heuristically conceptualized. As a whole-language activity, reading can only be practiced and understood in its multivocal, social context, in its particular ecology. As with the conceptualization of knowledge in pragmatism, comprehension in reading must be understood as situationally, functionally, and socially constructed. Reading occurs, says Constance Weaver (1988, 29), ". . . within a social and situational context. More accurately, there are a variety of social and situational factors, a variety of contexts, that affect the activation of one's schemas and the outcomes of the reader-text transaction." Rather than assign a definition to reading or elaborate an epistemology of it, whole-language practitioners recognize that reading may serve many functions, depending on the purposes and expectations of the reader.

As I have shown in Chapter 1, how one was taught to read determined to a large extent not only how one read but what one read and what reading was considered to be. The use of language in reading—and, as I will argue in Chapters 3 and 4, in any other context—can only be understood within the social context in which it is practiced and which it fosters, a context of community in which that language has come to have meaning and which sets the stage for meaning making.[2]

Originally, all first languages are learned, as James Gee (1990, 150) suggests, "in face-to-face communication with intimates which we achieve in our initial socialization within the 'family' as this is defined within a given culture." Shirley Brice Heath has shown in her study (1982, 366) that the uses of language and text—what we call literacy—are learned in the particular environments to which one belongs in a functional and pragmatic system. "[Because] the home patterns of language use are inextricably linked to other cultural features, changes in those language uses which so powerfully determine a child's success in school and future vocational orientation will come very slowly, and only in concert with numerous other types of change. The ways with words transmitted across generations, and covertly embedded and intertwined with other cultural patterns, will not change rapidly." For Heath, there are no correct or proper readings for her population; rather, there are the sanctioned and nonsanctioned readings and each results from the particular environment in which reading occurs. These categories, when understood metaphysically as correct/ incorrect, true/false, can only be understood as a particular social construct, and the unwillingness of the schools to recognize the existence of patterns and meanings of language use in the community in which that school resides produces educational failures.

This position on language learning and literacy is a position coincident with pragmatism. The pragmatist theory of truth, says Andrew Feffer (1993, 3) in his recent study of the Chicago pragmatists John Dewey, George Herbert Mead, and James Hayden Tufts, holds that "knowledge is relative to social and behavioral 'situations,' that it is provisional, and that it evolves as an instrument of problem solving . . ." Learning in school ought to occur as a result of this understanding. Randolph Bourne, who followed Dewey's pragmatic method

even after a break with his master over America's entry into
World War I, would write out of his pragmatism that "The
school might be a place where play passes insensibly to work,
and aimless experiment into purposeful construction" (in Blake,
1990). This philosophical perspective understands that language,
indeed all learning, must be conceived and constructed holistically not for itself but for its exercise in effect. John Mayher, an
English education researcher (1990, 104) asserts that "Tacit
learning [whole language] is holistic and top-down in the sense
that whenever analytically independent bits of knowledge and
skill are acquired they are mastered in the context of a meaning-
making task rooted in experience. In that sense they are acquired
in passing, on the way to doing something else which has a
meaningful integrity for the learner. Learning is not something
distinct from living but an integral part of all life processes."
Whole language asserts that education ought not to be
preparation for life; for whole language as for pragmatism,
education is life. "That education is literally and all the time its
own reward means that no alleged study or discipline is
educative unless it is worthwhile in its own immediate having"
(Dewey, 1916/66). Frank Smith argues (1988, 200) that children
learn language because it is meaningful, "because it changes the
world and is not arbitrary or capricious. . . . Children will not
stop learning anything that is meaningful to them. . . ." Thus,
whole language is more than a series of classroom practices;
whole language is a pragmatic system for diurnal existence
which not only has extension outside the classroom, but actually
functions there as well. Frank Smith (1988b, 128) states, "[T]hat is
what whole language is—a philosophy, not a slogan or a method
of teaching reading."

Whole language is situated on a philosophical base
separate and distinct from that of other approaches to reading
and language. Whole language argues, as does pragmatism, that
there is a distinction between what one intends to teach and
what is ultimately learned and that this difference is based in the
transaction between the potential learner and the material to be
learned. Both elements of the transaction must be understood in
their ecological context. "[M]eaning," says Dewey (1910/1991,
125), "thus signifies that we have acquired in the presence of

objects definite attitudes of response which lead us, without reflection, to anticipate certain possible consequences." Whole language believes that learning is a natural outcome of having questions and having the means to pursue possible answers. "All judgement," says Dewey (1910/1991, 119), "all reflective inference, presupposes some lack of understanding, a partial absence of meaning. We reflect in order that we may get hold of the full and adequate significance of what happens. . . . We think in order to grasp meaning, but none the less every extension of knowledge makes us aware of blind and opaque spots, where with less knowledge all that seemed obvious and natural." Whole language believes that language learning, which includes reading, is a natural activity that occurs in the course of daily living and is socially mediated by interactions and transactions with other language learners and practitioners. Gordon Wells (1986, 43) in his study of children's literacy development states that

> Children learn language because they are predisposed to do so. How they set about the task is largely determined by the way they are: seekers after meaning who try to find the underlying principles that will account for the patterns that they recognize in their experiences. At each successive stage . . . they are capable of dealing with new evidence of a certain degree of complexity and they are able to incorporate it into their developing language system.

Whereas subskill approaches to reading posit a series of incremental but absolute criteria—letter recognition, phonemic awareness, literal comprehension skill, vocabulary, decoding skills—the acquisition of which will lead finally to "reading,"[3] whole language as pragmatism argues that a criterion for knowing anything—criteria for knowledge—is so only, as Rorty says, because "some particular social practice needs to block the road of further inquiry, halt the regress of interpretations, in order to get things done" (1991, xli). Criteria in whole language and pragmatism are recognized as arbitrary and socially mediated realities and not absolute entities. To read anything requires first the existence of doubt and question; this uncertainty will constrain what may be produced in reading. For the pragmatist, as for the whole language practitioner, meaning is constructed in the exercise of living and absolute concepts such as objectivity, subjectivity, conventionality, or emotionality are not really categories of truth. Language is experienced as a process of social and personal invention from the outset, and it is originally learned from whole to parts. Goodman (1986, 19) writes that "scribbling, reversed letters, invented spellings, creative punctuation, and reading and writing miscues are charming indications of growth towards control of the language processes."

Of course, like everything else, whole language is only theory and represents an alternative perspective on life. "Theory starts," says Rorty, "when somebody has doubts about what everyone has always believed, and suggests that there is another way of looking at the matter" (Rorty, 1991, 25). So conceived, whole language is a theoretical perspective on the practices of everyday life. It is ultimately a means of reflection, of thinking, and of making reality. But in this sense, and as a pedagogical methodology, whole language/pragmatism makes possible the creation of selves alternatively produced than those selves developed under other pedagogies.

Whole language may be understood as deeply embedded in American pragmatism, a method which argues, as Cornel West (1989, 198) says of Rorty's pragmatism, "not that the world is not out there, only that the world does not speak our descriptive language of it. The world can cause us to hold certain beliefs, but these beliefs are elements of human languages, and human languages are our own creations—creations that change over time and space." The ideal notions of Truth or Knowledge do not exist for the whole-language theorist/pragmatist; rather, these categories are understood as a construction against uncertainty and doubt. For whole-language theorists/ pragmatists, our creations are always a product of our theories, which must always be known to be a result of and realized in the exercise of an activity. I will argue in Chapters 3 and 4 that this is a way of understanding a psychology of reading and of formulating an ecological basis for reading pedagogy. For now we acknowledge that a theory is a different way of being in the world; theories are partial attempts to understand the way the world is. Or as Rorty (1991, xlii) himself says of the pragmatic

method: what links Dewey and Foucault, James and Nietzsche is
". . . the sense that there is nothing deep down inside us except
what we have put there ourselves, no criteria that we have not
created in the course of creating a practice, no standard of
rationality that is not an appeal to such a criteria, no rigorous
argumentation that is not obedience to our own convention."

Both pragmatism and whole language are concerned
"about the holistic consequences of beliefs and actions when
[believers] seek to clarify meanings, . . . inquire into what is true
(small t) and false, good and evil, and beautiful and ugly"
(Cherryholmes, 1993, 26). Both whole language and pragmatism
argue, with William James, that truth happens to an idea and
does not inhere in it. To deny that is to deny the meaning-
making potential of the individual whose language produces
meaning. In her work as teacher, Cynthia Lewis (1993, 460)
comes to understand that in her efforts to help her student, Rick,
learn to read, she has inhibited the recognition and development
of his authentic voice by the imposition of *her* meaning on *his*
text. Trying to force her meaning of a fable on the reading of her
student, Lewis alienates Rick as he comes to understand her
denial of *him* in her denial of *his* meaning. Their respective
meanings had derived from the whole of Rick's life as well as her
own and from the cultures in which both functioned. "For it was
not just Rick's voice and my own that filled the room that day,
but many others, including the voice of *authority*, in the form of
interpretations sanctioned by middle-class social codes and
school culture, as well as the voice of *resistance*, both mine and
Rick's." Therefore, as does pragmatism, whole language places
the meaner in the center of activity, of knowledge production,
and the interest of whole language is in the *process* of meaning
making and not in the *product* of it: the product is always a point
in a process of further meaning making. This is the essence of
pragmatism.

Both whole language and pragmatism posit words as
resources and not as answers. William James (1907/1970, 46)
asserts that to follow pragmatism is "to use words to work
within the stream of personal experience . . . as a program for
more work, and more particularly, as an indication of the ways
in which existing realities may be *changed*." Whole-language

classroom teacher Timothy O'Keefe (Mills & Clyde, 1990, 92) asserts that

> I have learned how valuable it is to follow the children's lead in creating a learning environment that is exciting and interesting. This, of course, does not imply throwing up my hands and allowing the children to do whatever they want. By planning open-ended invitations and questions, using strategy sharing sessions, allowing meaningful choices, and instilling in children the notion that they are competent learners with much to share, we can help children go easily and confidently beyond what they currently know.

Whole language and pragmatism are methods of inquiry and hence methods of learning. "Ideas are true," says James (1907/1970, 49), *"just in so far as they help us to get into satisfactory relations with other parts of our experience to summarize them and get about among them by conceptual short-cuts instead of following the interminable succession of particular phenomena."*[4] Truth is an activity of making connections between what I will refer to in Chapter 5 as the phenomena and the root responsibility. Whole-language classrooms operate on the belief that "Language seems to develop to meet the needs of each individual as required for thinking, for communicating, for expressing ideas, and for learning," says John Mayher (1990, 135). "This process is largely unconscious and responds naturally and automatically to appropriate experiences. What is conscious and intentional are the goals of language use: Participating in the family conversation, telling or understanding a story, describing what happened on a recent trip, or explaining how something works" (135). Identity, as I will later argue, occurs in the process of language activity, of reading and making connections, and in the knowledge of the consequence of the relation between things "whose role as necessary elements in one another is appreciated for what it is" (Ollman, 1988, 68). Pragmatism and whole language accept knowledge as derived from relations in the activity and conscious awareness of those relations. Whole-language classrooms accept that children develop language practices in activity and in concert with other language users and not that they are given those practices. Indeed, Vygotsky (1988) has clearly shown that concepts cannot be taught; rather, they can only be learned.

These connections between pragmatism and whole language offer some insight into the development of reading pedagogy in the twentieth century. I believe that the political roots and position of pragmatism in the United States during this time may have defined the marginalization of pragmatism and the marginalization of reading practices that derive from that pragmatism in what has come to be known as whole language in the latter part of the century. As I have suggested in Chapter 1, the roots of whole language extend far deeper than the nineteenth century, but it was during that time in American educational history that a philosophical system—or as Rorty (1991) and West (1989) would contend, an anti-philosophical system—arose that offered an alternative perspective on educational practice that had developed in American culture. What Goodman, Shannon, and others call the New Education (1987) had advocacy and practice in the nineteenth century, but its marginalization is an historical phenomenon whose roots might be traced back into the late nineteenth and early twentieth century. Whole language, as a philosophy, has recently received acknowledgment as having pedagogical credibility, but still, it is only a marginal acceptance. It is still true that 85 percent of language arts elementary classrooms are organized around the use of basal reading programs. The historical conditions that led to what West (1989, 4) refers to as pragmatism's "emergence, development, decline and resurgence," its unacknowledged alignment with American populism, and the confluence of pragmatism, populism, and whole language help uncover the suppression of whole language and pragmatism in the twentieth century.

Pragmatism and Politics

First let me acknowledge pragmatism's situation in politics. Since I have suggested links between pragmatism and whole language, the identification of pragmatism with politics will situate whole language as well in politics; in this way its marginalization in the twentieth century might be historically understood. Dewey's pragmatism, as Deborah Meier (1992) notes, was ineffective by the mid-1950s. Dewey himself complained that he could never get anyone to give up his/her beliefs in epistemology—the study of knowledge. For the pragmatist, as for the whole-language practitioner, there could be no path to knowledge because knowledge existed in experience and was contextual and ever changing. But traditional Philosophy and Pedagogy, ever lovers, persisted in their beliefs in the presence of absolute Truth and Reality and Knowledge. Reading pedagogy during the twentieth century, as I have suggested, continued to secure its belief that knowledge *could* be defined and that the path to it could be known for all pursuers of it. Reading became knowing the meaning of words, and words became the concatenation of letters. Comprehension of text was a product of proper reading and not the very process of reading itself. An epistemology of reading argued for the necessity of acquiring the subskills that the greater whole— comprehension—may be produced. Language arts instruction in the schools followed this skill approach and developed methods and evaluative procedures to organize instruction. "I have piped my own song," said Dewey, "and few have listened, and fewer yet have found a melodic theme. There seems to be little belief in the need of any new musical mode" (in Westbrook, 1991, 137).

This choice of methodologies of reading instruction is not a merely pedagogical one; rather, as I have suggested, pragmatism represents a different theory of the world, and its marginal- ization must be acknowledged to be not a result of its lesser validity but a result of political power. Historical forces more dominant than those of pragmatism/whole language marginalized these practices because they did not accord with the prevailing ideologies and, therefore, presented a world that made their continuance unviable. Pragmatism, as an educational philosophy, argued for the development of a rational self; in that rationality, what we have come to know as reflective thinking, the individual could come to produce him/herself. "For derived and refined products are experienced only because of the intervention of systematic thinking," Dewey (1929/1971, 7) says in *Experience and Nature*. What we know is what we have constructed; who we are is the one who, in the process of construction, comes into being. Whole language, too, posits the ability of all to learn in a natural, functional environment. Both whole language and pragmatism argue for a democracy and a democratic process, which threatens the power of those structures in which privilege inheres and, therefore, threatens to dissipate that power and deconstruct those structures. To understand the marginalization of pragmatism and whole language requires situating pragmatism in its historical and political context.

Pragmatism, as Cornel West (1989) and Andrew Feffer attest (1993), was always a political force. In Chicago, where the pragmatists worked within the academic and overtly political establishment, pragmatists actively engaged in the public political arena, seeking to effect changes that would further the development of democracy and end the inequities that had developed as a result of the burgeoning industrial capitalism and the nascent monopoly capitalism of the late nineteenth century. George Herbert Mead's work with the Chicago city government and Dewey's Lincoln Park laboratory school arose out of their pragmatism, and the school actively promulgated the policy in its curriculum. Politics also led to Francis Parker's firing as head of the school. John Dewey incessantly linked politics to education, and Dewey's followers, such as Randolph Bourne and the Young Americans, understood that the pragmatic method exercised in the practice of education could be a tool for democratic community building; arrayed, as Bourne declared, as a "moral equivalent for Universal Military Service" (Blake, 1990, 97). Like Dewey, the Young Americans believed in "the ideal of a democratic community grounded in critical discourse and free communication" (Blake, 1990, 86). In this sense, pragmatism may be understood in its essential nature as political. Feffer (1993) argues that pragmatism in politics, arising out of the terrible discord produced by growing industrialism and the centralization of society, attempted to create a new social situation that maintained greater harmony in action. Cornel West (1989, 212) argues that pragmatism's three themes—provocation, power, and personality—were always politically situated issues; in his book, West calls for the construction in the present of a contemporary pragmatism that must be explicitly political. "This political mode of cultural criticism must recapture Emerson's sense of vision—his Utopian impulse—yet rechannel it through Dewey's conception of creative democracy and Du Bois' social structural analysis of the limits of capitalist democracy." West's (213) "prophetic pragmatism" posits a society and culture ". . . where politically adjudicated forms of knowledge are produced in which human participation is encouraged and for which human personalities are enhanced." This political agenda to be realized in pragmatism represents as well the project of whole language: "Learning in a holistic program is seen as making sense of the real world, finding order in it, and solving the problems of coping with it" (Goodman et al., 1987, 398). In my view, whole language cannot be divorced from its political roots, and its fortunes during the present century can be understood by situating whole language in politics and producing a narrative that might trace its marginalization during the twentieth century. Whole language represents a political project that contradicts the rise of technological culture upon which the ideology of American progress has been based during the twentieth century.

Of course, the notion of the political is itself a point of political contention; educators prefer to consider themselves idealistically above the political fray. Pragmatism, on the other hand, does not avoid its situation in political discourse. Rorty (1991, 229) acknowledges that the split between analytical philosophers and pragmatic (anti-)philosophers might be called ". . . a *political* split because both sides think of themselves as looking out for the interests of the global *polis*. . . . Further, this division into the 'scientific' and the 'unscientific' intellectuals is related in all sorts of ways to all sorts of issues which are 'political' in narrower and more familiar senses." It is an argument in which I have engaged in Chapter 1, where I argued that the method of teaching reading defines not only the practice of reading and what may be read, but sets the very idea of reading into a social and hence political context. James Gee (1991, 191) writes, ". . . that mainstream Dominant Discourses in our society, and, in particular, school-based Discourses, privilege us who have mastered them and do significant harm to others. They involve us in foolish views about other human beings and their Discourses. They foreshorten our view of human nature, human diversity and the capacities for human change for development." This is the result in part, I believe, of mainstream discourse in education, which promotes a subskill approach to learning to read and which derives from the technological thrust of American ideology. This approach creates reading groups based on normalized scales of anonymous readers, most of whom do not belong to the language community of the school. It creates the scope and sequence of learning to read despite absolute ignorance of the knowledge and interests of students, and when these students fail to achieve at the normalized rate, it declares the individual learner disabled, absolving the structure's implication in the child's condition. This ideology reifies the reading process as something external to the reader, transforming a natural activity into an unnatural one and therefore denying independence and competence to the emergent reader. This ideology creates exemplary texts that might be studied so that certain standards of beauty and morality and values might be learned (Block, 1992). But the divergent schools of reading pedagogy can easily be situated in politics by merely referring to the title of Chall's often cited book, *The Great Debate* (1967). How one teaches reading determines what one teaches reading to be and finally determines what may be taught by the materials that may be chosen.

Thus, the political nature of politics and pragmatism cannot be avoided. In *The American Evasion of Philosophy*, Cornel West (1989) explores the various manifestations of pragmatism from its immanence in the works of Ralph Waldo Emerson. Acknowledging that from its beginnings pragmatism was absolutely embedded in the political, West explores how various exponents of pragmatism either diverted it from actual political praxis or led to a particular nondemocratic practice.[5] Both Andrew Feffer and Cary Nelson Blake, too, explore the development of pragmatism and the political uses and abuses of it. David Hollinger (1980, 104) would write that pragmatism was so spare a philosophy that

one could believe in it while entertaining a whole range of
other beliefs, ancient and modern, idiosyncratic and
conventional. Hadn't Papini said pragmatism was not so
much a philosophy as a way of doing without one? There
was much to this, even if only because people sympathetic
to pragmatism so much enjoyed quoting it. Critics also
quoted it, voicing thereby what was eventually to become
the standard critique of pragmatism: that pragmatism was
too shallow to accomplish anything and that its adherents
had mistaken vacancy for liberation.

Situating pragmatism and whole language as intrinsically
political goes far in promoting an understanding of the
marginalization or dismissal of both as viable educational
philosophies.

Politics sits at the center of the pragmatic enterprise. West
(1989, 213) writes that

> The political motivation of the American evasion of
> philosophy [pragmatism] is not a mere cloak that conceals
> the material interests of a class or group. Rather, the claim
> is that once one gives up on the search for foundations and
> the quest for certainty, human inquiry into truth and
> knowledge shifts to the social and communal circum-
> stances under which persons can communicate and
> cooperate in the process of acquiring knowledge. What
> was once purely epistemological now highlights the
> values and operations of power requisite for the human
> production of truth and knowledge.

No doubt whole language, based in pragmatism, must also be
understood as deeply embedded in politics, for it is the function
of whole-language learning to situate knowledge in the social
and the contextual. As a way of being, this literacy learning is, as
Henry Giroux states in his introduction to Freire's text (1987, 7),
"inherently a political project in which men and women assert
their right and responsibility not only to read, understand, and
transform their own experiences [to produce meaning], but also
to reconstitute their relationship with the wider society." Whole
language, as is pragmatism, might be understood as a form of
populism, itself an overtly political expression in American
history. It is by situating pragmatism and whole language in
politics that we can understand the exceedingly vocal

vituperative attack against whole language by advocates of the subskill approach to reading, which is itself steeped solidly in mainstream quantitative science—the dominant and organizing ideology in American society today that is largely responsible for the curriculum decisions made during the past 100 years. These whole-language critiques can be thus understood as more than merely a pedagogical difference of opinion; they represent a wholly different and antagonistic world view.

Whole Language and Populism

In separate articles in the *Elementary School Journal* (1989), both Ken and Yetta Goodman refer to whole language as a grass-roots movement. Ken Goodman declares that "Whole language is a grass-roots movement among teachers that is based on research" (205). He asserts (208) that "Whole language is a dynamic, evolving grass-roots movement. For that reason there is considerable variability among views of whole language held by its advocates and among whole-language classrooms." Yetta Goodman states emphatically that "Whole language is a grass-roots movement" (115). She claims that "Many groups of teachers, administrators, teacher educators, and researchers are participating in a network of study and discussion groups, raising questions, researching, writing articles, and coming to conclusions resulting in a dynamically conceived conceptualization and definition of whole language."

Patrick Shannon's book *The Struggle to Continue* (1990) makes a similar argument. Situating whole language in local practice, Shannon describes in a historicized perspective alternative literacy philosophies and applications that developed in opposition to the dominant rationalized and technologized pedagogy advocated and practiced in the United States in the late nineteenth and early twentieth centuries. His work attempts "to build coalitions between and among reactors and resisters in order to improve the chances of success" (1990, x). Shannon's work continues the efforts not only to identify whole language as a grass-roots movement, one which grows from the native soils of individual communities and which is based on the ecologies of those environments, but to build coalitions between communities as well.

In the sense advanced by the Goodmans and Shannon, whole language is a political movement. Each portrays the whole language philosophy as oppositional to the rationalized and industrialized model of twentieth-century educational practices. As Goodman (1982, 311) only somewhat facetiously warns: "I think that government agencies are pressuring school administrators to regiment teachers and pupils so that time, space, movement, deployment of staff, allocation of materials, decision-making procedures, and authority all take on a precision characterisitic of a military manual or a Ford production schedule." Whole language, as does populism, situates itself in political opposition to this order and not only offers a different educational perspective but demands a more encompassing and extensive reordering of social priorities.

I think that this emphasis on the grass-roots aspect of whole language correctly identifies the philosophy as coincident to the populist program evident throughout United States history and prominent in the late nineteenth century. Which is not to say that the research findings reviewed by the Goodmans and Shannon, and which extend at least as far back as the seventeenth century and Comenius, are not a strong foundation for whole language but that whole language can be linked to a movement more extensive than merely pedagogical and can be identified with the development of a democratic ideal, which John Dewey epitomized in his work *Democracy and Education*. Whole language ought to be understood as a political movement if its place in the American curriculum is to be appreciated,[6] and when viewed politically, whole language may be linked to populism and pragmatism. In a strongly worded polemic, Ken Goodman (1982, 348) declares

> I must reject the skill sequences as arbitrary and baseless. I must reject the 'mastery learning' programs as unfounded in learning theory, empty of language content, dull and dehumanizing and subject to the ancient law of diminishing returns. I must reject 'direct teaching' as contradictory to much of what we know of language learning. I must reject legally mandated minimal

competency requirements as irrelevant to the realities of literacy achievement and punitive to the students they are supposed to help. I must reject simplistic phonics programs and other assorted back-to-basics propositions as reactionary, negative and rooted in ignorance and superstition. I must reject the evaluation establishment that dominates the teaching of literacy through tests. I must reject the federal and state guidelines that mandate tests and technology and lock out knowledge and humanity.

Rejecting the pedagogical theory and practice that organizes the majority of reading instruction in the United States today, Goodman rejects as well the beliefs that have given rise to the notion of validity upon which this pedagogy is based and the ideology it both represents and sustains. He rejects the educational establishment, its mandates for education, and the materials it selects to achieve those mandates. Not deeply hidden in Goodman's strident and somewhat angry remarks are the politics, populism, and pragmatism of whole language.

Populists, suggest historians Lawrence Goodwyn (1978) and Christopher Lasch (1990), argued for the efficacy of small-scale production within the large-unit systems of industrial and monopoly capitalist production. Arrayed as what Goodwyn calls "social heretics," populists saw the world that was forming and did not like it.

In an age of progress and forward motion, they had come to suspect that Horatio Alger was not real. In due course, they came to possess a cultural flaw that armed them with considerable critical power. . . . Once defeated, they lost what cultural autonomy they had amassed and surrendered their progeny to the training camps of the conquering army. All Americans, including the children of populists, were exposed to the new dogmas of progress confidently arrayed in the public school and in the nation's history texts. (Goodwyn, 320)

In opposition to the development of large, impersonal corporate entities, the populists argued for the democratic possibility of local and small-scale control and development. During the early days of monopoly capitalism in the late nineteenth century and in the technologized society of the twentieth century, this grass-

roots form of organization and production was—and still is—
antithetical to the economic and social development promulgated by the dominant powers. Recognizing their own power in
the mass meeting held on Alliance Day, populist farmers,
Goodwyn (296) notes

> ... saw their own movement: the Alliance was the people,
> and the people were together. As a result, they dared to
> listen to themselves individually, and to each other, rather
> than passively follow the teachings of the received
> hierarchical culture. Their own movement was their guide.
> Fragile as it was, it nevertheless opened up possibilities of
> an autonomous democratic life . . . the Populist essence
> was . . . an assertion of how people can *act* in the name of
> the idea of freedom.

Like populism, pragmatism and whole language argue for the
primacy of the particular ecology of the learner in learning.
Dewey (1929/1971, 248), describing the conditions under which
the illusion of objective reality exists, maintains that it is "Only
when vanity, prestige, rights of possession are involved does an
individual tend to separate off from the environment and the
group in which he, quite literally lives, some things as being
peculiarly himself." In this description, we hear the critique of
capitalism and the market economy that governs American
society in the twentieth century, and we hear as well a critique of
those whose interests benefitted from the ideology of progress,
which operated to their material benefit, and who aspired to
marginalize the discourses of populists operating in the elective
political arena or in the educational milieu. And in Dewey's
critique we hear as well the pragmatic idea, held equally by
whole-language advocates, that truth is something that occurs to
an idea and not something that inheres in it. Whole language,
like pragmatism, situates academic knowledge production in the
particular environments of local schools and communities. In
these environments, learning is natural, organic, and functional.
"The role of literacy instruction in school," Goodman (1982, 246)
writes, "is to facilitate the use by learners of [the natural]
resource . . . already present in the child. To be successful,
instruction accepts and expands on the base of literacy already
begun in the established community from which the child

derives and in which the school should function. The school's focus should be on expanding the awareness in the learners of the personal-social functions written language has for them." This learning is democratic for it is situated in the ecology of the learner, and it accepts the legitimacy of that ecology and its efficacy in the learner's development. Too, this pedagogy acknowledges the production of self and community in literacy education and both represents and promotes democratic ideals. It makes learners active and competent and creates community in that process. "Our identification with our community—our society, our political tradition, our intellectual heritage—is heightened when we see this community as *ours* rather than *nature's, shaped* rather than *found*, one among many which men have made. In the end, the pragmatists tell us, what matters is our loyalty to other human beings clinging together against the dark, not our hope of getting things right" (Rorty, 1991, 166). Whole language insists that that community comes into being in human interaction and is not an entity into which humans might enter after having acquired the requisite learning. "I have always insisted," says Paolo Freire (1991, 144), "that words used in organizing a literacy program come from the word universe of the people who are learning, expressing their actual language, their anxieties, fears, demands, dreams. Words should be laden with the meaning of the people's existential experience, and not of the teacher's experience." Based as it must be in the community of the learners, whole language is a populist program steeped in populist ideals and politics. "I want to proclaim a revolutionary doctrine," writes Ken Goodman (1982, 232). "The revolutionary doctrine is that literacy has to be the natural extension of language-learning, not something new, not something different, but something that grows out of and builds on the natural human tendency to communicate." This revolution acknowledges a "total change of vantage point from the traditional one that we have used" to examine learning to read. This is a political enterprise no less than the overtly political agenda of the populists who challenged the developing corporate state and its ideology of progress and its support of those practices that would further that progress. That challenge requires, as well, a new model of research and study rather than that which has been traditionally employed by reading researchers.

Science, Politics, and Whole Language

The Goodmans (1989) have summarized the nature of research out of which whole language has arisen as a movement and which supports the activities of whole-language classrooms. The nature of this research is an alternative to that of the dominant paradigm that is steeped, as I have shown, in experimental science and quantitative measurement. As the Goodmans both acknowledge and as I have suggested above, whole language is a philosophy and is consequently situated in politics; the research base upon which it sits must also be understood as located in politics. Whole language is, the Goodmans claim, humanistic and, because it is humanistic, it is also democratic.

> What we take from humanism is respect for, and positive attitudes toward, all learners regardless of their ages, abilities or backgrounds. What we take from science are the discoveries in psychology, linguistics, and socioling-uistics that are part of the current knowledge explosion concerning how students learn, how they learn language, how they use language to learn, and the influences of the individual, peers, teachers, and various cultural institutions on language learning and on using language to learn. (Goodman, Y.M., 1989, 125)

What I will argue in Chapters 3 and 4 is that this research all points to the precedence of the whole over the parts. Whole language, therefore, represents a critique of the prevailing ideology and the research on which it draws and offers a powerful criticism of the educational establishment that develops out of and as a part of the dominant social fabric. Like populism, whole language might be understood as a revolt against the encroaching dominance of technology. That technology has also promulgated a model of research against which pragmatism and whole language argue. Of this nonpragmatic, scientific method Dewey (1929/1971, 12) argues:

"It has upon its hands the problem of how it is possible to know at all; how an outer world can affect an inner mind; how the acts of mind can reach out and lay hold of objects defined in antithesis to them. Naturally, it is at a loss for an answer, since its premises make the fact of knowledge both unnatural and unempirical." I have discussed some of these issues in the first chapter. I would like to further situate these issues directly in politics for from the premises of the nonpragmatic method arise the methodology and findings of contemporary cognitive sciences. Thus, the research that Chall (1991) exalts might be understood as itself situated in politics.

In their companion articles, Ken and Yetta Goodman (1989) reviewed the research and curricular foundations of what is commonly referred to as whole language, situating the research in a nontechnological and broad-based qualitative research frame. Yetta Goodman, in "Roots of the Whole-Language Movement," argues that research and practice of whole language have a long, extensive, and secure historical base. Goodman explores the pedagogical influences on the whole-language movement situating these influences in curriculum studies (Dewey and William Kilpatrick), in linguistics (M.A.K. Halliday), in psychology (Jean Piaget and Lev Vygotsky), in literary studies (Louise Rosenblatt), in language studies (James Britton), in composition (Donald Graves), and in reading (Frank Smith). Finally, Yetta Goodman is able to situate the foundations of the whole-language movement in the pedagogies advocating integrated curricula and cross-disciplinary studies:

> The history of whole language shows that many groups and individuals have made continuous attempts to consider issues such as curriculum; individual differences; social interaction; collaboration; language learning; the relation between teaching, learning and evaluation; and their influences on the lives of teachers and students. (122)

She concludes that whole-language practitioners discover their roots in the humanistic and scientific beliefs of those who preceded them and that the roots of those who follow them will be found in the work of those currently practicing. In this way, she situates research in the activity of whole-language instruction in an extensive cross-disciplinary matrix, and she grounds educational philosophy pragmatically in the ecologies of those engaged specifically in education and in those directly involved in classroom practice.

In his article "Whole Language Research: Foundations and Development," Ken Goodman (1989) too, argues that the whole-language movement develops from and rests upon a strong and broad base of research steeped in a multi- and interdisciplinary milieu. "The practice of whole language is solidly rooted in scientific research and theory," he writes. "While it owes much to positive, child-centered educational movements from the past, it goes beyond them in integrating scientific concepts and theories of language processes, learning and cognitive development, teaching, and curriculum decision making" (205). Arguing that whole language rests on a separate paradigmatic basis from other approaches to teaching and learning, Goodman insists that it cannot produce answers to the questions posed by traditional research. Indeed, whole language asks different questions; therefore, its answers must be different. "Whole language starts with the premise that the whole is more than the sum of its parts; it cannot be studied or evaluated by reducing what happens in whole-language classrooms to what also happens to skill-based classrooms" (208).

The research in language learning, of which reading instruction is one mode, argues from a holistic basis, as I have suggested in Chapter 1. Contemporary language theorists continue the tradition we have observed at least as far back as Francis Parker. Arguing from what would now be called a whole-language perspective, Parker condemns the traditional reading pedagogy as irrelevant and unproductive. "The 'A, B, C' method, the countless phonic and word-building methods, the systematic, prescribed and predestined object-lesson, are all the bad results of ignorance in regard to this powerful, persistent, and spontaneous action of the mind" (Parker, 1894/1969, 113). That action of the mind to which Parker refers is the perception of the whole from which the parts may be then derived through analysis, rather than, as was generally held, the identification of the whole through the conscious combinatory act of mind of the various parts. Contemporary whole-language researchers, observes Ken Goodman, "start with the premise that the whole is more than the sum of its parts . . . whole-language teachers operate from an examined theory of how language, thought and knowledge develop holistically and in support of each other" (1989, 208). Given these premises, Goodman argues, whole language cannot be studied or evaluated by reducing what happens in whole-language classrooms to what also happens in skill-based classrooms. In other words, the research that inspires skill-based classrooms does not have primary applicability to whole-language classrooms; the two rest upon different assumptions. Skill-based classrooms operate on the assumption, as I have said, that reading can be broken down into a series of subskills, which are then somewhere assembled into the whole process. Each skill is then measurable; each whole skill could be further divided into isolable skills until we have reached the smallest possible graphic and phonemic unit—the letter and phoneme—and lost the whole purpose of reading, the production of meaning.

Goodman's use of the word "science" is, of course, a response to the critique of whole language as lacking authoritative research validity (see Chall, in Rothman, 1990), which is to say, that which has come to be defined *by* science *as* science. Science has been the hallmark of objectivity and validity during the twentieth century and has been the standard by which education has been measured and mandated. This is so for a number of reasons.

As I have said earlier, nineteenth-century science posited a world distinct from yet knowable by human consciousness. Science demystified the universe and made it knowable. Science offered the possibility and methodology of control by its discovery of the parts that comprise the whole and promised control of the whole by the subsequent manipulation of the parts. This notion gained credibility under the force of the factory system and the developing corporate structures. Order became the means and definition of progress. In the development of the factory and the rise of monopoly capitalism these standards were advanced as primary and efficacious. Increased production promised the possibilities of higher standards of living for all and not just the already-rich.

Technology supported by science promoted the myth of progress. Arguing that the modern conception of progress differed radically from the traditional millenarian and apocalyptic Christian view of history, Christopher Lasch (1990, 48) suggests that progress offered not utopia but the "promise of steady improvement with no foreseeable ending at all. . . . We take our cue from science, at once the source of our material achievements and the model of cumulative, self-perpetuating inquiry, which guarantees its continuation precisely by its willingness to submit every advance to the risk of supersession." Science, which becomes the model of and impetus for progress, becomes also the model by which knowledge may be validated. Science becomes objectified and its knowledge rendered atheoretical. Science becomes the definition of knowledge and the means of progress.

Applied to mind, experimental science promised to quantify and therefore isolate the parts of human consciousness and, thus, to suggest methods for strengthening the parts that the whole might be better. Likening the study of the mind to the work of cartographers, Cattell, in 1893, suggested that the work of psychology ought to be the mapping of the mind, the creation of a

> mental geography describing the contents of the mind . . .
> a mental mechanics demonstrating necessary relations of
> thought. [T]he mind is the beginning and the end of
> science. Physical science is possible because the mind
> observes and arranges, and physical science has worth
> because it satisfies mental needs. (in Jonçich, 1968, 114)

Cattell's charge to psychology was to chart the mind as if it existed apart from the particular ecology in which it develops and in which it exists. He suggested that the mind might be understood in the same fashion as the mind understood nature—as a concatenation of parts comprising a whole, much as a cartographer constructed the whole from the sum of its parts. Cattell's charge, of course, can be understood as progressive insofar as it demystifies the natural world and human conduct, but it perpetuates the split between human and nature and fosters the belief that a scientific psychology can isolate and define mind in opposition to nature. Dewey comments upon this tendency in philosophy that "The things of primary experience are so arresting and engrossing that we tend to accept them just as they are—the flat earth, the march of the sun from east to west and its sinking under the earth" (1929/1971, 15). We do not see these events in their ecological perspectives. Similarly, William James will note the proclivity to objectivity in modern society: "The low thermometer today . . . is supposed to come from something called 'climate.' Climate is really only the name for a certain group of days, but is treated as if it lay behind the day, and in general, we place the name, as if it were a being, behind the facts it is the name of" (1907/1970, 66). On the other hand, Cattell will say that nature and the physical science that studies it is organized as it is because of the natural needs of the human mind. Cattell, thus, will make possible the belief that physical science and its discoveries are natural, that science is natural, and will render other research invalid as a result.

This belief and practice were facilitated by the development of techniques of measurement. The twentieth century has seen the rise of measurement as the tool of scientific validity and science as the hallmark of objectivity. "Never," writes William James in 1907/1970, "were as many men of a decidedly empiricist proclivity in existence as there are at the present day . . . our esteem for facts has not neutralized in us all religiousness. It is itself almost religious. Our scientific temper is devout" (23). Science in the twentieth century and its tools of measurement have become the means by which progress and knowledge may be measured. Writing just a few years later than James, Edward Thorndike in 1913 will assert that

> Tables of correlation seem dull, dry, unimpressive things besides the insights of poets and proverb-makers—but only to those who miss their meaning. In the end they will contribute tenfold more to man's mastery of himself. History records no career, war, or revolution that can compare in significance with the fact that the correlation between intellect and morality is approximately .3, a fact to which perhaps a fourth of the world's progress is due. (in Jonçich, 1968, 310)

Arguing the case for measurement, Thorndike would state that

> Whatever exists, exists in some amount. To measure it is
> simply to know its varying amounts. Man sees no less
> beauty in flowers now than before the day of quantitative
> theory. It does not reduce courage or endurance to
> measure them and trace their relations to the autonomic
> system, the flow of the adrenal glands and the production
> of sugar in the blood. If any virtue is worth seeking, we
> shall seek it more eagerly the more we know and measure
> it. (in Jonçich, 1968, 282)

Of course, Thorndike does not seem to recognize that
measurement defines what is being measured after the behavior
has already been identified: what counts as courage or as a
response to beauty must be predefined that it might, indeed, be
measured.

This positivism, the hallmark of the dominant twentieth-
century science, will attempt to reduce language as well into a
quantifiable system and, in so doing, define it by statistical
measurement. Reading specialists' faith in science derived from
the ability to measure, a product of positivist science; they rarely
attempted to reconceptualize science. "With the advent of
instruments of measurement it was possible for the first time to
obtain scientific information about the effectiveness of reading
methods and materials and of administrative arrangements for
teaching reading in the classroom. As a result, more innovations
in reading instruction issued forth during this period than in all
the centuries of the past" (Smith, 1986, 157–8). Of course, as the
philosophers of science have shown in the twentieth century,
what counts as science is socially determined, and one
development of scientific theory during the post–World War II
years has called into question the notion of the atomistic nature
of reality.

As I have stated in Chapter 1, many factors account for the
rise of science as a dominant power. To those I would now add
the power of politics to objectify the knowledge derived from
science and the resulting hegemony that organized education in
general and reading pedagogy specifically. Certainly, the rise of
industrial and monopoly capitalism and the development of
technology made order and structure seem most beneficial to
advancement and progress. Christopher Lasch has explored this
myth of progress in his book *The True and Only Heaven* (1990). As

Lasch observes, the ability to measure, to develop diachronic structures for the sake of efficiency came to be equated with progress. The greater the quantity of production, the more progress the society seemed to make. Centralization and control became dominant ideologies because they seemed to produce and therefore sponsored continuous advancement. Even evolution and its orderly and measurable progress promoted belief in the order of science and its tools of measurement.

The scientific method—to observe, record, and to predict—placed emphasis on measurement. From this scientific religiosity arose the field of measurement, impelled by Edward Thorndike, an educational psychologist at Columbia University, whose work in statistical measurement and analysis continues to dominate the field of education. "Substitute science for the rule of thumb," for tradition, and for philosophy was Thorndike's argument for the development of an experimental psychology based on quantification and measurement. Once dependent on introspection, Thorndike meant to ground psychology in a positivist element, arguing that learning was a response to an organism's total environment. Geraldine Jonçich, in her biography of Thorndike, has written that in order to do so,

> Taylorites and Thorndikeans seek precise measurements and the analytical reduction of either bricklaying or learning to spell into all its calculable atoms of behavior. The disciples of Thorndike's *Introduction to the Theory of Mental and Social Measurements* are building statistical laboratories in university departments of psychology and education, founding research bureaus in city school systems and state departments of education, and calling in survey teams; like sociologists and psychologists, educators are possessed of what can be called an obsession with quantified observation. (1968, 308)

As I argued in the first chapter, science began to replace religion as the source of spiritual belief. This faith was realized in the belief science promulgated regarding the powers of measurement to attain truth. Cattell's work at Columbia, where he supervised over fifty Ph.D.s, most of whom would become experimental psychologists, said that "Psychology cannot attain the certainty and exactness of the physical sciences unless it rests on a foundation of experiment and measurement. A step in this direction could be made by applying a series of mental tests and measurements to a large number of individuals" (in Jonçich, 1968, 113). As empirical science dominated psychology producing experimental psychology as the paradigms of psychology, education fell under the sway of experimental psychology with quantification and measurement as the paradigms of educational studies. If learning could be measured, argued Thorndike, then its pieces could be isolated, ordered, and strengthened as desired. This belief would lead to Thorndike's laws of learning which have served as the basis for almost all the basal reader series in classrooms today as well as the paradigm for organizing curriculum instruction in schools. In a sense, of course, Thorndike's work supported the myth of progress, for he was claiming that all people could learn to be good or bad, as the case may be. This avoided the fatalism that had assumed secular support in social Darwinism or the natural development of the child movement, of which G. Stanley Hall was a major proponent. The practices of science seemed progressive, and their application to psychology gave this discipline the mantle of scientific objectivity. Indeed, in 1934, when Columbia created the Ed.D. degree, statistics was retained by the educational psychology program and dropped from educational studies. The early reading experts came almost unilaterally from the discipline of educational psychology. For example, Arthur Irving Gates, whose tests still are administered in the schools, was a student and colleague of Edward Thorndike. As Thorndike's student he learned that

> All errors in reading, as in any other kind of thinking . . . require for explanation just three simple mechanisms: underpotency or overpotency of elements, dislocation or disrelation of elements, and wrongness or inadequacy of connections (in Jonçich, 1968, 395).

From this statement much of quantitative reading research would derive. William Gray, in 1937, though he espoused comprehension as the purpose of reading, wrote for the Committee on the Economy of Time that the proper pedagogy of reading was a matter of efficiency. As I have shown in Chapter 1, this theory is based, positing as it does a definitive locus of arrival and meaning, solidly in the belief in the existence of truth and the reality of the path to it. Reading was an end to a product and not a process itself. Thorndike, Gates, and Gray and the plethora of reading specialists who define reading by its quantification continue the dualism that we have traced back at least to Plato.

Education rapidly fell under the sway of science. Muckrakers such as Joseph Mayer Rice decried the chaos that seemed to exist in education and created the ideological space for science to occupy as the structured alternative. Science not only offered in its discovery of order and the method for creating that order a means to rationalize schooling, but also promised a way to break the control of the strong family and give that control to the state. Under the influence of scientifically organized education, the unruly and seemingly unmanageable immigrant population could be organized by education, which was itself organized by positivist science.

> To Americans the "natural man" and the uninstructed child are alike objects of dread; both recall those fears of barbarism and anarchy which run through American social and political writings from the days of the first settlement at Jamestown. The man to be trusted is the man both enlightened and restrained by education, and every child must diligently be taught the rules to reach that state; spontaneity and emotionalism might erupt in the tendency toward revivalism in American religion, but these are not tolerated in the schoolhouse. (in Jonçich, 1968, 45).

Science offered a means of establishing rules of learning—indeed, this was the end of Thorndike's work—and, hence, of controlling the means of education in American society. The paradigm of research was positivist science whose atomistic view of the world determined the questions.

Dewey's pragmatism too fell under the sway of the dominating influence of science. Part of the problem seems to be in Dewey's own use of the term science and the scientific method. Was science for Dewey a model for the industrial society, in which case the school should model itself after that society as the technologists and social efficiency experts would aver? In this sense, the school should prepare students for life in the industrialized society and should mirror that society in its internal organization. Today, this belief might be heard in that large section of the reading field that organizes instruction around the needs of the marketplace and the preparation of future workers. Reading, as was the rest of curriculum, was compartmentalized, and reading became fetishized as an objective discipline.

Or, as the child-centered educators argued, if school learning ought to be integrated into the processes discovered in child development, then those processes could be discovered by quantitative methods developed by science. Hence, again, measurement becomes the model of research and pedagogical practice. Both social-efficiency experts and scientific managers would call upon Deweyan pragmatism as a model to socialize the industrial working classes.

Of course, these groups may have misinterpreted Dewey. This is the argument Robert Westbrook makes in his biography, *John Dewey and American Democracy* (1991). Westbrook believes that Dewey never intended the school to adapt itself to industrial society, a society that Dewey criticized until the end of his life, but that society offered the primary objects for reflection. Arguing not that education ought to facilitate adaptation to the industrial society, Dewey claimed

> The price that democratic societies will have to pay for
> their continuing health is the elimination of an oligarchy—
> the most exclusive and dangerous of all—that attempts to
> monopolize the benefits of intelligence and of the best
> methods for the profit of a few privileged ones. . . . These
> distinctions will disappear the day that, under the
> influence of education, science and practical activity are
> joined together forever. (in Westbrook, 173)

Indeed, rather than education following the model of science, Dewey proposed that science would be influenced by pragmatic education. This is the argument that whole-language theorists make regarding learning in whole-language classrooms. "An education which acknowledges the full intellectual and social meaning of a vocation would include instruction in the historical background of present conditions; training in science to give intelligence and initiative in dealing with the material and agencies of production; and studies of economics, civics and politics to bring the future worker in touch with the problems of the day and the various methods proposed for its improvement" (Westbrook, 1991, 177). In this way, Dewey proposed, all children would be given tools of social intelligence. In such a manner, the result in the social system would not involve an adaptation of the existing system but a radical change in educational foundation and aim: This is the very revolution called for by Kenneth Goodman (1982). That it has yet to be realized is no secret in classrooms where reading is exercised today.

NOTES

1. I use the term "philosopher" though it is technically a misnomer. Pragmatism eschews the notion of philosophy because of its metaphysical taint. Rather, pragmatists would prefer to be known as anti-philosophers. "Pragmatists," says Rorty, "keep trying to find ways of making anti-philosophical points in nonphilosophical language." This argument is similar to that of Cornel West in his exploration of pragmatism entitled *The American Evasion of Philosophy*.

2. For a perspective on this issue see James Gee (1991).

3. See, for example, the discussions that argue that phonemic awareness is a necessary condition for learning to read or the arguments for the necessity of a phonics approach to beginning reading. Or see the new basal reader series that posit "advanced reading" starting in the fifth grade. What could that possibly mean?

4. This represents the difference between algorithmic and heuristic thinking.

5. For example, Sidney Hook (1974, 25) claims that "Pragmatism, as I interpret it, is the theory and practice of enlarging human freedom in a precarious and tragic world by the arts of intelligent social control." That social control must be organized by those considered intelligent. This seems to me a typically liberal argument. Right-wing thinkers come in two varieties: neoconservative and neoliberal.

6. Herbert Kleibard's book, *The Struggle for the American Curriculum,* explores the development of the pedagogical in an explicitly political framework. I have learned a great deal from this book, and I hope the perspective I offer here may expand the vision offered by Kleibard.

CHAPTER 3

A Psychology of Reading: Foundations

Reading is a *sociopsycholinguistic productive* process. Which is to say that reading occurs as a transaction between the cultural, social, personal psyche of the virtual reader, already a complex textual subject, and the verbal text. The purpose and the effect of this transaction is the production of meaning. Meaning is identity: The way I organize meaning is the way I represent me. The making of meaning is the means by which self is produced. Self is what is represented. Meaning is representation. And what is this self which your representation is about? It is, Daniel Dennett (1991, 429) exclaims, "nothing more than, and nothing less than, your center of narrative gravity." My self is my representation; my representation is a matter of narrative strategies and resources. Or, as Dewey (1929/1971, 251) says, "Consciousness, an idea, is that phase of a system of meanings which at a given time is undergoing re-direction, transitive transformation." Against Derrida's dictum that there is nothing outside the text, I offer, "The world, including me, is a text that I may, indeed must, read, and write." Reading—and writing—is the exercise of narrative strategies that produce texts of self and world. Dewey (244) notes that "Formulated discourse, of which reading and writing may be considered types . . . is mainly but a selected statement of what we wish to retain among all these incipient starts, followings up and breakings off." A psychology of reading must account for the production of meaning without resort to mere information-processing models, which are based primarily on the conscious selection of goals and the conscious combining of elements *by rule* to reach those goals. Consciousness must be understood as an event and effect rather than a first cause. A psychology of reading must account for the production of both text and self outside of rules and in which goals are realized in action and are ever evolving and reformulating. Reading is a social activity that when engaged in results in the production of the individual. The individual, says Dewey (178), is a novel reconstruction of a preexisting order.

And so to characterize reading, I borrow the word "transaction" from Louise Rosenblatt (1978) who argues convincingly that reading is an event in time and not an object or an ideal entity. Reading is a process that arrives at no end. Rather, reading "happens during a coming together, a compenetration of a reader and a text" (12). During that compenetration, the text becomes a work and the reader, in conscious purpose, achieves self. Thus, reading is never over but becomes the reader, adding the possibility of novel narrative strategies in subsequent compenetrations: In the last line of Italo Calvino's novel, *If on a winter's night a traveler,* the reader announces, "Just a moment, I've almost finished *If on a winter's night a traveler* by Italo Calvino"(Calvino, 1981, 260). The reader is always a complex of multiple goals often diverse and contradictory and unrealized until the transaction occurs. Hence, reading never ends because in the transaction both text and reader have in the production of meaning been changed, and the text and reader are always original when meaning has been produced. Information-processing systems, which begin with a single conscious problem, misrepresent the virtual reader by assuming the end of reading to be the solution to the problem. Reading is understood in this model as an end and not a means. It is a process aimed at getting the meaning from the text, at comprehending the author's meaning. But, says John Dewey (1929/1971, 182), conception of meaning "may be mine rather than yours; yours rather than his, at a particular moment; but this fact is about me or you, not about the object and essence perceived and conceived." In the psychology of reading, I propose reading occurs as a transaction between the reader and the text and is understood as an ongoing process in which the elements or factors are aspects of a total situation, each conditioned by or conditioning the other. How the reader attends to a text activates certain elements in the reader's past experience that are somehow linked to the verbal symbols resulting in the production of meaning. In other words, the selection of what to attend to in the environment and the organization of responses to that environment are dependent on the assumptions, the expectations, and the sense of possible structures that the reader brings out of his/her stream of life. There is nothing in the text until the reader creates that text. To return to Derrida again, if there is nothing outside the text, then self is nothing but the creation of text in the active production of meaning. Reading is a transactional process that produces both the text and the reader in the activity itself.

Finally, I borrow the word "virtual" as the descriptor of a reader from Daniel Dennett (1991) because reading is, as I hope to show, an active process of a conscious mind, and Dennett argues that "conscious minds are more or less virtual machines implemented—inefficiently—on the parallel hardware that evolution has provided for us"(218). A virtual machine is what we commonly know as "software," a set of highly structured regularities—hundreds of thousands of instructions—that are imposed on the underlying hardware that give it a "huge set of interlocking habits or dispositions to react" (216). It is a virtual machine because it is not one itself but only acts as one. And those instructions/regularities are a function not only of the nature of the hardware itself, which is the product of an evolutionary process, but are as well the product of cultural development. Reading must be understood as an individual process in which the personal and cultural histories must be accounted for in the transaction with the text—in the case of reading a set of verbal symbols—to produce a work. And since no two conscious minds can be alike, no two readings can be identical. A psychology of reading must account for the production of the meaner and text before it accounts for any of the parts. Dreyfus and Dreyfus (1986, 28) argue that proficiency can be identified as the "intuitive ability to use patterns without decomposing them into component features." This is referred to as "holistic similarity recognition," and there is an effortless property about it. No detached choice occurs; no formal heuristic is followed. A psychology of reading that I will propose here will suggest that it is deleterious to focus on the parts before focusing on the whole because there is no meaning in the parts. The parts derive meaning as a result of the whole. George Dennison (1969, 92), in his study of children at the First Street Free School on the Lower East Side of New York City, argues that imitation cannot explain a child's communicative development because it is not discrete forms of behavior that the child wishes to reproduce. "The infant is surrounded by the life of the home, not by instructors or persons posing as models. Everything that he observes, every gesture, every word, is observed not only as action but as a truly instrumental form. And this indeed, this whole life of the form, is what he seeks to master. . . . No parent has ever heard an infant abstracting the separate parts of speech and practicing them. It simply does not happen." Rather, what is sought is the idea of game, of meaningful interaction out of which growth may occur but which is not integral to the interaction.

> A true description of an infant "talking" with its parents, then, must make clear that he is actually taking part. It is not make-believe or imitation, but true social sharing in the degree to which he is capable. We need only reduce this complex actuality to the relative simplicity of imitation to see at once what sort of loss he would suffer. The vivacity, the keen interest, the immediate sharing in the ongoing intercourse of others, and above all, the environmental effect—all these would vanish. His experience would be reduced to the dimensions of a chore. (Dennison, 1969, 93)

Hence, in our interactions with the world, we are readers from birth and reading the *verbal* text is merely the use of a different symbol system, which can be just as naturally acquired as learning to talk or to carry a tune.

Though I suggest that minds are virtual machines, they are not wholly explainable by the functionings of the software programs of computers, other types of virtual machines. The question is, as Dreyfus and Dreyfus suggest, not whether the brain is a machine that does information processing but whether the mind/brain is an information-processing mechanism. The difference of course, reflects one of purpose: The former assumes an already-conscious choice to process information, the latter assumes the inevitability of an unconscious act. Arguing against the notion of parallel processing systems, which account for meaning production by the processing of information by several parallel systems which must be collated in some central theater by a central meaner, Dreyfus and Dreyfus (1986, 56) declare that ". . . if human image processing operates on holistic representations that are not descriptions and relate such representations in other than rule-like ways, the appeal to parallel processing misses the point. The point is that human beings seem to be able to form and compare images in a way that cannot be captured by any number of procedures that operate on descriptions." Partly, this is a result of the wonderfully disparate physiology of the human brain. Physiologically, no two brains are alike. "Even identical twins with identical genes will not have identical brains at birth: The fine details of cortical circuitry will be quite different"(Sacks, 1993, 43). Hence, no two of us can originally perceive in exactly the same way, and thus, it seems to be that even perception is originally individualized. "Let us observe that in one sense the surroundings of a single animal are the same as the surroundings of all animals but that in another sense the surroundings of a single animal are different from those of any other animal" (Gibson, 1979, 7).

The very nature of the mind ensures variety and difference. "The most striking differences in human prowess depend on microstructural differences induced by the various memes[1] that have entered them and taken up residence. The memes enhance each others' opportunities: The meme for education, for instance, is a meme that reinforces the very process of meme implantation" (Dennett, 1991, 207). Hence, in what environment one develops and how one is educated will determine how one learns; how one is taught to read and what one is taught to read will determine how and what one reads. As I have tried to show in Chapter 1, our reading pedagogy has traditionally separated the reader from the text. But, the idea of the conscious mind as a virtual machine means that reading requires activation. Dewey (1929/1971, 153) notes that every ". . . sound, gesture, or written mark which is involved in language is a particular [singular] existence . . . but that each only becomes a word by gaining meaning which occurs when its use establishes a genuine community of action." There is no reader unless there is reading, and no two readings can ever be identical, even by the same person. "I, too," says the third reader in Calvino's novel *If on a winter's night a traveler*, "feel the need to reread the books I have already read, but at every rereading I seem to be reading a new book for the first time. Is it I who keep changing and seeing new things of which I was not previously aware? Or is reading a construction that assumes form, assembling a great number of variables, and therefore something that cannot be repeated twice according to the same pattern" (255). Of course, here the reader asks the same question twice: Reading produces both reader and text, and both are changed with each reading.

And so, I qualify reader with *virtual* because only this is reading: the production of identity in the transaction of reading. Identity is the totality of relations in which a thing engages. To read is to comprehend, to make meaning, a process effected in the transaction between text and reader. To read is to know that the sign expresses, and that that expression contains everything that has made possible the sign's appearance at this particular time and in this particular place, including what may now be called "me," which too, as a sign, expresses and contains everything that has made possible its appearance. Reading, as we will use it in this chapter, is a transaction between a reader and a verbal text composed of signs as words. The meaning of words derives from our experience in the world with them, which is never unitary. Words do not exist unless we assign meaning to them, and that process is an individual one. "The sense of a word," says Lev Vygotsky (1988, 146), "is the sum of all the psychological events aroused in our consciousness by the word. It is a dynamic, fluid, complex whole, which has several zones of unequal stability." And our experience with words in the world derives from the social aspects of our lives. "My own existence," says Karl Marx, "is a social existence" (in Fromm, 1966, 130). In that engagement with verbal symbols, identity is constructed as is constructed the text which is read. Unlike some modern views of reading, I see reading as a social activity, not only dependent upon society for its enactment but responsible as well in its engagement for society's construction. Describing José, a student defined by his reading problem, Dennison asks (1969,

76), "By what process did José and his schoolbook come together? Is this process part of his reading problem? Who asks him to read the book? *Someone* asks him. In what sort of voice and for what purpose, and with what concern or lack of concern for the outcome? And who wrote the book? For whom did they write it? Was it written for José? Can José actually partake of the life the book seems to offer?"

Sociolinguistics means to study the relationship between culture and language/discourse, and therefore, sociolinguists are concerned with the relationship between the language(s) with which an individual has facility and the cultures with which that individual engages. But because reading must take place as a production of the individual psyche, then it must be understood as a psychological process as well, hence the term sociopsycholinguistics. Vygotsky above suggests that the meaning of a word derives from a complex psychological process. Words do not exist outside of their psychological context, and their meaning is produced in the transaction between a reader and a text. A psychology of reading must explain not only that process by which language is produced and comprehended by the psyche of the reader, but the product of that process as well, the self. A psychology of reading that denies this relationship denies the self and denies the availability of reading. Again, speaking of José, Dennison (1969, 77) writes, "Obviously José has little skill in reading, but as I have just indicated, reading is no small matter of syllable and words. Then reading skills are no small matter either. They, too, include his typical relations with adults, with other children, and with himself; for he is fiercely divided within himself, and this conflict lies at the very heart of his reading problem. . . . José hates books, schools and teachers, and among a hundred other insufficiencies—*all of a piece*—he cannot read." To describe José as suffering from a reading problem is to deny everything about José except his response to printed letters. Rather, José "could not believe . . . that anything contained in books, or mentioned in classrooms, belonged by rights to himself, or even belonged to the world at large, as trees and lampposts belong quite simply to the world we all live in. . . . There has been no indication that he could share in them, but rather that he would be measured against them and be found wanting" (80). José, as a result of reading instruction, could only understand reading as a means of failure and not something in whose engagement he might partake and in the play of reading, create continuing selfhood.

For, in the activity of the process of reading, new products are continually created and new processes made possible within those new products. The products of reading are always identity. A psychology of reading must address both process and product and must address the constructivist nature of the reading process and product. "And so," said Edmund Burke Huey in 1908, "to completely analyze what we do when we read would almost be the acme of a psychologists's achievements, for it would be to describe very many of the most intricate workings of the human mind, as well as to unravel the tangled story of the most remarkable specific performance that civilization has learned in all its history"(6). To learn how we read would be to discover the mystery of consciousness. The psychology of reading that I will propose must first account for the whole—the reader reading, the conscious mind—before it accounts for any of the parts; and the psychology of reading I will propose must show how the parts derive from the whole and not, as is typical in much reading research, how the whole derives from the parts. The whole in reading is meaning: the conscious mind.

Of course, one can refuse to read, but that would mean a refusal to be self. I do not speak here of confusion, a state out of which a conscious mind would move. Nor do I speak of resistance, an act of reading as well. Rather, by a refusal to read I mean the unconscious mind which understands no symbols and is therefore denied self. Reading produces subject and object, and reading is then the essential act of living. "And what of José's failure to read?" Dennison asks (1969, 76). "We cannot stop at the fact that he draws a blank. How does he do it? What does he do? José's reading problem is José." The psychology of reading I will discuss is a productive process producing consciousness. "To know how reading occurs," says Huey (1908/1968, 6), "would be to know how almost any abstract representation of information—a traffic sign, a meter reading in the laboratory, or spoken words themselves—are evaluated and understood. It would be to know how people make sense of the welter of information from the environment and themselves with which they are constantly bombarded." People become selves when they are in the process of making sense of their environment.

Now, we may all be considered readers from birth: Infants, says Daniel Stern (1985, 10), are "predesigned to be selectively responsive to external social events and never experience an autistic-like phase." Newborn infants are aware of self-organizing processes, are from birth making hypotheses about their world and testing those hypotheses:

> From birth on, there appears to be a central tendency to form and test hypotheses about what is occuring in the world. Infants are also constantly "evaluating" in the sense of asking, is this different from or the same as that? How discrepant is what I have just encountered from what I have previously encountered. It is clear that this central tendency of mind, with constant application, will readily categorize the social world into confirming and contrasting patterns, events, sets, and experiences. The infant will readily discover which features of an experience are invariant and which are variant—that is, which features "belong" to the experience. The infant will apply these same processes to whatever sensations and perceptions are available, from the simplest to the ultimately most complex—that is, thoughts about thoughts. (42)

In other words, infants are from birth actively seeking cues from the environment and employing those cues to organize the self. It is what José has done all along; he has, however, organized the self in opposition to a hostile world against which he must maintain defense. Self is a social subjective perspective formed in the discovery of invariants. Self, says Daniel Stern (1985, 7), is an "invariant pattern of awarenesses that arise only on the occasion of the infants action or mental processes." Infants order the world by seeking invariants, understood as that which remains consistent when other things are in flux. This activity of seeking invariants appears to be innate. As we will explore in this chapter, this process of seeking cues and constructing meaning will be equated with the processes of reading. In this psychology of reading, as it is for a psychology for thought, the activity creates the self. Thought and reading will be shown to be equivalent processes. Some of us may be more efficient readers than others: We have learned how to better sample the environment for cues, to make predictions based on those cues, to confirm those predictions, and to integrate what we have confirmed with what we already know. And in this just-written sentence I have defined the nature of the reading process as conceptualized in the literature of whole-language philosophy and pedagogy (see Goodman et al., 1987). In this chapter, I would like to explore from psychogical perspectives this transactional/constructivist view of reading; which is to say, the idea that in the transaction that is reading we construct both the self and the text. A psychology of reading must account for those events. What happens to make reading occur and what occurs during the reading process are the questions of this chapter.

But reading, you might say, must involve print. And to an extent, this is true when we are discussing the reading of printed texts. This is the linguistic aspect of sociopsycholinguistics. Reading as a linguistic practice does concern the engagement with print. It is one of the particular environmental cues to which we must respond in reading print. We must look at the particular linguistic transaction with print to understand reading. And we must look for the presence of invariance in print to understand what might be sought in it. Recall that profiency is recognizing invariants without decomposing them into parts; therefore, a psychology for reading must account for the invariant aspects of language production/comprehension to explain the process. In the same sense that we do not hear words and then comprehend but, rather, comprehend as we hear words, in the same sense children do not learn words and then begin to hear and talk but, rather, learn to talk as they use and hear words, so might reading be understood as a natural language process that can only be learned in the activity of it. A psychology and pedagogy of reading must account for the natural aspect of the reading process. As the Goodmans have written (1982, 252):

> We believe that children learn to read and write in the
> same way and for the same reason that they learn to speak
> and listen. The way is to encounter language in use as a

vehicle of communicating meaning. The reason is need. Language learning whether oral or written is motivated by the need to communicate, to understand and be understood.

For the Goodmans, reading is a natural activity in need of support but not instruction. And what I will argue in this chapter is that this view of reading posits it as the prototypical activity for understanding the construction of human character and the world with which an individual transacts. I will show that what an infant does with the environmental cues in the construction of its self is no different from what we must all do with printed text and with the same result—the creation of self. This again is a psychological process and requires a psychology of reading for explanation.

Ontological and Ethical Aspects of Reading

I have said that a psychology of reading must account for the whole before it accounts for any of the parts, and I have said that the whole in reading is meaning. Though there are people who can bark at words, make "grunting sounds in response to print" (Goodman, K., 1971, 462), they are merely attacking words and short-circuiting meaning. They are able to recode the graphic symbol into a phonic one—these are children who have good word-attack skills, but in the process of attacking words they do not primarily address meaning, but merely recode one sign into another. Decoding is the going to meaning, and reading is making meaning. The Dreyfuses note (1986, 36) that "the conscious use of calculative rationality," or the use of, say, word-attack skills, produces regression to a primary-skill level and obstructs meaning production. A psychology of reading must account for the construction of meaning and meaner, or rather, the one who means, to avoid the metaphysical monster, the Central Meaner, the homunculus in the brain, before it accounts for, say, the derivative word-attack skills. What I would like to discuss here is how the construction of meaning—the whole—is coincident with the construction of the meaner—the whole reader. Then I would like to discuss how the parts must derive from this whole.

J. Hillis Miller writes in *The Ethics of Reading* (1987, 59) that "To live is to read, or rather to commit again and again the failure to read which is the human lot." Huey, quoted above, noted that reading is the exemplary activity for making sense of existence, and I have argued elsewhere (Block, 1989, 23) that "To live is to read texts but to be alive is to write them." Though I argued there that reading and writing were separate activities, I have now come to understand them as equivalent events, basically, as I will show, ontological and ethical in nature— ethical because ontological. Reading and writing differ only, perhaps, in the products of those events. As I have tried to show in Chapter 1, reading has historically been governed by the hermeneutical project of deriving meaning from a text rather than in constructing it, of exposing a text rather than creating one. Under the proper conditions and employing the right tools, it was claimed, meaning could be made to appear in the Cartesian theater for proper viewing and reviewing by a consciousness. Reading was governed by rule-based authoritative models, and meaning was predetermined and its discovery prefigured. Reading was deemphasized as itself a process for the elevation of its supposed product—meaning. Even in contemporary deconstructive criticism, which Denis Donogue (1993) in a recent issue of the *New York Review of Books* describes as primarily a writing project rather than a reading or speaking one, the practice of reading is defined in the exercise of writing. There, the text is exposed, discovered in all its inconsistencies and contradictions, and defined by these peccadilloes in its ideological necessity to be what it is and no other. Reading is the raw material of writing.

There is a voyeuristic element involved in all of this which may account somewhat for the reticence of some to engage in reading and to the fear often attached to the activity. Recall Hitchcock's *Rear Window* to understand the shame and dangers that accompany voyeurism. Or recall the secretive reading of banned books, sitting under the staircase studying selected portions of worn copies of *Lady Chatterley's Lover*. Reading traditionally has had a mantle of morality imposed upon it:

hence the dicta to read moral books, to read books for morals, and to read morally—which is to say, a reading true to the text. Reading has traditionally been viewed as consistent with the dualistic nature of existence, in which subject and object are separate. In Chapter 2, I showed how an alternative view of reading, one which held it to be a natural activity that was unnaturally and unnecessarily focused upon in educational policy, was marginalized by dominant powers who were able to monopolize the discourses on reading and pedagogy. This occupation made of reading a separate discipline and facilitated the invention of a vast array of intellectual and scholarly apparatus required for its pedagogy.

In all of this talk, the ethics and ontology of reading have been a neglected point. Rather, reading was understood as a skill to be practiced upon a text in which ethical positions could or could not be discovered by a reader sufficiently skilled to discover such positions. Dewey (1898a) criticized the traditional curriculum and its methodology for raising "a false educational god whose idolaters are legion, and whose cult influences the entire educational system," and believed reading ought to be understood "as servants of the intellectual or moral life" (39, 42), by which he meant that in the activity of reading, intellect and morality were constructed even as they changed.

So I would like, with Dewey and with Miller (1987), to look briefly at reading itself as an ontological and ethical act, for I believe that it bears on our discussion of the psychology of reading. Recall Huey's bold statement that to understand what happens when we read would be the quintessential achievement of the psychologist for then s/he would describe the intricate workings of the mind. And recall Dennett's statement that conscious mind may be partially explainable as a virtual machine that runs on a brain's parallel hardware. Finally, recall Dewey's (1929/1971, 247) discrimination between mind and consciousness, the former being the "whole system of meanings as they are embodied in the workings of organic life . . . [and] consciousness in a being with language as the active perception of meaning." Each view presents us with the idea that the activity of the mind producing consciousness is the activity of the production of self. The language activity we call reading, which is always and only the production of meaning, must be understood as an individual construction within a constrained context. Because there is no shared machine language between brains, because no two brains may be wired exactly the same, then all such attempts at sharing language must be social, context sensitive and to some degree self-organizing and self-correcting. All language experiences must be constructivist in nature: Reading, a language-based mode of meaning production—must be seen as an ontological activity that produces consciousness in the human brain. Language does permit us to communicate, to establish relations with an Other. In the act of communication, a behavior of which meaning is a property, we create the self that communicates. Conscious mind is self. The production of meaning is the production of self. And because it is ontological, reading must also be ethical. If we are to understand reading in its holistic sense, then we must acknowledge its role in the formation of self. Reading is not something a self does; rather, the self comes into existence in reading. Hence, the ethics of reading is concerned with the ethics of the creation and acceptance of self.

Traditionally, reading was a neutral means/skill to an ethical end: The substance read was held responsible for the ethical nature of the activity. Reading the Bible was ethical but reading *Tropic of Cancer* was not. Reading the Bible would offer ethical principles valuable to living; reading *Catcher in the Rye* or *To Kill a Mockingbird* would be deleterious to moral and ethical development. Reading was conceptualized as a window through which one could see, even discover meaning; learning to read was an attempt to get closer and closer to exact meaning to see more clearly through the window. Learning to read was understood as perhaps seeing "through a glass darkly," and the psychology of reading was an attempt to learn how information, what was in the text, was processed through the hardware of the brain so that it could be known. But the psychology of reading proposed here presents reading itself, regardless of subject material, as both an ontological and ethical act. Information is not processed; it is created. And reading creates the self and the world with which that self engages. Ethical discourse is traditionally founded upon the presumption of relationships.

And in its sociopsycholinguistic basis, reading is organized by relations. It is for this reason that I begin with the ontology and ethics of reading. As reading occurs in relationship with a mass of verbal symbols that must be constructed into a text and as the reader is constructed by that transaction with the verbal symbols and as the appearance of both text and reader is the reading event and as it is a relational act, then reading might be understood as an ethical project, even as it is simultaneously an ontological one. It is ethical for there must be some acknowledgment of responsibility, some assumption of accountability for the act of reading.

Miller (1987) states that the act of reading itself is an ethical project and inseparable from acts of living: As one reads so one exists. Reading is existence. Miller asserts, as did Huey almost seventy years before, that reading must take place; as I will show, existence is impossible without reading. Rather, as perhaps with José earlier, the greater the inefficiency of reading the greater the confusion, ineffectiveness, and lack of directing action possible to the individual. The greater the inefficiency of reading, the less possibility will be available to the reader, until finally the nonreader is reduced to virtual nonexistence. The greater the inefficiency in reading, the less conscious mind is produced. The ability to anticipate the future, to predict, is the central factor in conscious existence. "The key to control is the ability to *track* or even *anticipate* the important features of the environment, so all brains are, in essence, *anticipation machines*" (Dennett, 1991, 177).[2] Conversely, the inability to anticipate, to control or track—to discover invariants—precludes reading and condemns the self to the immediate present. In more human terms, the self in experiencing the incapacity to read, as I will show in Chapter 4, is incapable of choice and is condemned to nonexistence.

Now, ethics is usually defined by the possibility of choice. Tibor Machan (1985, 183) says that ethics is concerned with what is right or wrong "concerning human beings as such by virtue of their being human. And it concerns what is open to their choices. . . ." Madeleine Grumet (1988, 167) notes that "the object of ethical discourse is the discovery of those principles that can guide the moral conduct of persons who do not know each other." The ethics of reading I propose exists prior to this choice: If I am to be, I must already exist. An ethical discourse on reading, however, is also ontological and must also discuss those principles by which the self is organized, for that self comes into existence in relations. An ethics of reading, which I discuss here, does not presume a reader but constructs one. Its ethics is intrinsic to its activity: *I* must read, and it must be *I* who read. In this formulation, the act of reading itself may be considered ethical even though it is inevitable and seemingly beyond the notion of choice; and though the discourses of reading are not always about the discovery of those principles that guide the relational behavior of strangers,[3] nonetheless, reading as a language activity is relational. Reading is ethical because it takes place ". . . by an implacable necessity, as the response to a categorical demand in which one must attempt to make language referential, and in the sense that the reader *must* take responsibility for it and for its consequences in the personal, social, and political worlds" (Miller, 1987, 59). Reading must take place; it is living, and the reader *must* take responsibility for that reading. I may choose to see that wall as brick or straw, but *I* must take the consequences when *I* run into it. As I will argue, we have no choice if we are to live but to respond to the text—*be it in language or some other form*. We must walk on the road and not under it, unless there is another road below it. Or unless we are willing to make another road for our travels. But we must always acknowledge that response, that reading, *as the response of the individual to a text* if we are to assume the responsibility for self. We may choose not to read, though as Stern (1985) suggests, this may be contrary to our innate abilities. Or we may choose to read "against the grain," as Walter Benjamin (1969) counsels us to do. Only in so doing, Benjamin says, may the reader discover the horrible taint with which each artifact of culture is despoiled.[4] Or we may choose to read and wait for someone to tell us what we read. Or we may look at a verbal text and deny its existence, as does José, and that, too, is a form of reading. "What do you read?" the Reader asks Irnerio in Calvino's (1981) novel.

> Nothing. I've become so accustomed to not reading that I
> don't even read what appears before my eyes. It's not

> easy: they teach us to read as children, and for the rest of
> our lives we remain the slaves of all the written stuff they
> fling in front of us. I may have had to make some effort
> myself, at first to learn not to read, but now it comes quite
> naturally to me. (49)

But in each case, we will know—and be—things we could not be
without reading. To read, to choose to read, and to learn about
reading is to engage in the ethics and ontology of reading: "What
happens when I read *must* happen, but I must acknowledge it as
my act of reading . . . (Miller, 1987, 43). Without that act of reading, self does not exist. Self comes into existence in the act of
reading. I am what I read; I am when I read; I am by reading.

In the assumption of responsibility, the act of reading
becomes the means of the production of identity and is therefore
ethical. The act of reading becomes curriculum as the reader
constructs him/herself and the world in the engagement with it.
Our production of identity is, therefore, an ethical act in both the
political and ontological sense. For whatever reason *we* take
responsibility and in whatever form that responsibility is taken,
it is the *I* who must assume it. Reading then is a matter of ethics
because it is ontological; the process creates identity. Our
purpose here must be to come to some understanding of how the
brain builds self-representation in the activity of reading, so that
the bodies that the brains control are "responsible selves when
all goes well" (Dennett, 1991, 430).

As I have argued, how one is taught to read will determine
how one reads and therefore what identities are possible. This is
not to deny that reading is a productive activity and that what it
produces is self and world. Rather, it argues that we must be
aware of the significance of our reading pedagogies. I
understand in Miller's statement a description of reading that
seems to me closer to the actual experience of it. It argues as well
for the possibility not only of a reading pedagogy but of
reading's centrality to curriculum theorizing and praxis and
ultimately, to education. For Miller's formulation seems to
understand the world as text and conceptualized as text,
necessitating a reading to be originally perceived and
comprehended. Reading, in this formulation, is an ontological
activity: Reading becomes the act of living. The ethics of reading

for Miller is, then, also the ontology of reading. Learning to read may be understood as the function of education. As a forthcoming text will attest (Pinar, Reynolds, Slattery & Taubman, in press), this notion of textuality—and its correlative, intertextuality—is already a powerful movement in the field of curriculum theory and praxis. In that book, curriculum will be studied as a multidimensional text that can be realized in the act of reading. Curriculum may be conceptualized as the process of learning to read the text. Education will be a matter of reading pedagogy. The end product of education will be the development of the subject and the object, the subject as object. The act itself creates the actant and the activity. As Pinar and Grumet (1976) have written of curriculum in another context

> The track around which I run may be inalterably forced, but the rate at which I run, the quality of my running, my sensual-intellectual-emotional experience of moving bodily through space and time: all these are my creations; they are my responsibilities. The Regents may tell me what course to run, but whether the course is instructive or not, interesting or not, pleasurable or not, liberative or not, ultimately and immediately is my responsibility, and that of my fellow runners. (vii)

I would add to that image, that which runs and in what way—indeed, the decision to run at all—is productive of the runner or nonrunner. The track is only so when it is run upon, and when I run upon it I am the runner. Activity is, however, requisite and therefore demands reading. To have a picnic on the track makes it no longer a track. If I dine upon the track during the meet, I must take responsibity for the consequences of my choice. Reading, my transaction with the text, creates myself and my world—it is ethical in that I must take responsibility for it, and it is ontological in that I created myself and the world in the transaction.

   For Miller, reading—curriculum—is an ethical act, which is to say that it must be done and that *I* must take responsibility for *my* reading. My reading is a product of what I know, and it is I who knows. No one else knows what I know, has come to know it as I know it, and no one else can read this text as I read it now. In this sense, reading must be an ontological act: Selfhood is only achievable in the act of reading when both the creator and the creation are acknowledged in the singular act of reading. Reading creates the self: "What happens [when I read] is the experience of an 'I must' that is always the same but always different, unique, idiomatic" (Miller, 1987, 127). And because it is my self that must take responsibility for the reading, not according to some law but according to my self, then reading is truly an ethical act. A psychology of reading must account for and be responsible for the creation of this self and not for the processes by which an abstract and preexistent self processes information.

Miller's thesis epitomizes a view of reading not widely held in academic circles, where reading is traditionally theorized on hermeneutical models in which meaning is discoverable by employing the right skills, or where reading is conceived as occuring as a function of information-processing systems and the brain is likened to a computer. In the latter, reading is explained by the establishment of a system that transmits information for collation somewhere and by a central meaner. A failure to read is a breakdown in the system, as in dyslexia. In the former, a failure to read is attributed to a lack of skills, an inadequate self. Reading pedagogy is designed to train those skills, and school curriculum is based on those perceived needs. One learns to read so that one may read. As I have tried to show in the previous chapters and as Shannon has shown in his critical study of reading pedadgogy in the United States (1989), this pedagogy does not offer the open possibility of reading but rather, its constraint.

> If John Dewey was correct and "children learn what they do," then during these story-reading rituals, students learn that reading is the attempt to memorize text which someone else selects so that you can reproduce factual information when questioned and the passage's phonetics when asked to read orally—all under the watchful eye of the teacher/monitor. (96)

A psychology of reading premised on this model will produce an individual filled with doubt, self-hate, and fear. This pedagogy of reading denies the productive self and its meaning and supports the traditional and culturally correct meanings that historically have been given priority. When our meanings are denied, so too are our selves, and we learn to hate that self that produces falsehoods and lies. I would like to explore this notion briefly and look at the creative transactional nature of reading from the psychological perspective, explain the process from the vantage point of psychoanalytical theory, and suggest how a reading pedagogy that denies this process produces a self-hating individual.

Reading as Self-Production: A Psychological Perspective on Perceiving and Self

A theory of reading that separates the reader from the text not only falsifies the reading process and denies agency in the production of self but educates the reader to hate the self that is ultimately produced. Marion Milner (1987, 207), describing clients who came to Freud with emotional problems, suggests that the origin of their condition lay in the hegemony of positivistic rationalist thinking: "They had been trying to solve problems of feeling by means of the kind of thinking which divides what we see from ourselves seeing it, the kind of thinking which we call logical and for which we have formulated laws—the primary laws of logic; such as, for instance, that a thing is what it is and is not what it is not; or that something cannot both be and not be at the same time." This system accounts also for the predominance of psychological theories of reading based in cognitive psychology and information-processing systems. In this conception of reading based in cognitive science, a psychology of reading seeks to analyze the situation into context-free elements. Crowder and Wagner (1992), for example, are content not to "become paralyzed trying to define reading exactly," and offer instead ". . . to find out what goes on when a normal adult reads a newspaper article silently" (4). Needless to say, to try to define the reading process using the newspaper as exemplar could hardly explain the study of exegetical texts, the reading of a popular novel, the exploration of history, or looking for a number in a phone book, all of which are reading activities. Such an oversimplification denies the complexity of the nature of reading and of the self.

Recent information-processing models of reading (Crowder & Wagner, 1992; Just & Carpenter, 1987) have attempted to explore reading using the computer as exemplar. As justification for their approach, Just and Carpenter write that

> A theory of a complex cognitive skill can be quite cumbersome to describe because there are so many components to identify, explain, and relate. Furthermore, English and other natural languages are not well suited to describing information-processing operations . . . in cognitive psychology, theories are often expressed in the language of computer simulation models. Just as cardiac physiologists build hydraulic models of how they think the human heart operates, so do cognitive theories build computer programs as models of how they think the human mind operates. (10)

As Daniel Dennett (1991) argues, however, the computer software program might be a serial program, but the brain is a parallel-processing system, and the idea of consciousness may be only partially explained by any computer program. Information-processing systems using the computer as their model argue that it is possible to understand the whole from a study of the parts: "a theory of reading must not only explain how each component process operates but also how they all operate together" (Just & Carpenter, 1987, 261). This statement assumes that the parts are distinguishable from the whole and that the latter can be shown to derive from the individual parts. But the psychological reality of this makes no sense: "It follows," says Dewey (1929/1971, 268), "that theories which identify knowledge with acquaintance, recognition, definition and classification give evidence, all the better for being unintended, that we know not just events but events-with-meanings." Recognition assumes meaning and does not cause it. In other words, knowledge is never the parts but the parts contextualized into a meaningful whole that is no longer comprised of parts. "That a perception is cognitive means, accordingly, that it is used; it is treated as a sign of conditions that implicate other as yet unperceived consequences in addition to the perception itself" (263). Non-sense syllables are nonsense: That is ultimately the meaning of them as objects.

At least for now, establishing the existence of a pattern does not necessarily explain a system, given the present limits of our human abilities. Rather, the existence of a pattern indicates merely the existence of a consciousness creating a pattern. Information processing is an invention of the human mind and may not be intrinsic to that mind. The parts do not equal the whole but are derivable from that whole, which is itself not only ultimately irreducible but greater and different from the sum of the parts. Finally, a manipulation of any one of the parts will destroy the whole. Information processing requires the existence first of a discoverable system. John Searle (1992) has written persuasively that

> The brain, as far as its intrinsic operations are concerned, does no "information processing." It is a specific biological organ and its specific neurobiological processes cause specific forms of intentionality. In the brain, intrinsically, there are neurobiological processes and sometimes they cause consciousness. But that is the end of the story. All other mental attributes are either dispositional, as when we ascribe unconscious states to the agent, or they are observer relative, as when we assign a computational interpretation to his brain processes. (226)

Nor, as Jerome Bruner (1990, 7) has argued, does cognitive psychology's courtship with computer models deal with meaning or agency. In cognitive science, Bruner argues, "One did not have to truck with 'mental' processes or with meaning at all. In place of stimuli and responses, there was input and output, with reinforcement laundered of its affective taint by being converted into a control element that fed information about the outcome of an operation back into the system. So long as there was a computable program, there was 'mind.'" Hence, reading research is inundated with studies of nonsense syllables, as if reading nonsense could be equated with making sense.[5] Agency is here denied. Conceptualized in this way, reading is always an activity separate from the reader, a process about something that is not the reader. A psychology of reading premised on this model posits an activity but not a self engaged in that activity. There could be no ethics or ontology of reading in this view.

The notion of reading as a form of play, however, discounts both the skill-based theory and the informational-processing theory of reading and may help account for the ontology and ethics of reading I suggest. For it is in play that the self finds what it creates because, in play, the self exists in an environment where its omnipotence—the capacity to find what it creates with impunity—is accepted. Lev Vygotsky (1978) argues that play is central to the development of higher-order psychological processes. Play permits the child to give meaning to what is not there. Vygotsky states that "it is the essence of play that a new relation is created between the field of meaning and the visual field—that is, between situations in thought and real situations" (104). Play is a liberating activity, freeing the learner from the constraints of the immediate and immediacy. In the activity of play, things lose their determining force and are malleable. *"The child sees one thing but acts differently in relation to what he sees. Thus a condition is reached where the child begins to act independently of what he sees"* (97). In play, the family broom becomes my daughter's horse and my shirt her thick cascading hair. In play, the child creates the space wherein s/he exists and creates herself in that space. When my daughter puts hair clips in my shirt atop her head, she *is* a child with long hair. She is creating herself in that play and will never return to that original self. She will always have knowledge of the child with long hair.

Reading might be understood as a form of play and the text understood as the Winnicottian "transitional phenomena." For Winnicott (1986), transitional phenomena are the objects of play with which the infant creates the space where s/he lives—which is to say the potential space, the shape given to the area of illusion that there is actually an external reality that the child can create. My daughter's room is at times the ocean, a woods, or a bedroom. In that expanse and with the use of transitional phenomena, she creates the space in which she lives apart from her attachment to either myself or her mother. "In health, there is no separation [between the mother and child] because in the space-time area between the child and the mother, [in health] the child [and so the adult] lives creatively, making use of the materials that are available—a piece of wood or a late Beethoven quartet" (Winnicott, 1986, 36–7). Using transitional phenomena, the child and/or adult creates the space between and in which s/he can live creatively because it is the space s/he has created. "You be the brother," my daughter says to me when she wants to play house, and I am suddenly and willingly transformed into her creative space. In reading the text, and I speak here of written texts, the reader is able to take external reality—words, phrases, sentences, clauses—and make of it what she will in the act of play. A child who as yet has not learned to sample the written texts for graphophonic cues may create one story, while another who has learned such sampling strategies will produce another. In reading, the reader invents a world which s/he can know is not-me but which is created out of the me. That area of play invents both the text and the self and is the essence of cultural experience. This cultural experience, Winnicott (1986, 36) claims, "cannot be placed in the inner or personal psychical reality, because it is not a dream—it is part of shared reality. But it cannot be said to be part of external relationships, because it is dominated by dream." This cultural experience is, to use Rosenblatt's word, a transaction. Stern's pragmatism, which suggests that the child creates the sense of self in action in the world, argues similarly.

For Winnicott, it is the transitional phenomena—the text and its possibility—that make possible the child's separation from, yet linkage to, the mother/father and allows for the production of the me and the not-me. Now, I do not mean here to suggest that the infant exists originally in a natural undifferentiated state with the mother out of which it must develop. Rather, I would argue that the infant must become aware *through action or mental processes* of those invariants in the world out of which sense of self will arise. By mental processes I refer to the active, cognitive use of perception: This means, as Dewey says, that the perception "is treated as a sign of conditions that implicate other as yet unperceived consequences in addition to the perception itself" (Dewey, 1929/1971, 263). A perception is cognitive when its "active *use* is followed by consequences which fit appropriately into the other consequences which follow independently of its being perceived" (263). With regard to reading, this can only be realized in the production of meaning and not in the isolated identification of letters, nonsense syllables, or words. Transitional phenomena are not merely the breast's replacement, not *the means* of differentiation, a state which Stern argues is original to the infant, but rather, occasions of action by which invariants may be discovered and/or created. Using the text, the child/adult may produce the area of cultural experience and live creatively. "The child uses a position in between himself or herself and the mother or father, whoever it is, and there [in the potential space that is not there but which is created] whatever happens is symbolic of the union or the non-separation of these two separate things" (Winnicott, 1986, 134). In other words, what is created in that potential space is a product of all of the relations in which the child engages and yet is separate from those other relations. Recall that I said above that to read is to know that the sign expresses and that that expression contains everything that has made possible the sign's appearance at this particular time and in this particular place, including what may now be called 'me,' which too, as a sign, expresses and contains everything that has made possible its appearance. Therefore, in the creation of the space/text, the child has invented a self and space coincidentally. Hence it is that for Winnicott, though home is where we start from, it is in reading—in our play with the text—that we create the spaces wherein we live; wherein we produce ourselves in the creation of the other and in which we may reproduce all that we know of home. Reading the text is the essence of creativity and the experience of play and is the basis of health in this world. Milner (1987, 221) says that "there seems to have been a time when the faculty of consciousness itself was felt to be entirely creative, to be aware of anything was simply to have made it; all one saw was one's own, as Traherne said, and it was one's own because one had made it." It is only when what we have created is rejected, as we will shortly see, that we are disillusioned and experience self-hate. It is when we read and our creations are considered wrong that we learn to hate reading and ourselves who read.

Reading as Creativity

In reading instruction, we are taught to read outlines, to discover the letters, the words, etc. The predominance of subskill approaches to reading ensures this. In this approach, proficient reading is understood as the acquistion of developmental skills. These skills include the recognition of letters and words, the development of sight vocabulary, the identification of phonic principles to recode graphic cues into phonic ones, and the development of comprehension skills. According to this view, reading is a highly complex skill comprised of subordinate units that must be first mastered and integrated to form higher-order skills. In this view, reading is not a natural language process. Indeed, such reading theorists as Mitford Mathews declare reading to be the most unnatural language process (1966). Understood as an unnatural process, reading as an information-processing system remains separate from the real world. Dewey had said in another context that as long as a subject and an object were conceptualized as actually existing, then there could be the study by a subject who wants to know how it may be possible to know at all. In this dualistic division of subject and object arises what is known as epistemology, out of which will develop cognitive psychology. Describing what will become the project of cognitive psychology Dewey (1929/1971, 12) states,

> Therefore it has upon its hands the problem of how it is possible to know at all; how an outer world can affect an inner mind; how the acts of mind can reach out and lay hold of objects defined in antithesis to them.

In this view, the reader must acquire certain skills in order to gain the facility to read. The figure is separated from the ground, defining and changing the nature of both. "Reading," Eleanor Gibson and Harry Levin write, "is extracting information from text"(1975, 5). To be able to do so is to know the figure from the ground and to know where information is to be found.

   Now, I take this image of the figure and ground from Gestalt psychology and from the discipline of phenomenology. The ground may be considered all that is not the figure; it represents, according to Dreyfus and Dreyfus (1992), the outer horizon of our perceptual field. Employing a different terminology, Dewey (1929/1971, 254) describes the ground as the "remote, outlying field [which] corresponds to what does not have to be modified, and which may be dependably counted upon in dealing with imminent need." The ground may be thought of as the invariants in an event. The figure corresponds to the point of imminent need, of immediate urging. Now, the figure can only be perceived if the ground is perceived as well. The figure must be our perception of the specific object or pattern in question. When we look for words, we find words. But we cannot see the words if we do not know that they are organized on a page. We do not see the spaces between words or lines, though our ability to read assumes that we know they are there.

Marie Clay's *Sand: The Concepts About Prints Tests* (1972) assesses children's emergent sense of literacy, that is, of how books work. On one aspect of the test, Clay asks children to look at a page and to show her where they might find the words. Visually, the notion of the figure and ground permits us to see the profile when we look for the profile, to see the vase when we look for the vase, and to look for words when we seek words. We cannot, however, see the profile and the vase at the same time. Nor can we see the spaces between the lines and the words at the same time. This notion of the outer horizon permits us to understand how background information regarding a particular event may be ignored without being excluded. We cannot attend to the outer horizon or we might lose the figure, but the figure is only possible if we acknowledge the existence of the outer horizon. The outer horizon is our sense of the whole situation through which sense we may be guided in filling in details. It makes a world of difference whether a book is read at a school desk within the school building or it is read at home or in the public library. Context affects meaning.

Subskill approaches to reading suggest that the whole is comprised of the concatenation of the parts and though the whole may be ultimately greater than the sum of those parts, the whole can be reduced to them for analysis. As one book that advocates this subskill view of reading attests: "Where does meaning enter in? For skilled readers it seems that meaning, too, is largely the product of effortless and *automated* [emphasis added] activities" (Adams, 1990, 137). Adams adds that reading is a regular orderly and exactly definable process with a clear beginning and end: "The orthographic processor is the only one that received input directly from the printed page: The first important point of the figure is that, when reading, it is visual, orthographic processing that comes first and that causes the system to kick in" (137). Meaning in this schema derives from the processing of information, which must begin with the orthographic processor which "contains all of the individual letter recognition units and the associative linkages between them" (137). In this view, comprehension is a multilayered process starting at the bottom where each individual word must be comprehended, then collapsed into a composite interpretation. In a slightly different context, Madeleine Grumet (1988, 143) responds to this formulation in the following, and to me, wonderful way:

> The absurdity of this sequence would be matched only if I took out flour, sugar and butter, milk, eggs, vanilla, cardamon and baking powder, mixed them all in a bowl, observed the blend, noting its texture and flavor, applied this information to my previous experience, and hypothesized that I might be making either a cake, a pudding, an omelette, or a quiche, a blintz, a crepe, or a pancake.

In this conception, there is only the separated figure and ground. But of course, this conceptualization can little account for the production of meaning. It denies agency.

Reading is a whole procedure and the relationship between figure and ground is central in understanding the psychology of it. Reading occurs as a whole and not as a concatenation of parts and as a process may be largely explainable by Gestalt psychology, a psychology that recognizes the whole as different from and greater than the sum of any of its parts. A gestalt—the whole—defines what counts as the elements it organizes; the elements themselves are meaningless, defined independently of the gestalt, and the gestalt is nothing but the organization of the elements. If we only see letters it is because they make sense to us. There is a difference between

AAA and AA that goes beyond the number of letters, which are not recognized as letters but as the narrative of the organization, American Automobile Association or Alcoholics Anonymous. These organizations, and of course the letters that represent them, are only meaningful insofar as I have a relationship with them.

Letters and words may be defined by outlines, but as long as we understand letters and words to be products of separation, we deny the ability to read. And by separation I mean that letters and words are understood as distinct entities that must be *automatically and automatedly* organized and processed for the next stage of information processing in an increasingly complex system leading to meaning identification. The letters and words that we are taught to read are established by boundaries and are perceived as organized forms. As Marilyn Adams (1990, 63) argues, "The speed and accuracy of letter naming is an index of the thoroughness or confidence with which the letters' identities have been learned. A child who can recognize most letters with thorough confidence will have an easier time learning about letter sounds and word spellings than a child who has to work at remembering what is what." The assumption that reading is recoding the graphic symbol into an aural one organizes this psychology of reading and solidifies both the forms of the letters and the *rules* for their combinations. This system defines the figure and ignores the ground. My four-year-old daughter will recognize only three capital As and not the title of an organization when she comes upon AAA. In this system, forms as singular entities are specified by outlines—visual and aural— and represent separation. "How do you figure out a word you don't know?" a child is asked, and 95 percent of the time s/he will answer, "I sound it out." Reading as the production of meaning is a by-product of this process and not its sole purpose. I believe that this distorts the psychology of reading, making it all the more difficult to read. In the separation of the whole into the parts, the reading process is distorted and the ability of the reader to produce self and meaning is constrained and denied. In the separation of the whole into the parts, a particular reader is produced who will know only a limited form of reading.

We know that identifying words does not equate with reading, with meaning production. As any teacher will attest, a student can read every word and still comprehend very little. Nor does merely recoding words phonologically enhance meaning production significantly. Patterson and Coltheart (1987) argue that research suggests that neither assembled phonology (synthetic phonics) nor addressed phonology (whole word) can account for word recognition or comprehension. Rather, they theorize, phonological representations *may* assist in meaning production as a facility for storing text in short-term memory until a prediction based upon language sense and meaning-construction strategies can be made, resulting in comprehension. Since speech is an earlier language system than reading, it would be productive to use strategies already in place for comprehending and producing oral language. "It would seem inefficient, not to say perverse, if the reading skills to be acquired failed to make use of the sophisticated and elaborate language 'equipment' already available" (441). Phonological representation, then, is already based upon knowledge maintained by the reader about language and does not itself account for word recognition or comprehension. In fact, phonological representations seem already based on tentative comprehension strategies premised on prediction. Furthermore, since reading takes place in a different time-space continuum than listening, then some recoding to phonological representation may assist in facilitating meaning production. But we must understand phonological representation as only a strategy for meaning production, not one required for it. As Ken Goodman (1971a, 462) argues,

> The listener has already learned a very efficient language process. He has become competent with the oral language to the point where he can go from that oral signal to the underlying structure, to meaning, efficiently and rapidly. He knows which cues to select and knows how to plug in to the grammatical system to pick up grammatical cues and get at the underlying structures. He can plug in the meaning from his experiences and from concepts that he has developed. All that is working already. Now if the difference between reading and listening is a matter of going from a written signal rather than an oral signal, what, in fact, he has to learn is not how to match letters to

> sounds but how to get from that written signal to the
> underlying structure in much the way that he has learned
> to get from the oral signal to the underlying structure.

The phonological parts only have existence as they are derived from the whole, which is meaning. By itself, phonological representation cannot account for meaning production. Rather, emphasis on phonological representation as a necessary process of meaning production represents an isolation of form from content, falsifying the relationship between the two and creating a hierarchy of subskills which short-circuits the production of meaning.

Forms are separate objects made so by outlines. Letters and words are separate entities in traditional reading instruction and are learned out of their natural context as words and connected text.[6] Outlines, in separating one entity from another, in essence create those entities. Now what is perceived as separate is forever lost to us as part of ourselves. It, the form, is not of 'I' but of the 'other'. Our fealty to outlines in reading, in our emphasis on knowing letters and words prior to meaning, affirms our belief in an external, solid, permanent world that is not of us but is, rather, separate from us. In Winnicottian terms, this practice denies the text as a transitional phenomenon and denies its use in creating the cultural spaces in which we may live. Rather, it creates the text as a self-contained form. Outlines confirm us as individual entities by their act of separation, but they also insist on our alienation in that confirmation. I have no part in the production of letters and words; rather, I must learn to perceive and process them that I—a mysterious *I* that precedes my act—may finally get meaning from the text I read. In this process we are the other of the Other; we stand over and against the text and we must struggle with it to attain its meaning correctly. Marion Milner, in her book *On Not Being Able to Paint* (1950/1990), explores the significance of outlines because her inability to paint seems tied directly to her relationship to outlines and to the objects they create. I intend to link Milner's inability to paint to the psychological reality of reading, to the ontological and ethical qualities of it, and to the ability to read or the failure thereof. For both reading and writing are productive activities relying on the relationship to outlines, to figure and ground.

Milner relates how when she paints her products appear either as counterfeit when she attempts to paint representationally, following the outline she saw; or appear as a different painting from what she had intended when she attempts to paint only from her thoughts. When she considers the nature of her failure to represent her vision, it is to the idea of a relationship to outlines that she ascribes primary responsibility for that inadequacy. It is, after all, these outlines that can match in the representation in her painting neither the external reality nor her internal mood. Not being able to paint results from the inability to either affirm the outline or deny it. Phrased another way, the inability to paint seems to result from an inability to form a relationship between the external and the internal world. Words are nonexistent unless meaning can be produced with them: In gestalt terms, words require a virtual reader with a horizon to enable perception of the figure. "As to be a tool, or to be used as means for consequences, is to have and to endow with meaning, language, being the tool of tools, is the cherishing mother of all significance" (Dewey, 1929/1971, 154). As an example: NOW is accepting membership of anyone who knows something about its political positions and can support those positions with action now. The first and last "now" are pronounced exactly the same, but only the latter is a word. Pronunciation, emphasis, and intonation are dependent on the horizon brought to the text. A person ignorant of the National Organization of Women would ask, "Now who is accepting membership?" Outlines are created and are not fixed.

For Milner, painting is the attempt to represent a piece of the world on canvas, but what that world to be represented actually is is called into question by her inability to paint: by a perceived absence of creativity. Whenever she defines her subject prior to painting, she seems unable to paint. And the inability to paint, despite the technical skill and her desire to do so, argues another explanation for her failure. Milner explores how not being able to paint—and the subsequent engagement in learning how to do so—becomes for her a study of the relationships that create subject and object, self and world, and is a question of outlines and of the discipline that forms them. Adam Phillips (1993) makes a similar argument in his essay "First Hates: Phobias in Theory." Using William James' notion of the truth of a state of mind as a "leading that is worthwhile," Phillips describes the agoraphobic as the compromised pragmatist, for the agoraphobic would be led somewhere but is unable to find out whether it is worthwhile to be led there. "The terror, or the inability to hold the terror, preempts possible future states of mind, and so precludes their evaluation. A phobia, in other words, protects a person from his own curiousity" (14). The phobic looks at a page and is terrorized by the knowledge of what the page is for, even what s/he must use it for. In that sense, the page ceases to be open and leads directly into the past, "into the old world," and precludes action. Prior reading instruction has denied the possibility of present reading by establishing outlines, parameters, and boundaries of the permissible and acceptable.

As for Milner in painting, the conflict in reading may be understood as a conflict of boundaries, of outlines, of discriminations between subject and object. The reader, as must the painter, produces an order out of the arrayed symbols; without the reader the symbols are simply not there. A young child will often say that reading is knowing a lot of words, without knowing also that those words have no meaning unless they can "represent sensuous, emotional and intellectual perceptions" (Rosenblatt, 1938, 52). Then, with the symbols as stimulus, the reader "marshals his resources and crystallizes out from the stuff of memory, thought, and feeling a new order, a new experience, which [is seen] as the poem" (Rosenblatt, 1978, 12). The new order and experience that is produced as the poem means, too, the new order and experience that is produced as the individual. It is new, though it arises from all that is not new. "Empirically," says John Dewey (1929/1971, 178), "the individual is a novel reconstruction of a preexisting order." Meaning exists neither in the text nor in the reader but in the transaction between them, and both come into existence in the event of this transaction.

Painting and reading, by their nature, are the desire to produce meaning on canvas or some other medium, and seem to have something to do with feeling aroused by the idea of space and time. There is a canvas: in reading we call that canvas a text. To read it is to call into question the whole notion of space—with what that yet-empty potential expanse must be filled?, and to call into question the notion of time—will this production be always correct? "The phobic person," says Adam Phillips (1993, 19), "is suspended between the first and the second degree of composition; he assumes, quite sensibly, that making the transition will break the frame rather than . . . making it a frame for something that seems true. He hovers in his terror, unable to make that decisive transition."[7] Milner discovers that learning to paint—to read—required courage because it concerned ideas of distance and estrangement, of having and losing. So too with reading. If what I read is separate from me, can I negotiate the distance safely and attain the right forms? Do I dare take the risk?

Hence, the ability to paint and to read are linked inexorably to ideas of separation and of risk. Painting and reading have to do with outlines: "So it became clear," Milner (1950/1990, 12) writes, "that if painting is so concerned with problems of being a separate body in a world of other bodies which occupy different bits of space: in fact, it must be deeply concerned with ideas of distance and separation and having and losing." Her inability to paint might be understood as a failure to negotiate feelings of distance and separation, of having and losing. These are issues central to existence and true equally for understanding the ability to read and to teach reading. Our ability or inability to read concerns feelings of distance and separation, of having and losing. Research shows that students do not so much dislike reading as they dislike reading what is assigned in school because it is boring. Boring, as Frank Smith notes, is not being able to ask any questions, to make of the text what is needed. "Though we were encouraged to read, students were not guided to take control of the text, but only to learn the author's message" (Bintz, 1993, 607). Reading represented separation and loss. Reading required a denial of self and the acknowledgment of the authority of others in representing the world.[8] Reading, too, traditionally removes the reader abruptly, and often definitively, from what s/he has lived through in reading the word.

Milner's inability to paint seemed to stem not from a lack of technical skill but resulted in large part from conflicted thoughts about the human condition: about issues regarding separation and loss and the concerns about her capacity as an individual to negotiate those often painful feelings. Resistant readers show similar conflict. Getting it right is what classroom reading requires and separates readers from the production of meaning, ultimately making reading impossible. Getting it right is discovering the outline, the not-me. For Milner, this felt inability to paint became a question of boundaries, of outlines, for it is they that seemed to her to effect separation and establish distance. Milner is intrigued by the notion of the outline and its effect on her, as it appears to function to establish the object and offer the illusion that the object is real. Painting might be understood as the drawing of outline, of getting it right. Reading, too, is getting it right: Recall Adams' description of reading above as the exact processing of stimulus input. Or Ron Carver's (1992) definition of reading as looking at the words and getting meaning. But in close observation, Milner discovers that outlines—that which appears as the object of painting and that which creates forms that are the painting—are not, as one is led to believe, real: "When really looked at in relation to each other . . . outlines were not clear and compact, as I had always supposed them to be, they continually became lost in shadow"(Milner, 1950/1990, 15). Try sometime to see an outline of an other without also seeing its immediate context, its *ecology*, and you will understand what Milner means. The reality of the solidity of objects dissipates, and the separation between the world and self begins to dissolve. As forms break up, fear of madness may rise as separation between the world and self vanishes, as what is inside begins to bubble and threaten the solidity of the external world of forms constructed of outlines. This danger is a learned fear and derives from the focus on outlines, on separation, on getting it right.

Outlines represent the world of fact, of separate, touchable objects; to cling to a belief in outlines is to cling to the distinction between self and other, here and there, then and now. Outlines organize spatial and temporal relationships in this world by identifying separateness. What is the alternative? If indeed, outlines do not exist, then objects are not fact but are our constructions, and reality is not out there to be perceived by a subject but is, rather, established by a subject in relationship to objects. That subject, however, only comes into being in that relationship. What we see is what we create; perception is not the beginning of consciousness but the result of it and is premised in prior knowledge. As Gregory Bateson (1972, 453) says:

> . . . any object contains [and is contained by] any number of differences. Of this infinitude, we select a very limited number which become information. In fact, what we mean by information—the elementary unit of information—is a difference which makes a difference, and is able to make a difference because the neural pathways along which it travels and is continually transformed are themselves provided with energy. The pathways are ready to be triggered. We may even say that the question is already implicit in them.

In other words, what we find is what we look for and this is a product of what we are already predisposed to know. This means that in the creation of the object—what is out there—the subject is also constructed, for everything out there must be acknowledged as my own construction—that for which I must take responsibility.

This is the situation Milner explores in order to realize the ability to paint—to be creative, to read, to invent the world and herself. These are spiritual issues, complex psychological issues not explainable by information-processing systems. Seeing was an act of the imagination. Seeing the outlines of things was difficult; seeing the inside of things was even more profound and frightening. Milner's inability to paint represented an inability to negotiate these fears and terrors. To attempt to paint representationally, realistically, by drawing outlines is impossible because any view of any object is always fortuitous. "The present-moment view of any object is always determined by accident of where one is standing at the moment . . . to know the truth of people you have to select and combine . . . to combine all the partial glimpses into a relevant whole. This requires imagination . . ." (Milner, 1950/1990, 14).

Hence, the world is not real in the sense that it exists outside of us and we must discover it; rather, it is a construction of our imagination, all that we have within us from all past relationships, along with that which is outside of us, whether realized as outside relationships or not. Reality, it would seem, derives not from outline, from separation, but from our creation of the world, in our recognition that it is our own construction that establishes objects by our relation to them. Living is a process of relationships: Experience is the interplay of vital forces, the activity of relating constantly, leading through fresh relatings to a new activity. Our activity changes as we engage in it and does not evolve from purpose to deed and from deed to purpose as if life moved as on a pulley, with only an "external wirepuller to account for the jerks" (1950/1990, 77). I am a runner not because I own running shoes but because I wear them on the road. I am a runner not because I think about roads but because I run on them. And I am a runner because I am running and not because I am finished running. Reality is created in engagement with it, and this always occurs in a relational act of construction between our imaginations and that part of the world that makes itself available to our actions. Descartes found himself alone in the room and could not doubt only his ability to doubt. But Jo Anne Pagano (1990, 35) discovers, unlike Descartes, that "I am alone in the house, and I too am thinking. But my version of thinking takes place, literally, in a world of cats and puppies and husbands and vegetables and oven times. My version claims the world and acknowledges the world's claim on me." For Pagano, her horizon always is part of her thinking; she is not apart from the world. She is part of it. After all, if outlines do not in fact exist, whatever form we see is a product of those outlines we create based on our own needs, wishes, and dreams. "The substance of experience," Milner attests, "is what we bring to what we see, without our own contribution we see nothing" (1950/1990, 27). The power to endow the world with our dreams is creativity. Our action creates the world, and then it is our world and not that of common sense.

But this world, which does not coincide with the world of common sense, threatens our belief in a commonly taught common-sense reality, threatens belief in our sanity, and is usually summarily rejected. The belief in outlines staves off the madness that we are made to fear would result by losing our hold on the solid earth. Madness is what we fear by the loss of separateness that would result from the dissolution of outlines. Outlines represent the world of fact; belief in them protects one against the world of the imagination. But it does so at great price. If we accept our role in the creation of objects, then that object cannot be separate from us. To accept outlines is to endure separation and loss, an extremely painful condition. And so, Milner wonders, how is it possible to have remained so long unaware of this fact concerning outlines, and why does it take such a great mental effort to see the edges of objects as they actually show themselves rather than as she had always thought of them in the common-sense view of reality? From where does that common-sense view derive?

I believe that learning to read is equivalent to learning to paint. Experience is the establishment of a dialogic relationship between the external world and our own wishes and dreams. In painting, that relationship establishes a canvas; in reading, it establishes, in Louise Rosenblatt's terms, a poem. In life, that relationship establishes experience. The world is blank until we paint it on a canvas. A painting is never reality but one's creation of it. Creativity is a reciprocal relationship between dreams— what is inside—and what is outside. To learn to read is to learn how to endow the objects of the external world with a spiritual life, with action appropriate to their nature. "Meaning," Grumet (1988, 143) notes, "is something we make out of what we find when we look at texts. It is not in the texts." One seeks, says Milner, to find a bit of the outside world that is willing to temporarily fit in with one's dreams. In that illusion occurs a moment in which the inner and outer seem to coincide, in which a unity is achieved, and world and self are one and of our creation. It is in those moments that one begins to believe in the life of action, a life in which one could seek to rebuild, restore, recreate what one loved in actual achievement. In creativity, we come to understand that the outside world actually wants what we have to give; we fill the gap by creating the gap. This is what Winnicott meant by transitional phenomena and is what, I hold, makes a book exactly that. In painting and in reading, we may deliberately restore the split between subject and object and bring together the two into a new unity. In reading, the world is altered, distorted from its natural shape to fit the inner experience. One becomes whole. We are the world.

Of course, to deny this imagination is to deny the child and to deny reading. The child is denied hope of establishing creative and healthy relationships, as those relationships are delivered predefined and predetermined. "One of the great tragedies of contemporary education is not so much that many students leave school unable to read and to write, but that others graduate with an antipathy to reading and writing, despite the ability they might have. Nothing about reading or its instruction is inconsequential" (Smith, 1988, 177). As a result of this despair, the student may become a dictatorial egoist who actively denies the wishes and needs of the other (and this may include the physical earth as well as other people) and tries to make his/her own wishes alone determine what happens. Here is one who wholly denies the demands of an external world. Or one can become a passive egoist, retreating from public reality and taking refuge in a world of unexpressed dreams, becoming remote and inaccessible. Or finally, to avoid conflict, the individual permits the outside world to become a dictator, fits him/herself into the external world and its demands and results in doing what others want and betrays one's own wishes and dreams.

Reading the text may be understood as the essence of creativity *and* the experience of play. "Cultural experience," Winnicott (1986, 36) says, "starts as play, and leads on to the whole area of man's inheritance, including the arts, the myths of history, the slow march of philosophical thought and the mysteries of mathematics, and of group management and of religion." Winnicott (1971, 41) says that "playing is neither inside by any use of the word [which would be fantasy] . . . nor is it outside, that is, it is not a part of the repudiated world, the not-me, that which the individual has decided to recognize (with whatever difficulty and even pain) as truly external which is outside magical control." Playing is the activity that exists in the potential space that constitutes the greater part of the infant's experience and that "throughout life is retained in the intense experiencing that belongs to the arts and to religion and to imaginative living, and to scientific work"(14). We experience life in the area of transitional phenomena, "in the exciting interweave of subjectivity and objective observation, and in an area that is intermediate between the inner reality of the individual and the shared reality of the world external to individuals"(64). This is what Milner refers to above as the essence of creativity, of being able to paint. It also makes possible the ability to read. A psychology of reading that is not based upon this creative whole will only misrepresent the possibility of reading and hinder the ability to read.

The act of reading is, in its essence, a creative act. Reading produces something out of nothing, produces the reader and the poem, to use Rosenblatt's (1978) term for the creation that derives from a text. Out of the arrays of stimuli in the trans-action, the reader and the text come into existence: Regardless of her own insights, the reader reads according to her own temperament and no other. What is created is present meaning. "The creative impulse is therefore something that can be looked at as a thing in itself, something that of course is necessary if an artist is to produce a work of art, but also as something that is present when *anyone*—baby, child, adolescent, adult, old man or woman—looks in a healthy way on anything or does anything deliberately, such as making a mess with faeces or prolonging the act of crying to enjoy a musical sound" (Winnicott, 1971, 69). Reading is the active process of looking at and doing with a text and is an act of play and creation. Louise Rosenblatt (1978, 18) states that "In ecological terms, the text becomes the element of the environment to which the individual responds . . . each forms an environment for the other during the reading event." Of course, in a society whose emphasis is on product, the object, the *process* of reading is not only easily lost, but even denied as well. Further, in such a society as ours, product comes to determine process, object and subject are separated, and the resources that are brought to the creative process, indeed that *are* the creative process, are denied. Too often, Winnicott (1971) cautions, "the creation stands between the observer and the artist's creativity" (1971, 69). But it is the process and not the product that constitutes creativity: it is the process that is reading and in which creativity may exist. Unlike hermeneuticists and traditional reading specialists, who argue for the exactness of the process, reading is an imprecise activity and, hence, creative.

NOTES

1. A meme is a "cultural unit which can replicate itself with reliability and fecundity" (Dennett, 1991,201). A meme is an idea— categories.

2. For example, Dennett notes how the sea squirt eats its own brain after it has found its comfortable resting place. Consciousness needs a brain.

3. I am reminded here of Blanche DuBois's statement in Tennessee Williams' *A Streetcar Named Desire:* "I have always relied on the kindness of strangers."

4. See my book *Anonymous Toil* (1992) for a study of how our notion of literature is built upon the suppression and marginalization of other literary productions.

5. I am reminded here of the Talking Heads film, *Stop Making Sense*. To my mind, they did not mean to become unconscious but, rather, to stop following the hegemony of the rules of logic.

6. The lack of significance of meaning in the majority of studies of reading may be attested to by the number of studies employing nonsense syllables and words.

7. The first degree of composition is establishing the frame; the second degree of composition brings into the frame what is outside it.

8. A class of disaffected New York City area readers once voraciously read *A Streetcar Named Desire* when Blanche DuBois was perceived as a bag lady, a phenomenon then easily understood in that particular environment. This compared to the image of Blanche as a decayed Southern aristocat, partial victim of her own romantic idealizations and the encroaching postwar industrial America, neither of which conditions made much sense to these potential readers.

CHAPTER 4

A Psychology of Reading: Toward an Ecological Theory

The psychology of reading I have proposed above insists that reading is a creative event that involves a negotiation of space and time and in which event, reader, and poem may be produced. "The concept of the poem [is] the experience shaped by the reader under the guidance of the text, a series of signs interpretable as linguistic symbols" (Rosenblatt, 1978, 12). Reading is a productive process in which is produced the whole—reader and text—and not a reductive process in which meaning is a final, aggregate step. From this whole, the parts may be derived; from meaning, the translation from one code into another or *re*coding[1] may be enacted. Contrary to the traditional view of reading, which posits reading as a *de*coding process, I suggest that the only decoding involved in reading is to meaning and that the latter may only be understood as the transaction between virtual reader and text, resulting in the production of the poem and reader. A correctly deciphered— recoded—text does not ensure meaning production; conversely, our finest readers create meanings that were not possible to others. Louise Rosenblatt cogently asks what could the title *Hamlet* or *Moby Dick* mean apart from a reader except a set of black marks on a white page. Reading is a meaningful language system that can only make sense "against the background of common human concerns" (Dreyfus & Dreyfus, 1986, 76) and can only be understood as essentially creative. It is a whole process, greater than and different from the sum of any of its parts. Information-processing systems of explaining reading seek the parts upon which the whole is built and seek the forces that act on the parts. These parts must always be isolated out of context and outside of the background of common human concerns. As two cognitive psychologists state, "The most prominent characteristic of a cognitive approach is the focus on the processes underlying a cognitive skill . . . to describe how information is processed, the theory must also specify how the information itself is mentally represented" (Just & Carpenter, 1987, 9). But I will here assert that no matter how we look at those forces, they must be understood in a holistic sense against that backdrop of human concerns and cannot be explained by the various aspects and subparts. What counts as information can only be defined against the background of common human concerns. These forces and parts cannot be understood outside of a whole context. To do so would only misrepresent reading and its pedagogy. As Dewey (1929/1971, 277) said,

> As far as it is assumed that modes of consciousness are in themselves already differentiated into sensory, perceptual, conceptual, imaginative, retentive, emotional, conative (or may be so discriminated by direct inspection), physiological, study will consist simply of search for the different bodily and neural processes that underlie these differences.

From such beliefs derive the myriad research studies investigating such processes and trying to devise methods to control them. But, as it is itself a meaningful system, reading presumes a meaningful world and cannot be explained by analysis into parts. We never approach a book unless we intend to make meaning, though we do not know when we approach it exactly what meaning that may be or who we will be when meaning has been made. Words in disconnected discourse may make sense in a phone book but not in a normal text nor in a testing situation, except perhaps, in the context of the testing situation, which is not a normal reading condition. Regardless of our facility with language, James Joyce's *Finnegans Wake* is presumed to be a novel written in English. Decoding is understanding the novel and not merely grunting at its words, some of which are the very nonsense-type words so popular with reading researchers. To attempt to read Joyce's novel by sounding out words would not enable comprehension but inhibit it. Dreyfus and Dreyfus (1986, 36) note in this regard that,

"The conscious use of calculative rationality (combining component parts to obtain a whole) produces regression to the skill of the novice or at best, the competent performer." Word-attack skills are a form of calculative rationality and do not represent development in reading instruction. Indeed, this subskill approach understands reading as the recoding of the written code first into a phonic code and then a subsequent decoding of that into meaning. This view of reading separates the process from the production of meaning and sees it rather as an endlessly regressive systematic process of recoding. Is it "mares eat oats and does eat oats and little lambs eat ivy," or is it "Mairzy Doates and Doazy Doates and little Lambsy Divy?" Of course, it matters.

Jeanne Chall, in *Learning to Read: The Great Debate* (1967, 137) says "Under a code emphasis, the child shows, from the very beginning, greater accuracy in word recognition and oral reading; this may or may not give him an advantage on reading-for-meaning tests ... [at the very beginning] the child seems to read more slowly because of the greater stress on accuracy." Her assumptions are revealing. Chall suggests that a child must have word-attack—recoding—skills so that word recognition may be achieved, but that word recognition does not necessarily facilitate meaning production. She suggests as well that the desire for accuracy, which derives from a pedagogy of subskills that must be mastered, reduces the opportunity to make meaning. Slow oral reading challenges the short-term memory where items are stored until meaning can be made of them. Short-term memory has a limited capacity (see Miller, 1956, below) and concentrating on accuracy of pronunciation and phoneme recognition exhausts this capacity. Accuracy and meaning production may be antithetical goals. Furthermore, if the subskill approach is valid for beginning reading, then why is it not also true for beginning listeners? Must we teach a child to attack words in oral speech before that child can understand? Must we teach children to hear by first teaching them to discriminate between sounds?[2] How is it that the young child will hear its mother's voice and not the vacuum cleaner whirring in the background? The feat of long-term recognition for a voice or a face, of which an infant is capable, is unlikely to be an accomplishment of feature recognition but is rather the result of a construction that is meaningful: The human voice is constructed in an interaction of the infant with the environment in which that infant constructs the sound of the voice, say, from the myriad array of other stimuli that the voice shares with other physical stimuli.

But, for Chall, this first stage of reading is referred to as the Decoding Stage. "The essential aspect of Stage I is learning the arbitary set of letters and associating these with corresponding parts of spoken words" (1967, 16–17). However, as I have explained, recoding words into another symbol system could not facilitate reading any more than recoding a foreign language into speech facilitates its comprehension. I have asked a roomful of college juniors and seniors to read aloud Edgar Allan Poe's story, "The Cask of Amontillado," and observed how recoding the words into even accurate phonic terms could not facilitate comprehension. Whether students pronounced the words correctly or not, the only way that they understood the word was in its context, and for this, no recoding was necessary. Rather, decoding, *the movement to meaning*, was required, and then, accurate pronunciation was not important.

This subskill approach assumes that reading is an unnatural language process. Yet, listening and speaking, our two other language processes, are learned without teaching. Furthermore, children learn to sing without instruction in the stretching and compression of the vocal cords. No child is denied the right to sing until s/he can carry a proper tune, except perhaps in schools in which choruses require tryouts. Only in schools are children denied the right to read meaningfully until they have acquired the right skills. The result, of course, is inattention, resistance, and/or self-hate. Chall quotes one researcher's observation of an elementary classroom using a basal series:

> the [editor of a basal reader] series described a recent visit to a first-grade class in which the children were using one of the supplemental systematic phonics programs. He was shocked by the amount of scratching and masturbating that went on in the room during the phonics lesson. (1967, 60)

Outside of meaningful text and meaning making, providing and practicing rules for reading serves little purpose and is easily dismissed as a waste of time by perceptive students. Frank Smith (1985, 129) notes that "Most of the drills that children are given to help them to read become useful—and easy—only after skill in reading has been developed. Better readers are always more efficient at knowing the alphabet, knowing the 'sounds of letters,' and blending letter sounds together to make words, because these are all tasks that become deceptively simple with experience in reading. *But they are all difficult if not impossible before children understand what reading is* [emphasis added]." Learning to read must be made as easy as is learning to speak. It is accomplished as part of the natural functioning of daily life and is, indeed, a product and by-product of human survival in the twentieth century.

Marilyn Adams' book, *Beginning to Read* (1990), continues this advocacy of the subskill approach to reading with a strong emphasis on phonics-based reading instruction. Adams suggests that reading is the result of a complex parallel processing system.

> Skillful readers do have and use knowledge about word patterns, orthographic redundancy, and have complete spellings; they can and normally do produce spelling-sound translations; and though they seem not to use it to avoid visual processing, they are highly attuned to the semantic and syntactic constraints of text. Each of these sorts of knowledge and skills is a real asset for the skilled reader—all the more, if they work in concert with rather than displacement of one another. (105)

For Adams, skillful reading is "the product of the coordinated and highly interactive processing" (107) of different information systems. She suggests that reading is possible because the brain processes information in parallel processing systems that represent orthographic, phonic, and semantic information. Where these different information systems come together and under whose aegis is left unaddressed in Adams' schema, but seem directly linked to the Cartesian dualism spoken of in Chapter 1. Assuming, as she does, that reading begins with the perception of letters, this processing proceeds from parts to whole, albeit in a complex parallel processing system. This system assumes that processing occurs not linearly but in a more interactive parallel model.[3] Here again, perception begins at an elemental level: visual features of letters which activate words that contain these letters which activate phrases/sentences which contain such words. Again, meaning is a construction from the parts rather than the derivation of the parts from the whole meaning. And the processing of information assumes the nature of that information as well as the delivery and processing of that information to the proper address via known procedures and pathways.

However, we have discussed in Chapter 3 that a psychology of reading must first define the whole to account for reading and that only from the whole may parts be discernible. Reading proceeds from whole to parts and occurs in a transaction between a virtual reader and text, in which event the poem and self are produced. There are no parts until the whole is known. Using the metaphor of dance popular with quantum physicists, Constance Weaver (1985, 313) states that

> Meaning, the poem, may be viewed as an ever-fluctuating dance that occurs more or less simultaneously on and across various levels: letters, words, sentences, schemata; writer, text, and reader; text/reader and context; the present reader with other readers, past and present, and so forth; all connected in a multidimensional holarchy, an interlocking network or web of meaning, a synchronous dance in which there is no clear distinction between what is and what happens.

Reading—making meaning—occurs wholly and in whole images. When you read the sentence, "The horse grazed in the soft summer fields," do you see the words or the horse? The question remains, as Dreyfus and Dreyfus (1986, 56) note, if human *image* processing [compared to information processing which must occur in discrete parts] operates in some situations of which reading might be considered a primary one, and if those images are realized in holistic representations and are not only descriptions or even propositions, and if these representations are related in ways other than merely rule-like, then even parallel information-processing models miss the point. Information is not being processed at all; images—Weaver's multidimensional holarchy,[4] the interlocking network or web of meaning, and synchronous dance in which there is no clear distinction between what is and what happens—are produced whole. A reader's primary subject matter "is the web of feelings, sensations, images, ideas, that he weaves between himself and the text"(Rosenblatt, 1978, 136–7).

I would argue further that that primary subject matter is indeed the reader contextualized, and that all interpretation is merely an attempt to describe *in some way* the nature of the lived-through production of the work. Understanding of the whole text is always the perception of the text as whole image: Without a reader there is not text. Texts are created wholly. "Under the magnetism of the ordered symbols of the text, [the reader] marshals his resources and crystallizes out from the stuff of memory, thought, and feeling a new order, a new experience which [is seen] as the poem" (Rosenblatt, 1978, 12). Derivation of the parts from the whole is an algorithmic device that may facilitate meaning production but always assumes a holistic framework of meaning within which work proceeds. I may not comprehend a philosophical treatise, but I also never search it for its story line. For Dreyfus and Dreyfus (1986, 56), processing is a device necessary only when humans come upon a situation with which they are unfamiliar. "People too reason things out in the explicit, step-by-step way computers do *if they must think about relationships they have never seen and so cannot imagine* [emphasis added]." Frank Smith (1988) also asserts that phonics is a valuable tool for those who already know the words. He states that "phonic rules look deceptively simple when you know what a word is in the first place. . . . Teachers often feel convinced that phonic rules work because letter-sound correspondences seem obvious if a word is known in advance; the alternatives are not considered" (137). It is only after the whole is comprehended that the parts may even be discerned.

Language, oral and written, is a thoroughly familiar environmental factor for humans. People know that language must make sense and know how it is used to form meaning. Indeed, learning to mean is learning how language functions. Michael Halliday (1975) notes that language learning is learning the functions of language. In an intensive and extensive study of his infant son's language development, Halliday describes how learning to talk is learning how to mean. Learning how to mean is gaining mastery of certain basic functions of language and developing meaning potential in each function. This can only be done in social interaction. Learning to talk is learning to mean and is a holistic process from which the parts will derive. "But text is not made of sounds or letters; and in the same way it is not made of words and phrases and clauses and sentences. A text is a semantic unit, realized as lexicogrammatical units which are further realized in phonological or orthographical units" (Halliday, 1975, 124). In other words, unlike Adams' schema, in Halliday's language model the parts derive from the whole rather than vice versa. The whole—meaning—cannot be described by a mere description of the individual processes that comprise it.

The same is true of the code that comprises written text. It is a whole from which derive the parts; the text is a semantic unit: It is meaningful or it cannot, indeed will not, be read. Words have no meaning outside of meaningful text; letters are meaningless outside of words. We have all experienced the situation when we have been able to read all of the words in a passage, even know their conventional definitions, but have been unable to produce meaning. And we know that, at times, we have not actually read passages and yet have understood them thoroughly, as probably occurs frequently in reading comprehension tests when the passage is fortuitously about a subject with which we are familiar. Our knowledge exists as functions of a whole. "The point is that human beings seem to be able to form and compare images in a way that cannot be captured by any number of procedures that operate on description" (Dreyfus & Dreyfus 1986, 56). Meaning production cannot be explained by a reduction into its artificially derived component parts.

Thus, I would like to account for meaning in a holistic sense and then to note the parts that may be derived from meaning production. The question now concerns how we can show that reading—producing meaning—is a holistic process and that it can only be understood in its ecological sense and only occurs ecologically. First, we must show that thinking is a natural holistic process that itself occurs ecologically. Second, we must show that reading is thinking, and then we must account for the perception of the whole rather than the parts: to note how that whole is larger than and different from any of those parts. And finally, we must suggest a pedagogy of reading that accounts for its holistic basis. This, of course, is the easiest section.

Thinking and Reading

As I have said above, reading occurs in the moment when self and text are created in the act of comprehension. Reading only occurs when comprehension is achieved; comprehension, as I will show, produces the self, indeed, may be the self. Comprehension is the production of new knowledge and is an act of thought. The question then is: What is thinking? I will argue that thinking is what we do in the activity of making sense of our world, using the available symbols that are subjectively ordered in a specific way by the individual thinker but governed by the complex environmental conditions in which the individual exists. Making sense of the world is what we do in order to survive in it, given that complete knowing is neither possible nor even a consummation devoutly to be wished. "Everything has to be taken on trust," says the Player in Tom Stoppard's play *Rosencrantz and Guildenstern Are Dead* (1968, 67), "truth is only that which is taken to be true. It's the currency of living. There may be nothing behind it, but it doesn't make any difference so long as it is honoured. One acts on assumptions." Comprehension is what happens when we can make sense of our experience based on what we already know. Certainty—certain knowledge of the world—is unknown and impossible. All knowledge is ultimately incomplete, impelling further action and further learning which is then available for use in eventual action. Knowledge of the world is attained in action in the world, which must occur in regular practice.

In *The Quest for Certainty* (1929, 26), John Dewey explores how traditional Western metaphysics, of which reading research, as I have shown in Chapter 1, partakes, developed in part from the evidence of contingency in the world. He also examines how metaphysics and epistemology were an attempt to ground knowledge in certainty, to find a realm where contingency based in external conditions was inoperable and certainty could be discovered. What occurred in practice produced changes; therefore, practice produced evidence of the impermanent and contingent. What was real had to be immutable; truth could only be known outside of practice. "Greek thinkers saw clearly—and logically—that experience cannot furnish us, as respects cognition of existence, with anything more than contingent probability. Experience cannot deliver to us necessary truths, truths completely demonstrated by reason. Its conclusions are particular, not universal."

Thus, from the Greeks we derive the distinction between the empirical or observational sciences and the rational sciences, the former dealing with the immediate and inexact—such as analytical psychology—and the latter dealing with eternal and universal objects and possessed of necessary truths. I have tried to show in Chapter 1 how the field of reading research and pedagogy has been occupied by rational science. Means for gaining meaning—truth—could be isolated and defined, recombined to act effectively, and could then be taught as a method of comprehension, of truth seeking. Absent from this schema was the intrinsic and inescapable role of practice—the actual exercise of behavior—in the making of meaning. Truth was something that must be attained outside of practice; practice was denied its role in reality. "If a thing changes, its alteration is convincing evidence of its lack of true or complete Being. What *is*, in the full and pregnant sense of the world, is always, eternally. . . . That which becomes merely *comes* to be, never truly is. It is infected with non-being; with privation of being in the perfect sense. The world of generation is the world of decay and destruction. Wherever one thing comes into being something else passes out of being" (Dewey, 1929, 19). Meaning, it was believed, must be certain. However, daily practice is contingent and its meanings cannot, therefore, be accepted as truth. Thus it is that schools have found it necessary to engage in a pedagogy characterized by a subskill approach to education, of which reading is one subject, that often denies meaning production of students practiced daily and effectively and instead promotes a pedagogy that seeks permanent truths. Thinking and reasoning skills need to be taught. Reading as a skill must be taught so that it can be practiced.

"Thinking," says Frank Smith (1990, 30), "is not an occasional activity; it goes on all the time, without awareness. Thinking organizes reality for us, and our own place in those realities, and creates alternative realities that we might hope to achieve (or to avoid)." Theory and practice, says Dewey, are merely two modes of practice. Robert Sternberg (1991, 287) states that "learning that is related to intelligence is the kind that occurs in our everyday interactions with the environment, rather than the very simple kinds that have often been studied in the laboratories of experimental psychologists." Thinking occurs in the regular interactions with our environment as we attempt to make sense of it. As has always been known, it is never possible to know anything but a small piece of the world, and therefore we must produce and act upon hypotheses about the world that work in the present. Reading is merely thinking, using written text as an element in the perceptual field. Frank Smith (1988, 7) argues that we all carry about with us a theory of the world, "a *theory* of what the world is like, a theory that is the basis of all our perceptions and understandings of the world, the root of all learning, the source of hopes and fears, motives And expectancies, reasoning and creativity. And this theory is all we have." This theory has been described by many people and given many different names. Frederic Jameson (1981) has called it "the political unconscious," and Terry Eagleton (1991) has described it as ideology. Daniel Dennett (1991) refers to it somewhat facetiously as the memosphere, the place where memes thrive. Memes are cultural units that can replicate themselves with reliability and fecundity. To all, however, this theory of the world refers essentially to hypotheses about the world that we all carry about and act upon in our daily lives; hypotheses about what the world is like, about what is possible in the world, about what *we* can do in the world, and therefore what *we* are like. We are constantly moving about in a world that we expect to make sense. But because of contingency, it can only be a theory of the world, requiring constant hypotheses: We expect the sidewalk to be there when we step down, but that does not mean necessarily that it will be there. Recall Holden Caulfield's terror in the penultimate chapter of *Catcher in the Rye* when he anticipates the fall from the curbside. We know that in the rain forest every step could be fraught with danger, and so there we walk with careful deliberation. Our hypotheses about the world determine how we proceed.

Now, this theory of the world must be acknowledged as only theoretical because it is impossible to ever know everything there is about existence: Uncertainty is the original state of the human organism. "The world of concrete personal experience," says William James (1907/1970, 27), "to which the street belongs is multitudinous beyond imagination, tangled, muddy, painful and perplexed." Uncertainty is the only certainty in this contingent universe. "As expressed in Heisenberg's uncertainty principle, the physicist can never predict with absolute certainty which possiblity will be actualized and which other(s) will be negated; the physicist can only calculate the probability of certain possiblities being actualized or negated in the transaction that results in the quantum leap" (Weaver, 1985, 301).[5] John Dewey has written (1910/1991, 12) that one of the conditions of thought is uncertainty: "The origin of thinking is some perplexity, confusion, or doubt." We are always more interested in the future than in the present or the past. Indeed, the present may not be thought about at all: It may only be thought about in a future. The past itself exists only in the future.

The origin of self exists in this doubt, and that self is realized in the act of reading/thought. Indeed, doubt might be the natural state of human life. For example, Daniel Dennett (1991, 54) notes how interesting it is that our peripheral vision is severely limited, that we cannot see much beyond two or three degrees from dead center, but that that deficiency is not readily apparent because our eyes are constantly darting about "in an incessant and largely unnoticed game of visual tag with the items of potential interest happening in our field of view." We are, as George Miller (1956) has said, "informavores," organisms who actively explore both the environment and themselves. We actively seek information, but what counts as information has its origins in doubt. There is not only more to the world than we can know, there is at any moment more to the world than we wish to know. Therefore, the individual must begin with a question—a doubt—so that information, which we may define here as *whatever reduces alternatives* (Smith, 1988), may be actively sought so that further decisions can be made. Doubt distinguishes between inefficient behavior—the random and chance activity of organisms in the environment, the sea squirt searching for a resting place and having found it eating its now useless brain— and efficient actions—the purposive and directed behavior that originates in doubt. "Where there is thought," Dewey (1910/1991,14) notes, "things present act as signs or tokens of things not yet experienced. A thinking being can, accordingly, *act on the basis of the absent and the future.*" Doubts orient the creature in the environment to direct it towards potential satisfaction.

I mean to distinguish here between traditional Cartesian doubt, which validates existence by the act of doubt itself, and pragmatic doubt, which seeks effects and impels action. For the rationalist, the world of appearances is deceptive, and therefore, for the rationalist, knowledge must be based on certainty, grounded on an unshakable foundation. Our senses may deceive us, claims the rationalist, and our sense of the world may be a product of that deception. Our truths, says the rationalist, ought to be based on firm principles that reason has confirmed to be true. Here we also recognize the argument of reading ideologues who say that reading is getting the author's meaning. Interpretation is governed by acts of reason by which meaning may be derived from printed text, premised on definable principles of thought: We take from the text, emptying it so to speak, and consider that meaning as now part of the reader. This view of the reading process denies both text and reader, as if robbing from Peter to pay Paul is a valid method of returning debts and establishing relationships.

Doubt is, therefore, the impetus for all action. For the rationalist, doubt is the principle of reflection, but Dewey (1991, 11) tells us that the "demand for the solution of a perplexity is the steadying and guiding factor in the entire process of reflection." For the pragmatist, doubt impels reflection but is not

itself reflection. Piaget (1968, 3), too, has argued that disequi-
librium is the motive force in all learning:

> The psychological development that starts at birth and
> terminates in adulthood is comparable to organic growth.
> Like the latter, it consists essentially of activity directed
> towards equilibrium. Just as the body evolves toward a
> relatively stable level characterized by the completion of
> the growth process and by organ maturity, so mental life
> can be conceived as evolving toward a final form of
> equilibrium represented by the adult mind.

Disregarding the notion of completion which experience and
modern thought have called into serious question, Piaget's
principle still can account for the development of thought. From
the discomfort of uncertainty, the organism seeks an equilbrium
with his/her environment. As deconstruction has taught us,
what *accounts* for our notions of equilbrium is cultural, and as
Freud (1963) has noted, we must all discover the means of our
own salvation; nonetheless, thought that leads to comprehension
must begin in doubt. Stern (1985), too, claims that doubt leads to
movement and consciousness: leads to self. The child is
constantly seeking from its environment what is invariant in the
event and what is not invariant. The self, says Stern, is a product
of the awarenesses of invariant patterns—what remains
unchanging in an experience—and may arise only through
action, through hypotheses testing in the environment. "I am
suggesting that the infant can experience the *process* of emerging
organization as well as the result, and it is this experience of
emerging organization that [is] called the *emergent sense of
self*"(45). The self as product is a function of process.

    Which is not to say that unreflective thought is not
characteristic of human activity. Of course, one may act and
"read" without engaging in reflective thought. For it is possible
to bark at words even as it is possible to have relations with an
environment that remains confusing. One can read and
comprehend very little, which is to say, to not read at all—"I
read the chapter but I didn't understand a word." And, of
course, everything that is produced by our brains is thought. But
Dewey (1910/1991), for one, distinguishes between reflective
and unreflective thought. One can follow a sequence of ideas,

but reflection is a matter of a *con*sequence of ideas, "a consecutive ordering in such a way that each determines the next as its proper outcome, while each in turn leans back on its predecessors" (2–3). Dewey suggests that reflective thinking is only that operation in which "present facts suggest other facts (or truths) in such a way as to induce belief in the latter upon the ground or warrant of the former"(9). Reflective thinking is making connections. Making connections creates images, creates the image-maker. This is a description similar to the contemporary notion of cognitive mapping or cognitive schema theory. This is also similar to Peirce's (1991, 247) discourse on signs:

> The whole purpose of a sign is that it shall be interpreted in another sign; and its whole purport lies in the special character which imparts to that interpretation. When a sign determines an interpretation of itself in another sign, it produces an [e]ffect external to itself, a physical effect, though the sign producing the effect may itself be not an existent object but merely a type.

All thinking occurs in signs: "only in external signs can thought be known at all—and since all thinking is in signs, every thought must address itself to some other, must determine some other, since that is the essence of the sign"(49). In reading, one aspect of the sign is the printed word.

Thinking is an aspect of consciousness, and consciousness produces future which is always an hypothesis. Oliver Sacks (1993), quoting Gerald Edelman's recent book *Bright Air, Brilliant Fire: On the Matter of the Mind* says that

> Primary consciousness is the state of being mentally aware of things in the world—of having mental images in the present. But it is not accompanied by any sense of [being] a person with a past and a future. . . . In contrast, higher-order consciousness involves the recognition by a thinking subject of his or her own acts and affections. It embodies a model of the personal, and of the past and future as well as the present. . . .

Thinking and reading require this sense of a past and future as we attempt to integrate the present world into our cognitive structures and theories. Comprehension is making sense of the world and is inseparable from our prior knowledge of it. Consciousness is not what makes the difference between our theory of the world and the world; consciousness is the process of making the difference.

Prediction deriving from original doubt may be the explanation for much of what we know as consciousness. Dennett (1991, 144) notes that "the brain's task is to guide the body it controls through a world of shifting conditions and sudden surprises, so it must gather information from that world and use it *swiftly* to 'produce future'—to extract anticipations in order to stay one step ahead of disaster." Dennett, citing physiological evidence that the brain works by prediction, declares that in the contingent world "in order to cope, an organism must either armor itself . . . or else develop methods of getting out of harm's way and into the better neighborhoods in its vicinity" (177). The key to control is the ability to track or even anticipate the important features of the environment. As Stern said of the infant learning, we must learn what is invariant in the environment—what is permanent in the experience and what is not part of the experience. Both Stern and Dennett posit the brain as anticipation machines (Dennett, 177).

Certainly, prediction is central to Frank Smith's views of thinking and reading. Smith argues (1988, 1990) that prediction is the basis of all thinking and reading, and hence of thought. He offers three reasons for this claim. First, since our position in the world is protean, we are almost always more concerned with what is going to happen than with what has already occurred or is even happening at present. The past may sometimes be a clue to the future, but no two circumstances are ever alike nor can we ever be identical in two circumstances, and we call up the past only to help us in the present with the future. James Britton (1972, 26) has written that "Experience is kaleidoscopic: The experience of every moment is unique and unrepeatable. Until we can group items in it on the basis of their similarity we can set up no expectations, make no predictions; lacking these we can make nothing of the present moment." Without prediction, Britton claims, we are trapped in the particularity of the here and now, of the unique present. Therefore, prediction is that which releases us from the immediate. As Dewey (1910/1991, 15) said,

"To a being who thinks, things are records of their past, as fossils tell of the prior history of the earth, and are prophetic of their future, as from the present positions of heavenly bodies remote eclipses are foretold." We move through the world predicting our way, often suppressing our doubt because our theories of how the world works function so well. Nonetheless, though I expect my car to start every morning, there is no surety that it will; and though my theories of the world cause me to believe that that noise down the road is an eighteen-wheel semi truck, it could be a stampeding herd of buffalo. Prediction is, as Smith suggests, the prior elimination of alternatives and makes life possible. One function of the present is its potential use in the future.

Second, because reality is so protean, so complex and multitudinous, there are too many possible choices, too many ways to view things, so that we must limit those ways available to us if we are not to be overwhelmed. We do this through the prior elimination of alternatives, by prediction. We thus are able to find that for which we look, or we are mightily surprised when we do not. Harmony between the knower and the known, says John Dewey (1929/1971, 252) "is always an attained outcome of prior inferences and investigations." What I really want to know about this beautiful golden ring is not by whom and what process it was mined and produced (though knowing these things *may* affect my decision to purchase), but how much it costs. Knowing as well its human cost may put me off buying it. We wear our cotton garments not considering how they were made and by whom and at what human expense. I do not eat my dinner looking for the suffering efforts of the migrant workers who helped bring this food to the table. Prediction permits us to move through the world because it reduces the number of alternatives at which we must look and about which we must think.

Finally, because there is so much uncertainty in the world, the brain would be overwhelmed trying to choose amongst alternatives. The brain requires time to make a decision as to what it has seen, and the fewer alternatives the quicker the decision can be made. Not that quick decisions are always requisite, but unless the brain acts relatively quickly, the possibilities for comprehension will be minimized. Tunnel vision, the incapacity to make a decision about a perceptual event, makes comprehension impossible because it precludes contexualization, which is a necessary and sufficient condition for it. Tunnel vision, says Dreyfus and Dreyfus (1986, 37), is "maintaining a perspective in the face of persistent and disquieting evidence; failing to recognize potential new perspectives that better explain past events and better dictate future actions." To experience tunnel vision is to deny the reality of doubt and be incapable of comprehension. "Prediction," Frank Smith says, "brings potential meaning to texts, reducing ambiguity, and eliminating in advance irrelevant alternatives. Thus, we are able to generate comprehensible experience from inert pages of print. . . . *Prediction is the prior elimination of unlikely alternatives*" (1988, 18). Though the words '"table" and "chair" refer to pieces of furniture, they may also refer to the actions of an organizational functionary performing tasks of daily business in the service of those members who may be sitting and working on those chairs and tables. Words, too, are protean, and comprehending them requires the prior elmination of unlikely alternatives. Vygotsky (1988, 245) teaches us that "The sense of a word is a complex, mobile, protean phenomenon; it changes in different minds and situations and is almost unlimited." To delimit possibility and facilitate comprehension, prediction is requisite. But that prediction requires prior knowledge: "The word is a thing in our consciousness," as Ludwig Feuerbach put it, "that is absolutely impossible for one person, but that becomes a reality for two. The word is a direct expression of the historical nature of human consciousness" (256). Prediction is the only way to comprehend words.

Now, when the world is making sense, or rather, when our hypotheses are confirmed, we are comprehending. Our theory of the world is proved accurate. But when our hypotheses are not confirmed, then what we expect to find in the world is not found, and we are confused. The world is no longer contiguous with our theory of it, and to proceed we must adjust our theory of the world with the world itself. We may do this in two ways: We may change the world or we may change our theory of it. To effect the first requires that we assimilate that part of the world into our preexisting theory, as when the child calls every animal a dog. This may work for a short time but oversimplifies the world and does not finally serve facile movement in the world. Or we can accommodate our theory to that part of the world that confuses us and bring the two into greater alignment. In this way, our theory is changed by the world in our relationship to it. We are changed in and by the new theory. We are our theories. Dewey (1929/1971, 257) tells us that ". . . to get a new meaning is perforce to be in a new attitude. . . . Perception or consciousness is literally, the difference in the process of making . . . intentional change in the direction of events is transforming change in the meaning of events." We hear also Piaget's schema for childhood learning in these terms. Of course, this schema is equally true for adults as well. Saying some of my best friends are Jewish though I wouldn't want my son to marry one is assimilation; practicing multiculturalism is accommodation.

Prediction is the acknowledgment that what is presently known is based only on partial knowledge; recall, the brain is in the business of producing futures:

> The brain's task is to guide the body it controls through a world of shifting conditions and sudden surprises, so it must gather information from that world and use it *swiftly* to "produce future"—to extract anticipations in order to stay one step ahead of disaster. (Dennett, 1991, 144)

Learning—reading—is the activity that facilitates the movement out of confusion. It is the testing of hypotheses and the assimilation of their results. The opposite of confusion—the incongruence of the world with our theory of it—is comprehension—the integration of the world with our theory of it. That integration produces world and self.

Reading, Thinking, and Prediction

Uncertainty produces thought, produces the possiblity of self. But it is always a theory about the world upon which our hypotheses are constructed and not certainty about it. And that is why J. Hillis Miller also may argue, as indeed he does, that reading must be understood as a failure to read, the impossibility of ever knowing whether our reading is the true one. And this failure must be understood, too, as intrinsic to the creation of self and must be accepted in a psychology of reading. Miller declares that to read is always to fail to read, to be imprecise, incomplete, and uncertain, and that that imprecision is at the origin of reading and of living. Miller argues that though everything we do is reading, our pain stems from the uncertainty of reading, of having to read but of "having no way whatsoever of knowing whether or not we may have in our discursive wanderings and aberrancies stumbled by accident on the right reading"(1987, 59). There is always more to the word than our understanding of it, more to the world than we already know. Shoshana Felman (1982, 31) argues that knowledge exists in the admission that knowledge is "untotalizable," and that "Textual knowledge—the very stuff the literature teacher is supposed to deal in—is knowledge of the functioning of language, of symbolic structures, of the signifier, knowledge at once derived from—and directed towards—interpretation." Finally, however, that knowledge is impossible and is not a substance at all, but is, rather, contained in the dynamic between the virtual reader and the text. It is impossible to know ultimately, and there is an element of failure in this lack of exactness that is the impetus to further learning. As Miller asserts, the element of failure is intrinsic to reading—to thinking—and this too must be accounted for in a psychology and pedagogy of reading.

The psychology of reading of which I speak does not ignore letters and words; indeed, without letters and words reading verbal texts would be impossible. Rather, the psychology of reading I offer here must account for reading as it actually occurs—in comprehension. This psychology of reading must account for the creation of both the reader and the text, neither of which can exist without the other. It must account for a pedagogy of reading as well. Reading, the testing and assimilating of hypotheses, making meaning, is taught by reading. Reading occurs because of what one knows; the more one knows, the more can be comprehended; the more that is comprehended, the better able one is to read.

In Marilyn Adams' *Beginning to Read* (1990), a text that follows in the tradition of Jeanne Chall's enormously popular and inordinately influential book *Learning to Read: The Great Debate* (1967), Adams eschews this approach for one that actually discounts the genuine reader. Summing up her review of the research Adams notes:

> If mature readers do not recognize words holistically, *even though that's what they look like they do*; and if mature readers do not use context to help them recognize words, *even though that's what they feel like they do*; then we must at least consider the possibility that they recognize words by sounding them out, *even if that's not what they look or feel like they do* [emphasis added]. (103)

In other words, Adams is willing to discount the actual experience of the reader's reading in order to validate a psychological approach to reading that views reading as a processing model separate from a reader and irrespective of text. Stern (1985) notes that it is impossible to separate cognitive from affective results in children, and it is no less so in adults. I prefer to offer a psychology of reading that begins with the reader and the text, to show how the transaction creates both, and how the subskills are created by the holistic practice. Such an approach makes reading and thinking, as Huey suggests (1908/1968), equivalent processes.

Reading and Pragmatism: Reading as Holistic Practice

First, we must assert that though there are many definitions of reading,[6] the one we mean to hold to here concerns the comprehension of written text. Comprehension is establishing answers to the questions we pose in interaction with written text but not limited to or by that text. Reading a phone book is as important as reading a novel, only its purposes—the questions we ask and the answers we seek—are disparate. In the latter we require primarily experience, in the former predominately information. Both require reading, however. This is not to say that the reading of the phone book, or dictionary for that matter, may not produce meaningful experience or that a novel may not produce information. Indeed, reading is such a complex process that it may never be explained in such simplistic terms. Separating reading into these isolated categories falsifies the process. Yet, advocates of subskill approaches to reading, such as Harold Herber, will argue that "Reading to learn *is* different from learning to read, both for the learner and for the teacher" (1984, 227). In their advocacy of the subskill approach, theorists will argue that first you must learn to read before you can learn anything from reading. Using similar logic, first you must learn to talk and then you can learn to understand what you are saying.

Rather, all reading is premised on having questions for which answers will be sought. Comprehension is achieving answers to those questions. Thus, all texts potentially provide information because the virtual reader may ask specific questions of the text. Even the hagiography of Malcolm X suggests that his reading the dictionary was premised on having questions about a predominantly exclusionary white language. He asked certain questions of the dictionary and was able to read it by searching for answers to those questions. In the process, he learned to read even as he read to learn. The question and motive force for reading were determined by the reader: The true and the evident were determined by the reader transacting with the text and were not contained in either the text or the virtual reader.

Second, we must note that comprehension is an act of consciousness. And that consciousness itself is an event and not an organization of materials prepared for viewing on a central stage by a central meaner. Consciousness occurs in a particular environment and is never replicative. Daniel Dennett (1991) proposes a theory of consciousness which he names the multiple drafts theory. Consciousness in this view is a single draft of a continually developing document called reality. A conscious mind, Dennett says, is "an observer who takes in a limited subset of all the information there is" (101). This definition is useful because it establishes reality as the event of consciousness, and yet it is clear that neither consciousness nor reality is an ideality.

Reality is what it is possible to produce from what may be available. The question then is, how does one establish that particular subset? Clearly, it is a matter of what may be perceived, which, as we have noted above, is an active process based on prior learning. The multiple drafts theory provides a sense of how and why this might happen and equates with Smith's version of comprehension, which will lead us to understanding reading.

In Dennett's model visual stimuli come in, say, from a book, and these stimuli evoke a chain of events in the cortex of the brain that yield discriminations with greater and greater specificity. At different times and in different places on the cortex, various decisions or judgments are made; parts of the brain go into states that discriminate different features, like the onset of the stimulus, then shape, location, and then perhaps color. Each excited state transmits effects to other places, and every time a discriminative state is transmitted further discriminations become possible. This is referred to as the Pandemonium Model of Feature Recognition (Crowder & Wagner, 1992). Now, as soon as any discriminated state is accomplished, it becomes available for either eliciting some behavior or for modulating internal informational states. In the former, consciousness is experienced in actual behavior, and in the latter, consciousness may be experienced as the establishment of what are traditionally called mind sets. As emendations occur in this multitrack process, "something like a narrative stream occurs which can be thought of as subject to continual editing by many processes distributed around the brain" (Dennett, 1991, 134–5).

Consciousness is the precipitation of a particular narrative upon the stimulus of a particular problem. Consciousness is an event: It is, as Dewey might say, the meaning of events in the course of remaking. Consciousness occurs as comprehension; it is reading. At any one place a draft is incomplete—there is always more to the world than we know. A probe is merely the result of a particular interaction within the environment. I sometimes know I am sitting on a chair, but I am not unconscious of the chair when I do not "know" I am upon it. And when I know I am on the chair, I do not always feel my glasses on my nose. It is very much like the relationship between figure and ground discussed above. But consciousness becomes here an event: What I am conscious of depends on when I probe the stream. We must probe that stream in order to precipitate a narrative, and the nature of that probe will have great influence on the nature of the narrative. Hence, Dennett's multiple drafts theory: "Since these narratives are under continual revision, there is no single narrative that counts as the canonical version, the 'first edition' in which are laid down, for all time, the events that happened in the stream of consciousness of the subject, all deviations from which must be corruptions of the text" (136). As Dewey (1929/1971, 182) said, "Recognition of an object, conception of a meaning may be mine rather than yours; yours rather than his; at a particular moment; but this fact is about me or you, not about the object and essence perceived and conceived." There is no reality outside relations. Nor is there a definitive reality. That is equally true for the meaning of texts.

The probe, which produces consciousness, is predicated on our capacity to hypothesize about the world. "As emendations and overwritings occur this stream brings certain content to the surface, gets revised, contributes to the interpretation of other contents or the modulation of behavior (verbal and otherwise) and in the process leaves traces in memory which then eventually decay or get incorporated into or overwritten by later contents, wholly or in part" (Dennett, 1991, 136). There is no truth involved here; all reality is merely a draft copy. Dewey said the same thing almost fifty years before. Distinguishing between mind and consciousness, Dewey (1929/1971, 247) wrote

> Mind is contextual and persistent; consciousness is focal and transitive. Mind is, so to speak, structural, substantial, a constant background and foreground; perceptive consciousness is process, a series of heres and nows. Mind is a constant luminosity; consciousness intermittent, a series of flashes of varying intensities. *Consciousness is, as it were, the occasional interception of messages continually transmitted, as a mechanical receiving device selects a few of the vibrations with which the air is filled and renders them audible* [emphasis added].

Meaning is always contextual and is produced by the transaction between stimuli and receptor. The latter must educate him/herself as to how and what to perceive. This is basically a natural process that does not reveal meaning but rather, produces it. Psychologist J.J. Gibson (1979, 51) agreed with Dewey's earlier views of perception and meaning. Gibson argued that the perceptual system could only be defined in its context as "a pair of eyes set in a head that can turn attached to a body that can move from place to place." This system is never "stimulated," as would subskill approach theorists argue of the reading process; rather, this system goes into activity in the presence of stimulus information. This ecological theory makes the reader and the environment reciprocal terms. The environment of the reader must include his/her entire past life— the theory of the world.

As for Dennett, so too for the pragmatist for whom knowledge is only possible by action in the world and is only knowable in activity. Says William James, "Truth *happens* to an idea. It *becomes* true, is *made* true by events. Its verity *is* in fact an event, a process" (James, 1907/1970, 133). James continues, saying that "*Such simply and fully verified leadings are certainly the originals and proto-types of the truth-process* . . ." (136). In this view, truth—meaning—occurs in the transaction. A psychology of reading that is based on the rationalist model must account for the process of reading by a reader, separating the process from the processor, reducing reading to the processing of information by defining textual units—letters, words—as the separate building components of meaning. Information is in the text preexistent to a reader, and the reader must approach a text already skilled in extracting that information. Marilyn Adams (1990, 54) notes that "the most critical factor beneath fluent word reading is the ability to recognize letters, spelling patterns, and whole words effortlessly, automatically, and visually. The central goal of all reading instruction—comprehension— depends critically on this ability"(54). Reading is conceptualized as a concatenation of subskills leading to comprehension. Reading is an exact procedure.

Towards an Ecological Theory

In traditional reading instruction, the correct answer, the true meaning, the proper and accepted understanding is sought. To achieve any one of these equal objects, there are prescribed abilities and techniques that may be employed and that can therefore be taught—rule-like processes amenable to explanation by information-processing systems which lead to a true reading. Of course, this view posits a hierarchy of skills and of skill-users and establishes a body of authority to which one must turn for instruction and validation. The role of the individual and his/her knowledge is minimized for those of the authorities. We have explored the history and rationale for this model in the first two chapters of this book. This view, says Christopher Lasch (1991), derives in part from Enlightenment thinking: "Beginning with Descartes, philosophers took up a new task: to analyze and make explict the procedures that governed clear thinking. Once critical analysis had reduced phenomena to their simplest components, they believed, it could reassemble those components in the form of laws having universal validity." Here we have the rationale upon which information-processing theory rests and upon which reading research and pedagogy is based.

But for the pragmatist, the true and the evident, what is sought for in traditional reading instruction—the correct answer, the true meaning, the right understanding—are not defined so as external realities but are so, rather, because they exist in a relationship between the things and the speaker and the person addressed. "If 'existent' is a name in the logical sense, i.e. a word which names a thing, a thing which is judged affirmatively, it is a relational word. I use it to indicate that I am thinking of some thing as corresponding to my thinking [and also, naturally, that I am thinking of myself as thinking correctly]"(Brentano, 1930/1966, 69). The true and evident are so because I think they are. I am reminded of Sir Thomas More in Robert Bolt's drama, *A Man for All Seasons* (1962, 53), who, when asked why he persists in a behavior that must lead eventually to his execution, replies, "No, it is not because I *believe* it, but because *I* believe it." The true and evident exist in the relationship between the believer and the thing believed: The believer comes into existence in the believed and vice versa. I may think of a unicorn and that unicorn is real because I think it and because I think myself thinking it correctly. The true and evident—reality—are a construction of thought, but thought constructs the thinker as well.

Reality is multiform and diverse, a construction in which universal truths and first principles are impossible. Psychologist J.J. Gibson (1979, 254–5) has written that

> What we see *now*, refers to the self, not the environment. The perspective appearance of the world at a given moment of time is simply what specifies to the observer where he is at that moment. . . . To perceive is to be aware of the surfaces of the environment and of oneself in it. . . . The full awareness of surfaces includes their layout, their substances, their events, and their affordances.

Reading, even by traditional standards, begins in perception of the written matter, but perception may not be considered the beginning stage of reading or the reader. Perception is the particular act of creation in which the perceiver and the perceived are produced. The matter that may be read is a specific book on a specific table in a particular location, each of which has surfaces that specify the environment and the self in it: The words are originally black marks on a page. What may be perceived is dependent on the age of the perceiver, how and in what manner s/he is motivated to perceive, and how well s/he has learned to perceive.[7] There is a context to reading that extends far beyond the written language but which must be accounted for to comprehend reading. Both thought and reading, the latter a mode of thought, are ecologically based. Reading always occurs as the result of a particular pair of mobile eyes that are set in a head that can turn and that is attached to a body that can and has moved from place to place. No two perceivers can perceive alike.

That the world offers no first principles to which reading may turn for its rationale and pedagogy is asserted as well by the American philosopher/psychologist William James (1907/1970, 137, 145), who argued that "Truth lives . . . for the most part on a credit system . . . our thoughts and beliefs 'pass' so long as nothing challenges them, just as bank-notes pass so long as nobody refuses them . . . the true is only the expedient in the way of our thinking, just as the 'right' is only the expedient in the way of our behaving." The world cannot be explained by first principles, for "all theories are instrumental, are mental modes of adaptation to reality, rather than revelations or gnostic answers to some divinely instituted world-enigma" (127). Theories are all based in perception, and as we have argued, perception is a constructive, creative act.

Traditional philosophy, says James, has always attempted to describe a world more true and real than the everyday world of common sense. The world of traditional philosophy, says James, refers not to the actual world but to an addition to it, a structure built atop it, "a classic sanctuary in which the rationalist fancy may take refuge from the intolerably confused and gothic character which mere facts present"(27). But, says James, philosophy ought not to avoid the world that exists by positing abstract and general truths that have no relation to the world, but rather, ". . . to find out what definite difference it will make to you and me, at definite instants of our life, if this world-formula or that world-formula be the true one"(45). Philosophy is exercise in the real world and not exercise about it. The true, for James, is whatever proves valuable in the way of belief for definite and definable reasons. The pragmatic method is that of "settling metaphysical disputes that otherwise might be interminable," such as the search for Truth or true meaning, by interpreting "each notion by tracing its respective practical consequences"(42). The world of appearances, says the pragmatist, rather than being deceptive, is all that there is. And the appearance of the world is a product of the perceiver actively involved in perception and not the result of a passive reception of stimuli.

J.J. Gibson, in his work, *The Ecological Approach to Visual Perception* (1979, 63) states that "The world is *specified* in the structure of the light that reaches us, but it is entirely up to us to perceive it. The secrets of nature are not to be understood by the breaking of its code." For Gibson, perceiving is a keeping-in-touch with the world, an experiencing of things rather than a having of experiences. Getting the author's meaning is an example of the latter. Perception ought to be understood as an active process. Learning to read—to break the code—to discover the author's meaning is an impossibility. Dewey (1929/1971, 148) said that "The heart of language is not 'expression' of something antecedent, much less expression of antecedent thought. It is communication; the establishment of cooperation in an activity in which there are partners, and in which the activity of each is modified and regulated by partnership." Lev Vygotsky (1988, 141), working at the same time as Dewey, would say that it is "not only the deaf who cannot understand one another but any two people who give a different meaning to the same word or who hold divergent views." A theory and pedagogy of reading that purports to achieve another's meaning discounts the very nature of language and the productive and creative nature of perception.

Such a theory also assumes a unity and consciousness of purpose in the writer that is impossible. Daniel Dennett argues, as a conclusion drawn from his multiple-drafts theory of consciousness, that all language production is a result of multiple nonlanguage goals finding opportunities in available language and of language finding appropriate goals to be embodied. Our available words seek content to be embodied even as our language goals seek words to be realized. In this process, the available words may actually change the content to be expressed. An author's meaning is not consciously predetermined but created in the activity of the brain. "Consciousness," Dennett (1991, 166) asserts, "is a *mode of action* of the brain rather than a subsystem of the brain. . . ." Psychology long ago taught us that what we say is often steeped in unconscious process and only partly known. And sociolinguistics has shown how language and its production is anchored in the environments in which it develops, is indeed, a product of the interactions between the environment and the organism. Linguist James Gee (1990, 85) says that "Words have no meaning in and of themselves and by themselves apart from other words. They have meanings only relative to *choices* (by speakers and writers) and *guesses* (by hearers and readers) about other words, and *assumptions* about contexts." The act of perception that occurs upon contact with the stimulus of one's own words or those of another is always creative and never determinable.

So may perception be understood from the psychoanalytic perspective. Psychotherapist Marion Milner, in her reading of Blake's prints of *The Book of Job* and her study of the suppressed madness of ordinary men says that "I think he [Blake] is saying that perception of the external world itself is a creative act, an act of imagination; without the imagination we would not in fact see what is there to be seen" (1987, 179). Reading is an act that entails perception, but unless perception is understood as an imaginative act, we deny reading and the self who can read. As I have discussed above, we can be taught to see specific outlines, letters, words, etc.; this pedagogy does not negate the act of self in perception; it simply determines it at great cost to the creative self. Reading must, of course, begin in perception occurring in relation to printed text: But we see what we expect to see, and in a large way, we expect to see what we have learned to see. As Dewey (1929/1971, 120) said, "Sensory data, whether they are designated psychic or physical, are thus not starting points; they are the products of analysis." Yet for many in reading research, sensory data are indeed, the beginning of the reading process. Charles Perfetti (1992, 151) notes that ". . . in real reading, as opposed to lexical decision tasks, it is hard to imagine what 'lexical access' can refer to except a point at which the reader is prepared to name the word or to make some judgment about its meaning. *(The reader certainly does not decide whether it is a word)* [emphasis added]." Yet, the research of Ferreiro and Teberosky (1982) suggests that preschool literacy indeed concerns learning what is and is not a word. We know that often typographical errors are read *as if* they were words, and Joyce's *Finnegans Wake* and Burgess' *Clockwork Orange* are studied by the reader producing meaning in typographical marks that are not English words. Rather, what we see is what we have constructed based on our prior knowledge, our nonvisual sense or what we have been taught to see. Beginning readers, Emerald Dechant (1991, 59) notes, "focus all or most of their attention on the fixated word and make only minimal use of the parafoveal and peripheral vision and thus have a reduced perceptual span." This statement addresses not necessarily the innate perceptual deficiencies of the beginning reader but the focus of early reading instruction—the autonomous word. An ecological theory of reading seems aware that the autonomous word does not exist. Everything exists as a product of the relations in which it is engaged. Harste, Woodward, and Burke (1984) suggest, indeed, that words may be conceptualized as placemarkers for meaning, which require the transaction of a reader to become active.

In this regard, young children must come to understand what a word is, ironically enough, so that in reading they may learn to avoid reading them. We cannot ignore, of course, what we do not know exists. Calling upon the findings of quantitative reading research steeped in the experimental psychology laboratory, Stanovich (1991, 20) notes that it has been shown conclusively that "*sampling* of the text during reading, as indicated by fixation points, is *relatively* dense; [and] visual feature extraction during a fixation is *relatively* complete [emphasis added]." Rayner and Pollatsek (1987, 329) state that "While a majority of the words in a text are fixated during reading, many words are skipped so that foveal processing of each word is not necessary." However, this acknowledgment that completeness is never wholly realized and that sampling does occur returns us to the idea that perception is a creative act depending on pick-up of information by a perceiver. What is picked up will depend on what is possible to be seen. What it is possible to see depends on the questions asked, and this is a function of what it is possible to ask.

Indeed, we may not even see what we do not know exists. How children come to recognize a word is crucial to the pedagogy of reading. Vellutino and Scanlon (1991, 202) report that ". . . the way in which a child approaches word identification and the word features to which she/he is attuned are largely determined by the instructional biases to which she/he is exposed." What we know to exist is always what comes to be meaningful in our relationship to it. What has no relationship has no meaning. "In truth, attitudes, dispositions and their kin, while capable of being distinguished and made concrete intellectual objects, are never separate existences. They are always *of, from, toward,* situations and things" (Dewey,

1929/1971, 195). Ferreiro and Teberosky (1982, 276) have shown that children come to their own knowledge of words and text without instruction in the natural course of their lives because print has meaning to them in their lives. "The data we have gathered from preschool children shows that at no time do they opt for pure deciphering [recoding] as the way to approach print." These children learn to know and to make sense of print because it is meaningful to them; they do not come to meaning after print is made meaningful. What we see must make sense to us: When it does not we must work at comprehension, accommodating our theory of the world with our experience in it and changing both in the process. And, in essence, creating both. Or, in our work as educators, we may create nonreaders. As Irnerio, a character in Italo Calvino's novel, *if on a winter's night a traveler* (1981, 49), says

> I've become so accustomed to not reading that I don't even read what appears before my eyes. It's not easy: they teach us to read as children, and for the rest of our lives we remain the slaves of all the written stuff they fling in front of us. I may have had to make some effort myself, at first, to learn not to read, but now it comes quite naturally to me. The secret is not refusing to look at the written words. On the contrary, you must look at them, intensely, until they disappear.

Reading pedagogy has as much to do with dissuading people from reading by purportedly teaching them to read.

The reader approaches a text with a wealth of experience that s/he must bring to bear in transacting with that text. Louise Rosenblatt (1978, 11) argues convincingly that it is the reader's attention to a text that activates certain elements in the reader's past experience that have become linked to verbal symbols. "Meaning will emerge from a network of relationships among the things symbolized as [the reader] senses them. . . . The selection and organization of responses to some degree hinge on the assumptions, the expectations or sense of possible structures that the Reader brings out of the stream of life." We see what we are looking for, what we are capable of seeing. The brain does not passively receive stimuli; rather, information is picked up in the environment. What we see is a result not of stimuli but of stimulus information available to the perceptual system.

> Just as the stimulation of the receptors in the retina cannot be seen, so the mechanical stimulation of the receptors in the skin cannot be felt, and the stimulation of the hair cells in the inner ear cannot be heard. So also the chemical stimulation of the receptors in the tongue cannot be tasted, and the stimulation of the receptors in the nasal membrane cannot be smelled. We do not perceive stimuli. (Gibson, 1979, 56)

Perception is not based in stimuli but on what information may be picked up from the environment. "It depends on the age of the perceiver, how well he has learned to perceive, and how strongly he is motivated to perceive" (Gibson, 1979, 57). Age is a factor not in developmental isolation but in correlation with the number of language encounters in which an individual can engage. What counts as information must be originally learned but is always based on questions/doubts of the learner.

In his work, neurophysiologist Walter Freeman (1991) shows how nerve cell assemblies learn to respond to the environment, and having once learned, not only are able to discern in the environment what they have previously learned, but are able to generalize that learning based on few stimuli. He notes that receptors in various areas of the recepting organ—say, the nose—may be stimulated and yet the brain recognizes that all the separate and disparate messages refer to the same stimulus—say, the odor of perfume. And it is equally true that the sensory organ foregrounds a particular sense and backgrounds the rest so that perfume is recognized as the dominant smell but the chocolate cake is not perceived. Freeman suggests that the nerve cell assemblies actually learn what to respond to, and having learned, generalize that learning and foreground it.

> If we are correct, the existence of a nerve cell assembly would help explain both the foreground-background problem and generalization over equivalence receptors. In the first instance, the assembly would confer "front-runner" status on stimuli that experience, stored in the Hebbian synapses, has made important to the individual.

> In the second instance, the assembly would ensure that
> information from any subset of receptors, regardless of
> where in the nose they were located, would spread
> immediately over the entire assembly and from there to
> the rest of the bulb. (82)

Thus, perception is conceptualized as an active process and not a passive one. "Perceiving," as Gibson emphasized (1979, 149), "is an act, not a response, an act of attention, not a triggered impression, an achievement not a reflex." Thus, contrary to subskill approaches to reading, reading does not begin with the perception of letters; rather, letters are produced as part of an act of thought.

> Even as simple a matter as recognizing letters of the
> alphabet begins with a question that we are asking—the
> predicted range of alternatives—and ends with a search
> for an answer on the page. And the answer is found in the
> marks on the page. (Smith, 1985, 102)

The act of thought seeks to comprehend: the reestablishment of a state of equilibrium. Perception occurs as a result of a preexisting state of doubt, the presence of "confusion," questions that are based in the relationship between our theory of the world and primary unreflective experience in the world. The act of perception is an active process and the result of learning. "A prior adaptation constitutes a threshold (better called a platform or plateau); what is consciously noted is alteration of one plateau; re-adjustment to another" (Dewey, 1929/1971, 255). We perceive what we have been taught to perceive.

> A man breaking his journey between one place and
> another at a third place of no name, character, population
> or significance, sees a unicorn cross his path and
> disappear. That in itself is startling, but there are
> precedents for mystical encounters of various kinds, or to
> be less extreme, a choice of persuasions to put it down to
> fancy; until—"My God," says a second man, "I must be
> dreaming, I thought I saw a unicorn." At which point, a
> dimension is added that makes the experience as alarming
> as it will ever be. A third witness, you understand, adds
> no further dimension but only spreads it thinner, and a
> fourth thinner still, and the more witnesses there are the

> thinner it gets and the more reasonable it becomes until it
> is as thin as reality, the name we give to the common
> experience.... "Look, look!" recites the crowd. "A horse
> with an arrow in its forehead! It must have been mistaken
> for a deer." (Stoppard, 1968, 21)

In schools we are taught to ignore what we have learned in order to seek for the viewpoint of the authorities; the process of reading is falsified and the reader denied. We are taught to recognize the outlines and forms of shapes in the structures legitimated by power. The creative role of the learner—and hence, the learner her/himself—is denied. Frank Smith (1985, 90) argues that "One reason children might have nothing to learn is very simple—they know it already ... [and] children exhibit the same symptoms of boredom not because they know something already, but because they cannot make sense of what they are expected to learn." Nonsense syllables may be, but unicorns are not usually, available to schoolchildren. Chomsky's famous sentence of easily recognized words, "*Colourless green ideas sleep furiously,*" which is held to be meaningless, reminds me of Dylan Thomas' lines "The force that through the green fuse drives the flower/Drives my green age." And I appreciate and comprehend both the Chomsky and Thomas lines because of what I know about language, about poetry, and about language in poetry. But my comprehension also has to do with my experience in the world. I know how something can be colourless but green, and I know, as did Macbeth, how "the innocent sleep that knits up the ravell'ed sleeve of care" can be furious.

Reading requires the organization of figure-ground spoken of earlier and explains the creative act of perception that is part of the reading process. But again, we must recognize reading as ecologically based: We see what we have learned to see. "Control of form," say Harste et al. (1984, 39), "is a social event. It is not to the white spaces we look when reading: students who look for meaning between the lines will never achieve meaning." "Overt action," says Dewey (1929/1971, 249), "the activity of reading, is an enstatement of established organic-environmental integrations." Reading is, to an extent, a matter of seeing; it is to print that we must respond in the reading situation. But, we must acknowledge that meaning is what is sought, and this is only incidentally a product of visual skills. "One great mistake in the orthodox psychological tradition is its exclusive preoccupation with sharp focalization to the neglect of the vague shading off from the foci into a field of increasing dimness."(249) Traditional reading theories posit it as a processing of information that begins in the identification and recognition of letters. I am suggesting that this is a subsequent step, that we see only what we expect and desire to see, and that reading is only incidentally visual. Most of what we read is a product of nonvisual information. Reading cannot occur without vision of some sort—the blind may read Braille—but reading is only minimally visual. We must turn now to a discussion of the incidental nature of the visual in reading.

Reading Is Only Incidentally Visual—
It Requires a Reader

I have argued that thought is produced by doubt; that conscious thought is produced by prediction; and that prediction is how we are able to move through the world. I have suggested that reading and thought are equivalent processes. I would like now to suggest that reading is organized by prediction and that it is only incidentally visual. We approach any text with questions about what we will find: These questions, as Frank Smith (1988) describes them, produce an array of global and focal predictions. The former concern larger, overriding qualities of an activity, issues of perhaps genre, content, theme, and style. Of course, they pertain to issues concerning the virtual reader as well; issues such as, why would I want to read this book, or any book for that matter? What else might I be doing other than reading this book? One has only to read Chapter 1 of Italo Calvino's novel, *If on a winter's night a traveler* (1981), to have some understanding of what global predictions mean to the process of reading. There Calvino describes all the "reading" that precedes and prepares for the actual engagement with graphic print and that is part of the production of the reader and the text. Focal predictions, on the other hand, refer to the more detailed predictions made during the actual engagement with print—"particular sets of local circumstances" it would be impossible to know prior to the actual engagement itself (Smith, 1988, 168).

> Semantic and syntactic information drawn from their world knowledge, their linguistic knowledge [which must of course derive from the world], and their memory for the text already read enables readers to form expectations about upcoming words in text, at least about a word's form class and semantic features if not the word itself. This information is coordinated with graphemic information when reader's eyes fixate on particular words. (Ehri, 1992, 57)

The interplay between global and focal predictions is the processs of moving through—creating—a text. The process of thinking—and reading—is the continuous call-and-response experience of asking questions and seeking answers to those questions based on prediction, itself based on prior knowledge, in an engagement with the environment.

> The more focal the prediction, the sooner it arises (because it is based on more immediate antecedents) and the sooner it is disposed of (because it has fewer long-range consequences) . . . predictions at various levels inform each other. Your comprehension of one sentence could change your view of a whole book. (Smith, 1988, 169)

Read Ford Madox Ford's *The Good Soldier* to see how global and focal predictions have influence on each other, how single sentences may subvert predictions and require re-views of entire perspectives.

Prediction, you will recall, is based on our theories of the world, all that we already know. Prediction is the prior elimination of unlikely alternatives. Prediction is a creative process and is inseparable from living. It is, as I have suggested above, a matter of picking up information in the environment. Reading the verbal text requires the engagement with written language, but reading may only be considered minimally visual. If we try to see each and every letter and each and every word we will be incapable of comprehension. The brain just cannot work that slowly. It is physiologically impossible to read without prediction, as I hope to briefly show, and, therefore, we must acknowledge that reading occurs not in seeing the text, but in the incredibly complex integration of what we already know with what we want to know. What we see now, Gibson (1979, 251) asserts, refers to the self and not to the environment. Reading is ecological because it involves the creation of the world in the word by a reader who comes to being in reading. Readers may fixate on words and may sample the visual array even densely, but what is seen—what it is possible to see—must derive from prior learning. "The recognition span, or the amount and the size of the unit seen, recognized, organized, and comprehended during a single fixation (its length in terms of words), depends upon readers' facility in word recognition, the difficulty of the material, their familiarity with the material being read or the knowledge of the readers, the physical characteristics of the material, and their ability to assimilate ideas" (Dechant, 1991 61). What is seen is what it is possible to see, and that is dependent on the virtual reader. Ehrlich and Rayner (1981, 653) conclude that "contextual information does allow a reduction in readers' reliance on visual information." Contextual information is everything the virtual reader may bring to the process and is nonvisual.

Paul Kolers (1968, 1970) has noted that reading is only incidentally visual. Most of reading occurs as a result of nonvisual information: what the reader already knows and that s/he brings to the text. In his study, Kolers identifies what are traditionally considered the three levels of reading: the first concerns the recognition of letters, the second the recognition of words, and the third the recognition of meaning.[8] Using this conventional categorization of the reading process into stages, Kolers asks at each level to what extent reading is dependent on visual processing. And at each level, Kolers discovers that recognition is dependent far more on prior expectations—what is already known—than on what is actually seen. What is visually perceived depends on what one expects to see, itself based on what one already knows. For example, in recognizing letters that have been geometrically transformed, respondents named letters based not on sound similarity (*t* was never substituted for *b*, *d*, or *p* though it sounds like bee, dee or pee), but on judgment of orientation (rather, *t* was substituted for *f*).

But subjects were not consistent in their responses: Sometimes a given letter was called *you* and sometimes it was called *en*. Depending on context—what was the orientation of letters that immediately preceded the test letter—letters would be recognized. "In general the data indicate that a judgment of the orientation of the letters is a precondition for their correct identification" (Kolers, 1970, 98). In other words, letters are recognized correctly because their orientation in space is presupposed, but this process lapses occasionally. These lapses result in the appearance of conditions known as dyslexia. Errors seem to be based on a small subset of letters and do not occur haphazardly. Certain letters are confused but others are never so. And the pattern of these errors indicates that the orientation of the reader to the letters is a variable and continuing process.

> In summary, we may say that, when subjects err while naming geometrically transformed letters, they tend to name a letter in terms of another untransformed one . . . and that the patterning of these errors reveals the prior judgment of orientation of the material. Further, this judgment of orientation is not made just once for the whole transformed page, but is a continuing aspect of letter identification, which lapses from time to time. (Kolers, 1970, 99)

Comparison is made by images and not by rule-deduced processing; reading is only incidentally visual.

But letters are usually seen in context, and Kolers and his associates asked to what extent letters are affected by the environment in which they are placed. On the level of the letter, Kolers has shown that readers see what they expect to see. But the question remains, during reading what does one see? To what extent are words seen as composed of letters? To what extent are letters seen in words? In another series of experiments, Kolers and his associates rotated in space examples of normally connected text only to discover that the simple geometry of the letters was not sufficient to explain the recognition of them. Subjects were shown this text and asked to name letters. Letters read from left to right were more readily recognized than letters read from right to left. Recall that English is a language oriented from left to right and that learning this orientation is part of the process of learning to read.[9] Thus, again, the actual reading of the letters cannot be accounted for by visual perception. "It should follow," Kolers concludes, "that as their geometry is not sufficient to explain their recognition, it surely cannot explain their being read" (11). Again, we must acknowledge that reading is only incidentally visual.

Cattell (1886) had earlier discovered that whole sentences of four or five words (approximately 25–30 letters) could be read in the same amount of time that it took to identify two unrelated words (approximately 10–12 letters) and that even two unrelated words could be seen in the same amount of time it took to see five unrelated letters. Clearly, reading could not be solely visual for, given the time needed by the brain to make a decision, it would be impossible to read whole sentences in the same amount of time as it takes to read five letters. Recent research has suggested it is the identification of letters that carries the greater burden in word recognition, arguing that reading was too rapid for context effects to have influence. This research has suggested that readers do, indeed, look at every word. Studies of eye movements during reading by Rayner (1987) and his associates have shown that good readers read every word. This research argued that if words could not be recognized by the context, then how could their recognition be accounted for in reading.

The default explanation turned to letter identification. This research, however, does not account for the existence of global predictions and the constant interplay between them and the engagement with the text—with focal predictions. It assumes that readers approach texts with neither expectations nor predictive abilities. It assumes that people cannot and do not constrain context on purpose. This may be true for schools, but it is true nowhere else. Huey (1908/1968), too, argued that since only a few letters could be seen during an eye fixation, reading must go on by means other than recognition of letters. "Blanchard, Pollatsek, and Rayner (1988) found that the word may be fully identified in the parafovea (and thus may be skipped), or it may be partially activated. The latter may speed later identification of the word"(in Dechant, 1991, 60). Visual acuity is limited to only about two to three degrees, and reading must occur by means other than exact ordered processing from letters to words to meaning. And we must distinguish between sampling the text—we know that fewer miscues occur at the beginning of words than in the middle or towards the end of words—to facilitate comprehension and laboriously combining even two words together at a time to make meaning. The latter procedure will not work for much other than a two-word sentence. Indeed, O'Regan and Lévy-Schoen (1987, 364) conclude that "word perception in reading is governed by three kinds of constraints: sensory constraints (acuity and lateral masking), oculomotor constraints, and processing constraints (lexical and linguistic)." It is in the ecological interplay of the three types of constraints that reading occurs.

Kolers discovered that the recognition of words, a second stage of reading, rather than being primarily a product of visual perception, is heavily dependent on grammatical structure. Because grammar involves relations and sequences of words it is impossible that reading could occur by the mere translating of graphemes (sounds written) into phonemes (sounds spoken). Levin and Buckley (1979, 147) note that "The size [of the eye-voice span] is determined in large part by the grammar and meaning of the text. EVSs are longest when constraints are highest, and by extension, we believe that all reading follows this generalization." Now, it is interesting that the EVS is the distance that the eye is ahead of the voice in reading aloud. It offers an interesting window on the reading process in two ways. Research has shown that our peripheral vision is woefully inaccurate, and yet the research reported by Levin and Buckley suggests that somehow in oral reading—and presumably in silent reading as well—the eye seems to jump meaningfully ahead of the voice. How can the eye know where to fixate unless it is predicting from prior knowledge of grammatical and semantic language contraints? O'Regan and Lévy-Schoen (1987) suggest that, in part, the eye jumps (saccades) unconsciously based on low-level information, but Freeman's (1991) work suggests that what is referred to as unconscious may actually be the product of prior learning.

Second, if indeed peripheral vision is unreliable, how could the eye actually see where to fixate at all? Huey (1908/1968) wondered why we do not see blurs during reading since the eye must make rapid jumps. On the one hand, Huey believed that based on prior knowledge the eye reorients itself to the page even when closed; on the other hand, Huey said, meaning takes care of fusion in advance and we see what we expect to see. Fusion occurs only when meaning is not produced from the data; in that case, consciousness arises from the data—the black and white sensation—and fusion occurs. Reading, we must acknowledge, occurs only incidentally visually. Huey (67) wrote that ". . . the larger the amount read during a reading pause, the more inevitably must the reading be by suggestion and inference from clews of whatsoever kind, internal or external. In reading, the deficient picture is filled in, retouched by the mind and the page is thus made to present the familiar appearances of completeness." We *may* see every word—though I know of few studies that give credence to the notion that we see every letter of every word—but only know meaning.

Third, even barring a subsequent fixation, how could the mind produce correct constructions without visual input unless the mind was actually creating those constructions based on what it already knew? There is no internal theater where images are projected as on a screen for viewing by the brain. All that enters the eye are light rays. The brain must construct an image, but it must know what it is looking for. Levin and Buckley (1979, 147) conclude that the reader will direct his/her attention to reading the textual material in the most economical way possible and that the information relevant to the reader's purpose is selected for priority of attention. That attention is organized by the reader's purpose, which originates in doubt and seeks information. The "patterns of eye movements [are] regulated by the reader to take advantage of the highest-order invariants in the text appropriate to the reader's purposes. Such a view shows reading to be an efficient, flexible, and adaptive process" (Levin & Buckley, 147).

Indeed, this is the same conclusion Kolers had earlier reached based on his study. In the third stage of reading, the direct perception of meanings and relations, Kolers' work suggests that readers perceive and remember words based on their meanings and not on their appearances or sounds; that readers could comprehend bilingual passages as easily as they could unilingual passages; and that in reading bilingual passages aloud, readers miscued by reading one language into another, saying, for example *porte* for *door*, Kolers concludes

> And so again I have shown that the skilled reader of a language is not operating in terms of a passive but faithful mouthing of the text before him. He is not trying to translate graphemes into phonemes, and he is not responding especially to the morphemic structure of the words. He is not even able to see all of the words on the page . . . instead, he is treating words as symbols and is operating on them in terms of their meanings and their relations to other symbols. (1970, 113)

This activity is, as noted above, called comprehension. It is also thinking. It is also learning.

Based as it must be on uncertainty, reading may be understood as a psycholinguistic guessing game, requiring not greater degrees of skill, but, rather, improved skill in prediction. Reading is not only incidentally visual, as studies have shown, but it is physiologically impossible without prediction. George Miller (1956), in a very important article, notes how the channel capacity—the greatest amount of information based upon absolute judgment that a subject can give about a stimulus—seems to rest at about seven, plus or minus two. "We possess," Miller writes, "a finite and rather small capacity for making such unidimensional judgments and that seems similar in all sensory attributes"(3). For example, in speech, Miller notes, each phoneme requires the recognition of eight to nine distinctive features (of sound), which would make comprehension impossible given the limited channel capacity. Recall that the brain requires time to make a decision as to what has been heard. If the brain does not act quickly, the sensory data are pushed out by subsequent sensory input. Miller's conclusion is that people must choose to be less accurate in absolute judgment when listening to speech. "Did I hear what I think you said?" Double takes in visual experience are also a complex product of strategies for handling limitations in absolute judgment. Similarly, since the recognition of any single word visually depends upon the recognition of distinctive features far in excess of that magical number, it is clear that there must be a psychological process that facilitates recognition of the whole prior to the parts.

Now, Miller discovers that the channel capacity for multidimensional judgments increases, but at a decreasing rate, by adding independent variables and that adding variables to the display increases the total channel capacity (the information reported) but decreases the accuracy. In other words, if we seek judgment based on initial letters *and* structural context we increase the possiblility for judgment, though we *may* increase the possibility of misjudgment.

> We might argue that in the course of evolution those organisms were most successful that were responsive to the widest range of stimulus energies in their environment. In order to survive in a constantly fluctuating world, it was better to have a little information about a lot of things than to have a lot of information about a small segment of the environment. (Miller, 88)

The more dimensions we may employ for judgment, the more information we may bring to bear on the decision. The more we know, the more we are able to know; the more we read, the more we are able to read. Reading is learned by reading in meaningful contexts: Reading must be ecologically based.

Organisms had to invent processes to facilitate judgment to get beyond the limits of the magical number seven, plus or minus two. Miller suggests three strategies: The first is relative judgment. We estimate based on prior knowledge. The second involves multidimensionality, as for example, making judgments based upon both visual input and a specific global expectation. The third strategy for increasing the limited capacity of short-term memory is the use of successive judgments: the constant revision of judgments spoken of above as the interplay of global and focal predictions. Each of these strategies is a function of predicting and produces judgments of greater range but less accuracy. "By organizing the stimulus input simultaneously into several dimensions and successively into a sequence of chunks, we manage to break (or at least stretch) this informational bottleneck" (95). Chunking is the organization of discrete pieces of information into a larger unit to facilitate short-term memory whose capacity is seven, plus or minus two. "Sohcatoa" is one word and not eight letters and so I can recall my geometric relations. The phone number I wish to remember exists in three chunks rather than ten numbers.

Reading requires each of these three strategies, each of which is based on the use of prior knowledge to produce futures. As Ken Goodman (1970) has written of reading in a seminal article on whole-language philosophy and research,

> Efficient reading does not result from precise perception and identification of all elements, but from skill in selecting the fewest, most productive cues necessary to produce guesses which are right the first time. The ability to anticipate that which has not been seen, of course, is vital in reading, just as the ability to anticipate what has not yet been heard is vital in listening. (Goodman, 1970, 260)

This uncertainty is intrinsic to reading, as it is to reflective thinking, as it is to life. As in J. Hillis Miller's (1987) ethics of reading, reading and thinking and living are equivalent activities, are ethical and ontological, ethical because ontological, ontological because ethical. I argue along with Miller that living and reading are commensurate and therefore equal activities. Reading—the experience of guessing—becomes not just necessary to living but the process of existence itself. I would like to argue, as well, that the failure to read, about which Miller speaks, is not equivalent to the illiteracy touted so highly by the ideological right as prevalent today, but is rather contained in the very nature of the reading process and can be viewed as the quintessential creative activity producing self and world in one endeavor. For as a guessing game, reading refuses exactitude, and opens up uncertainty as not only inevitable, but as absolutely requisite to freedom. However, I would like to argue as well that a real failure to read is rather a failure to exist. The psychology of reading that I posit is also a psychology of self.

A Pedagogy of Reading: Ecological Perspectives

In 1929, John Dewey wrote that "The use or intent of instruction, advice, admonition, and honest dialectic is to bring awareness— meanings hitherto unperceived thereby constituting their ideas . . ." (27). In an ecological theory of reading, the pedagogy of reading must offer assistance in discovering, to paraphrase Maurice Sendak, where the wild things are. What are wild things, of course, is particular to the individual. I have attempted to show above that reading could not happen by exact procedure, but occurs instead based upon interest, prediction, and confirmation. A pedagogy of reading must address these issues. It is to that I would like to turn now.

I have said that reading occurs on the basis of prediction, on what is already known. Reading is, as Ken Goodman (1970, 259) notes, a psycholinguistic guessing game. It is "a selective process [involving] partial use of available minimal language cues selected from perceptual input on the basis of the reader's expectations. As this partial information is processed, tentative decisions are made to be confirmed, rejected or refined as reading progresses." Thus, as has been stated repeatedly, the practice and pedagogy of reading depends on the prior knowledge of the reader and the ability of the teacher to facilitate greater and more accurate guessing. The most proficient reader is the most efficient reader: the one who can obtain the greatest quantity of cues from the environment using the least amount of information.[10] Since reading is minimally visual, the vast quanitity of cues exists ecologically: in the relationship between the virtual reader and the text.

Of course, this is not to say that the reader does not need to see the text, nor even that, as research shows, readers need not see every word. However, reading every word does not necessarily result in comprehension; that requires an integration of various cues from a variety of language and other sources, including the graphophonemic, syntactic, semantic, and pragmatic.[11] Thus, an ecological theory of reading would "help readers gain information from a cueing system that they may not be using adequately or that they may believe they should not use" (Goodman & Burke, 1980, 29). This does not preclude decoding skills, but rather, offers them as one alternative to getting one's questions answered. Indeed, even researchers steeped in subskill approaches to reading acknowledge that "Decoding rules of some sort are important in producing a backup process in reading never-encountered words. (Context has this value also.)" (Gough et al., 1991, 155). As Jerome Harste (in Mills et al., 1992, ix) has written, whole language has never eschewed phonics or the study of any graphophonemic system. Rather, he argues

> Where is the book that assures us that teachers who teach reading though a phonetic approach are making sure that children see reading as functional and meaningful? Where is the book that shows how phonics advocates are making sure that they are connecting kids with books for life? Where is the book that shows how phonics advocates have stopped silencing children through recognition that there are other cue systems in language that children already master and that they can build from this base? Where is the book that shows teachers how to counteract the negative ripple effect that phonics instruction has on reading comprehension?

No one would advocate that reading occurs in the absence of instruction. The question I raise here is what constitutes instruction. "Reading is a complex activity that requires familiarity with the patterns within and between words, and those patterns quite often need to be amplified by an adult. Just as talk about multiple stories allows children to increase their understanding of character motivation and diverse story genres, talk about the patterns of language enables children to decode familiar words, as well as unlock new configuations" (Wolf & Heath, 1992, 191). All that I argue here is that reading—the establishment of meaning—only occurs ecologically, and that therefore, a theory of reading must begin with this perspective.

NOTES

1. Ken Goodman distinguishes beween *re*coding—going from one code into another—and *de*coding—going from code to meaning.

2. For some answers to this question see Charles Read's "Preschool Children's Knowledge of English Phonology" (1971).

3. See Rumelhart, Hinton, and McClelland (1986).

4. The idea of the holograph as the manner of representation of ideas is interesting and is explored in some detail in Dreyfus and Dreyfus (1986).

5. The quantum leap is defined as the simultaneous actualization of one possiblity and the negation of all others. In other words, the observer makes reality by deciding what to observe. It is, perhaps, what Kierkegaard referred to as the leap of faith.

6. Charles Perfetti (1992, 34), for example, states that reading is "the identitifying of written words."

7. Rayner and Pollatsek (in Dechant, 1991) state that the first event in eye control necessary for reading is the striking on the retina of meaningful information. What they do not note is that it is a virtual reader who must determine what is to be recognized as meaningful information.

8. This is to be compared with Jeanne Chall's five-stage process of learning to read (1983). It may also be compared with Linnea Ehri's (1992) three stages of visual cue reading, phonetic cue reading, and deciphering, or decoding. Phillip Gough, Connie Juel, and Priscilla Griffith (1991, 1992) postulate three stages of reading acquisition as well. They define the paired associate learning stage, the cipher stage, and code reading (decoding).

9. For an excellent discussion of this event, see Marie Clay, *Becoming Literate: The Construction of Inner Control* (1991).

10. In the game of Clue, if one can guess that it was Miss Peacock in the dining room with the candlestick after a single question, then the game is over. This is not to say that reading is best accomplished with a single question—unless of course, you are looking for a number in a phone book. The experience of play—the game of Clue or reading *War and Peace*—is also part of reading, but first one must learn that that is, indeed, one purpose of reading. Having finished *War and Peace* is not as significant as what has occurred during the process or as who has now

finished it. In the same way as the winner of Clue is different than the player of Clue.

11. In their study, "The Intervention of Context and Parafoveal Visual Information in Reading," Balota, Pollatsek, and Rayner (1985, 387) conclude that "the data contradict a view of reading wherein expectations and predictions about forthcoming information are primary and visual information is there merely for confirmation." But it has never been the claim of whole language that the visual is only used for confirmation. That would substitute a different hierarchy for the one now advocated by the subskill approach to reading. Rather, whole language advocates argue that the visual is only one cueing system from which information may be picked up.

CHAPTER 5

Three Readers Reading: A Pedagogy

I have earlier quoted from J. Hillis Miller's *The Ethics of Reading* (1987, 59). There he said that "To live is to read, or rather to commit again and again the failure to read which is the human lot." I have explored in sufficient depth, I hope, what that might mean in a psychology of reading. I have tried to show how the act of reading might be understood as an original and natural creative act, how it is equivalent to thought, how it is, therefore, central to human existence. It is by reading that we may proceed through the world continuing to learn. Indeed, it is by reading that we *must* proceed through the world: acting upon our theory of the world by making predictions from the available data and then seeking confirmation of those predictions and integrating that new knowledge within our theories of the world. In these workings, we change our theories of the world as we change ourselves. We think. We learn. We create ourselves in reading. The process is all. A pedagogy of reading must provide space for experiment, for trial, for questions posed in an atmosphere supportive of these queries. This pedagogy of reading must support questions, inquiry, and the uncertain, and it must provide resources for finding the wild things. As John Dewey (1929/1971, 182) teaches us, "Freedom of thought denotes freedom of thinking; specific doubting, inquiring, suspense, creating, and cultivating of tentative hypotheses, trials, and experimenting that are unguaranteed and that involve risks of waste, loss, and error." As a language activity, reading must be supported by immersion in language that the latter's structures and resources and potentialities might be explored in an environment made risk free and available for experiment. Reading does not need to be taught but, rather, to be learned.

Reading written texts, Miller (1987, 59) has noted, takes place "by an implacable necessity, as the response to a categorical demand in which one must attempt to make language referential," but it is a response for which the reader must take responsibility in the individual, social, and political worlds. Ironically, then, as I have shown, in making language referential each individual creates the self and the world in which that self exists. Reading creates selves. Of course, as Miller also notes, we have no way of ever knowing certainly that we have accomplished the correct reading, so that reading is always finally a failure to read, but that failure is not one of process but of certainty. Though there is no authorized reading, there is authority in reading. "Every thinker puts some portion of an apparently stable world in peril and no one can wholly predict what will emerge in its place," declared Dewey (1929/1971, 182). Accepting the doubt and the final uncertainty is also acceptance of the self that creates the doubt and is uncertain. "No one discovers a new world without forsaking an old one; and no one discovers a new world who exacts guarantees in advance for what it shall be, or who puts the acts of discovery under bonds with respect to what the new world shall do to him when it comes into vision" (Dewey, 1929/1971, 201). We read, we think, we learn.

In the assumption of responsibility of and for reading, in making language referential, the self acknowledges the construction of itself and the world in the very engagement with and construction of that world. Reading, engagement with texts, creates us and connects us at the same time. Jo Anne Pagano (1990, 39–40) describes this process as the claim of philia, the claim of the individual coming into existence in and through community:

> The claim of philia is a claim on both men and women. The claim of patriarchy and its single-sided concern with certainty and totalizing discourses, its mistake regarding the nature and source of authority in the interest of repressing patriarchal anxiety and toward the end of turning from the primal love for the mother, transforms knowledge into a product lodged in the system of free-market exchange. Romanticized, ritualized, sentimentalized, theatricalized, privatized claims of matriarchy

similarly wedge knowledge into the cramped corners of commodity relations. My knowledge, not yours. The claim of philia turns us to genuine alternative practice, practice in which knowledge is a use value. It binds us together in common work. The claim of philia turns us to the text—the product—and the texture of our reading both. The trick is to appropriate the text and to let it continue to be itself—to be near yet separate. We can do this if we recollect the textures of our readings, if we appreciate the textures of others' readings. These readings will be unauthorized texts, and these are the basis, but not the sum, of our authority as readers and speakers.

For Pagano, as for Miller and myself, our reading is always *our* knowledge, but never Knowledge. Our selves come into existence—acquire agency—reading, in the acknowledgment of the word in the world, of the world in the word, and of ourselves in the word. Reading is formative even as it is performative. Reading has real consequences, as does the failure to read have serious effects. And so I would like to examine briefly three readers and their reading and to observe how the latter makes possible the appearance of the former. I would also like to explore briefly how their roles as readers may be understood as an expression of them, the means by which they manifest who they are, the means by which agency is produced. I would like to observe how their coming to being occurs in reading, in learning to read; and how their failures to exist, to have agency, arise from a denial of reading.

Stephen Dedalus

Toward the end of James Joyce's *Portrait of the Artist as a Young Man* (1966, 243) Stephen Dedalus explains to Cranly why he will not take communion even at his dying mother's request. "I fear many things; dogs, horses, firearms, the sea, thunderstorms, machinery, the country roads at night." Still puzzled, Cranly asks Stephen why he also fears the piece of bread that would satisfy his communion, and Stephen responds, "I imagine that there is a malevolent reality behind those things I say I fear."

This statement speaks to an acceptance of an absolute and material reality lying behind words, a reality that is merely represented by those words, a presence that not only paralyzes but alienates Stephen as well. At the end of *Portrait*, Stephen flees what he understands as constraints to his individuality—country, family, church, history—and imposes self-exile so that he might feel free to become the artist. But called home from France for his mother's funeral, Stephen realizes that he has failed in that endeavor to become an artist during his period of self-exile. He has been incapable of ridding himself of that malevolent reality represented in words. As Daniel Schwarz (1987, 73) says about Stephen in the first three chapters of *Ulysses*, "he is back where he was at the beginning of the last section of *Portrait* when, partly in response to the devolution in the family fortunes, his heart [was] already bitten by an ache of loathing and bitterness." He is incapable of doing much or establishing any relations. Stephen is incapable of being self-sufficient either emotionally or intellectually, and it is his alienation and dis-ease that drives him from his home on the morning of June 16, 1904, the now famous day on which the novel, *Ulysses*, takes place. "I will not sleep here tonight," Stephen declares as he leaves his residence at Martello Tower, and reflects as well, in language that reminds us of the conclusion of *A Portrait of the Artist as a Young Man*, that "Home also I cannot go" (1986, 19). Until Stephen can establish relations with the world that derive from freedom of thinking, Stephen is condemned to a lack of self-sufficiency which he so desperately desires but for which he has not the skill. When Stephen reads it is reality he seeks, not understanding that it is his creative power by which reality comes into existence.

Stephen is homeless and alone. Indeed, Stephen's fears—his readings of the world—as expressed in the final pages of *Portrait* are the basis, though not the sum, of his character, and they find expression again at the opening of the "Proteus" chapter in Joyce's next book, *Ulysses*. There, you will recall, Stephen is returned home from his self-exile from Ireland and is seemingly exiled at home as well, cut off from family, friends, and community, and filled with self-loathing. He is incapable of action. In "Proteus," the fear of this malevolent reality signifies the confused condition in which we find Dedalus, desiring desperately to be the artist, but finding himself still alienated from the world in which he seeks truth and which, in his art, he would represent. In "Proteus" Stephen declares his belief that it is impossible to avoid the visible, that to see is to experience thought. It is, of course, what we have argued earlier: The act of perception is an act of thought and not its beginnings. But in his conceptual frame, Stephen maintains the dichotomy between subject and object we have seen prevalent in Western thought since Plato and which has been responsible for the organization of reading pedagogy. To Stephen, what is visible is only the mask of reality: "Ineluctable modality of the visible, at least that if no more, thought through my eyes. Signature of all things I am here to read" (31). For Stephen, knowing reality is a matter of "reading signs," and it is in the act of reading that he would satisfy that quest to find the "word known to all men"(41).[1] When Stephen has acquired this word, or the skill to read it, then, he believes, he will know Truth.

Here, as in the earlier *Portrait*, Stephen assumes that the sign is a fixed form for an absolute and discoverable reality and that this reality exists outside of him. Stephen is incapable of play, an activity, we have said, in which things lose their determining force. In play, Vygotsky (1978, 97) tells us, *"The child sees one thing but acts differently in relation to what he sees. Thus a condition is reached where the child begins to act independently of what he sees."* In play, the child creates the world from what is available, as long as no one obstructs that creation. "Creation," Marion Milner (1987, 206) says, "is a struggle to let something happen in relation to a chosen material, that malleable bit of external world which can be shaped. And it is by this struggle with the material that the conscious mind disciplines the chaotic forces in the creative depths." Stephen believes that creation is being able to read the signatures so that he would know the Real which the signs represent—the Ideal, the word known to all men—and could then operate as that Reality would determine. Stephen would be an artist, but his idea of creation will not suffice: There is clearly no responsibility or ethics in his reading, and certainly no creative Stephen.

We may, of course, hear in Stephen's desire to learn to read the signature of all things the claim of the conservatives whose idea of reading Stephen here espouses. Theirs is a reading that searches for meaning existent outside of the self, whose attainment will (and you may choose one) enhance, organize, prepare, and/or complete the self. As meaning is situated outside of the reader, indeed, exists without the reader (pun intended), then there must be skills by which it can be discovered. Reading is defined as a series of discrete subskills, and a curriculum is subsequently organized about the teaching of those skills that make reading possible. "Signature of all things I must learn to read" (Joyce, 1986, 31). Frank Smith (1988, 75) rightly argues, I believe, that this form of learning is "the world turned upside down, that it is nonsensical, determined by the experimenter, and rel[ies] on data collected in controlled experimental conditions" rather than understood in its natural ecology. It is a pedagogy that Paolo Freire calls an academic approach to reading. "In this case," Freire says, "reading is viewed as the acquisition of predefined forms of knowledge and is organized around the study of Latin and Greek and the mastery of the great classical works" (Freire & Macedo, 1986, 146). Of course, this has been Stephen's classical education and reminds us that how one reads determines what one will read; what one reads is determined by the skills that define reading. In this perspective of reading and its pedagogy, the student is the empty vessel that must be filled to become a subject, to become viable in the present marketplace.

However, if Stephen is to become the artist who will ultimately write *Ulysses*, then he must first learn to know reading in a manner contradictory to that which he expresses in "Proteus." There, though having read the Greek and Latin classics and having adopted a Platonism which ought to have led him to the perception and creation of beauty, he is still incapable of artistic creation. "Creation from nothing," is what Stephen desires: the ideal recreation of the world as he wishes. Actually, however, and despite his readings, Stephen is yet no further along in his desire to be the artist. This conservative pedagogy will not suffice because for Stephen the forms in which reality is contained will not hold still. His despair throughout the

"Proteus," indeed, throughout the day, is a product of the changeableness of forms. His despair is symptomatic of an infantile condition which denies separation and hence, identity. As Vygotsky (1978, 97) says, "... *it is impossible for very young children to separate the field of meaning from the visual field* because there is no such intimate fusion between meaning and what is seen." Dedalus, tied to the form which will not assume permanent presence, is incapable of producing identity which is dependent upon his capacity to read. For even as Stephen fears the forms behind the words, a belief premised on the solidity of forms, so too does he fear formlessness, or rather, fears his own inability to be comfortable in that formlessness. Stephen insists on knowing reality, thereby separating himself from it and making his ability to create within it impossible. Indeed, reading requires that Stephen accept his role in the creation of reality and not merely its unmasking. It is only when Stephen can begin to accept the nature of the sign—its formlessness as changeableness and not formlessness—that he can establish a relationship to it that may be of service to him in the production of his identity as an artist.[2] This will mean that Stephen must come to accept that Truth exists not in Knowledge itself, nor in the signatures that can be learned to be read, but in a relation to knowledge, a relation to language.

In learning to read, Stephen will have the capacity to produce himself, will at least produce the Stephen capable of writing *Ulysses*—Stephen Dedalus, the artist, no longer a young and callow man. First, however, Stephen, the would-be artist, must learn the nature of language so that he might produce identity through its use rather than be resigned to discover himself in it. Explicating Jacques Lacan, the French psychoanalyst whose rereadings of Freud organized his practice, Anika Lemaire (1986, 54) declares that "Language is ... the precondition for *the act of becoming aware of oneself as a distinct entity*." It is language that establishes mediate relationships and in which the subject may be aware of herself; without language there is no distance between the self and others, between the self and the world. Without language there is no identity. It is this that Stephen must learn about language, about reading, and about himself. Then he will have learned the signatures of all things which he is here to read.

Reading, as we have said, is play. Play is the creation of what is not there out of what is present. As we have shown above, the text may be understood as a Winnicottian *transitional phenomenon*, a means by which the child or adult may produce the area of cultural experience and live creatively. Reading the text is the essence of creativity and is the experience of play and is the basis of health in the world. Winnicott (1986, 36) tells us that "Cultural experience starts as play, and leads on to the whole area of man's inheritance, including the arts, the myths of history, the slow march of philosophical thought and the mysteries of mathematics, and of group management and of religion." Reading, as we have discussed it, is the experience of play and is constitutive of creativity. "Playing," Winnicott tells us (1971, 41), "is neither inside by any use of the word [which would be fantasy] . . . nor is it outside, that is, it is not a part of the repudiated world, the not-me, that which the individual has decided to recognize (with whatever difficulty and even pain) as truly external, which is outside magical control." It is this *potential* space that constitutes the greater part of the infant's experience and that "throughout life is retained in the intense experiencing that belongs to the arts and to religion and to imaginative living and to scientific work" (1971, 14). Indeed, it is this potential space that is produced in reading. "We experience life," Winnicott (1971, 64) tells us, "in the area of transitional phenomena, in the exciting interweave of subjectivity and objective observation, and in an area that is intermediate between the inner reality of the individual and the shared reality of the world external to individuals."

The act of reading, as Stephen Dedalus must learn, ought to be understood as essentially the creative act—the act of the artist he would become. Reading is the active process of looking and doing with a text and is an act of play and creation. "The creative impulse is therefore something that can be looked at as a thing in itself, something that of course is necessary if an artist is to produce a work of art, but also something that is present when *anyone*—baby, child, adolescent, adult, old man, or woman— looks in a healthy way on anything or does anything deliberately, such as making a mess with faeces or prolonging the act of crying to enjoy a musical sound" (Winnicott, 1971, 69). Creation is what we do with what is available. In a society such as ours, whose emphasis is on product, process—reading—is not only easily lost but even denied as well. Further, in a society such as ours, product comes to determine process, and the resources that are brought to the creative process are denied. Too often, Winnicott (1971, 69) cautions, "The creation stands between the observer and the artist's creativity." But it is the process and not the product that constitutes creativity; it is the process that is reading and in which creativity resides. It is this that Stephen mistakes, searching by his reading for the product and yet missing the product in the process.[3] Stephen's quest is, I believe, an impossible one, but is not necessarily nobly so. He requires his reading to be true and defines his reading as the learning of the Real. But, as Ralph Waldo Emerson has asked, "What can we see, read, acquire but ourselves? Cousin is a thousand books to a thousand persons. Take the book, my friend, & read your eyes out; you will never find there what I find" (in Porte, 1982, 81).

It is this very notion of reading and identity that Stephen Dedalus cannot accept. Ultimately, Stephen must, however, learn to read the text, though he must acknowledge his complicity in that text from the outset. Michael Halliday (1975, 123) declares that "text is not made of sounds or letters; and in the same way it is not made of words and phrases and clauses and sentences. It is made of meanings, and encoded in wordings, soundings, and spellings." In the act of reading, the reader creates the very text he reads and the identity that is made possible by the reading of the text. It is what Miller described above as accepting responsibility for that reading in the social, political, and personal worlds of the reader. Stephen's education in *Ulysses* may be seen in this fashion as a pedagogy of reading: He exclaims in "Proteus" that "signatures of all things I am here to read," though he repeatedly fails to read. That he eventually does so during the course of this eventful but mundane day is evident in the penultimate chapter of *Ulysses*. There, Stephen's encounter with Bloom reveals his newly acquired understanding of self and the world and a new pedagogy of reading. Recall that in this chapter, referred to as "Eumaeus," Stephen is rescued by Bloom from the dangerous chaos of Nighttown and Stephen's own belligerent and antagonistic posturings, and is led home by the caring and loving older man, the two engaged continuously in conversation at cross-purposes. Neither is actually listening to the other. Bloom concernedly invites the drunken Stephen to spend the evening, but Stephen declines the offer. After the two walk outside for Stephen's departure, they stand outside Bloom's home in which lies his wife, Molly, and the narrator describes the two men as "silent, each contemplating the other in both mirrors of the reciprocal flesh of theirhisnothis fellow faces" (1986, 577). Here, apparently for the first time, Stephen recognizes a meaning that is contained not in signatures, in presence, but as a result of a relationship that derives primarily from absence and that creates presence in that absence. You may recall that Bloom has lost a son and is looking for one; Stephen searches for a father. Each creates in the other what he seeks for himself, creates the self in reading. As in "Proteus," but clearly without despair, form shifts here, and the encounter is not with the Real, but rather with the real mediated—produced—by Stephen's experience. It is a moment of creativity, of play, of reading the text. Stephen's identity is constructed in his relation to another, for to see his own in Bloom's face is to see himself as man of action, a man intimately tied to history, a man who is for the most part creative, and yet a man who has suffered, positions that Stephen has previously been incapable of or that he has outrightly rejected. In "Circe," Stephen had announced, "Personally, I detest action." Reading, however, requires action.

As Stephen learns that signs—external reality—have no ideal form, or rather, that their form is protean, he must learn as well how they acquire meaning: the sense of form that signs may take and that depends on reading. Meaning inheres in words which themselves have meaning only in context which is, itself, changeable, unpredictable, protean. Signs have meaning only as they exist in a particular context and as the reader is able to contextualize that context. Signs contain neither meaning nor truth; rather, truth exists in the relationship to signs, which is a function of history. Reading is, then, the establishment of relations between a reader and history.

History is perhaps another way of describing context, for history is all that comes before the actual inscription, be it literal, ideographic, or pictographic. However, once history is contained in language, once feeling moves through thought to language, it is based on absence and can only be expressed as metaphor. "*Ulysses*," Daniel Schwarz says (1987, 14), "is Joyce's inquiry into how language signifies; it is about the creation of metaphors and their importance as a means of understanding ourselves and the world we live in." Schwarz (13) defines metaphor as ". . . the use of words to suggest a resemblance between something that is part of the teller's focus of attention—part of his real or imagined world—with something that is not literally or actually a part of the phenomenon that is engaging his mind." Metaphor cannot function without history, for metaphor signifies only insofar as a relationship between presence and an absence can be established. Metaphor is the relational structure in which the signifier becomes the signified. But even metaphor is protean: "What any metaphor *says* or *means* or *does* will always be to some extent alterable by altering its context" (14). Hence, all meaning is dependent on relationships, and those relationships are in a continual state of flux. Marx tells us that ". . . history itself is nothing but the activity of men pursuing their purposes" (in Wolfe, 1964, ix). In that pursuit, all meaning derives from the relationships that are established and that determine knowledge. Meaning is the substance of identity; identity is achieved in relationships; reading depends on the establishment of relationships; reading is the production of identity.

Stephen's concern is with language: He seeks its meaning that he might use it as an artist. But if art is, for Stephen, ". . . the human disposition of sensible or intelligible matter for an esthetic end" (Joyce, 1966, 207), then Stephen's apprehension of the illogicality of signs precludes his ability to produce sensible or intelligible matter; hence, his ability to read the signature of all things. Signs must be illogical, as we have said, for they contain no form themselves. Signs are inherently substanceless. "The written signifier is always technical and representative," Derrida (1976, 11) teaches us. "It has no constitutive meaning." Because Stephen is incapable of accepting the protean nature of form— reality—he cannot attain to the vocation of artist. The continuing protean nature of form suggests that the nature of it is not static; this is antagonistic to Stephen's tenet that beauty depends on *quidditas* (1966, 213):

> When you have apprehended that basket as one thing and have then analyzed it as a thing you make the only synthesis which is logically and esthetically permissible. You see that it is that thing which it is and no other thing. . . . The instant wherein that supreme quality of beauty, the clear radiance of the esthetic image, is apprehended luminously by the mind which has been arrested by its wholeness and fascinated by its harmony is the luminous silent stasis of esthetic pleasure. . . .

But ideal form cannot exist if it can be so readily effaced; hence, form becomes substanceless. Or, as Stephen worries, if he cannot control his work's reception, what value can it have: "Who ever anywhere will read these written words. Signs on a white field" (1986, 40). For what is substance if it has no form? Stephen's quest for that word known to all men is a fruitless search, for no form exists absolutely and meaning cannot inhere in formless and substanceless space.

Rather, meaning exists in a relation to the sign, to what is an absence. Stephen's control over words is impossible in this schema, and no word can ever be known to all men for meaning exists not within a word, but rather, without it, in the relationships between words and humans who use those words. Stephen must first understand that it is not reality he must seek—not the word known to all men—but a relationship to words that will produce knowledge and his identity as the artist. Only when he accepts history can Stephen do this.

Knowledge is impossible without context, without a relationship between the sign and the perceiver of the sign. That relationship is an historical entity and is reading. Yet, Stephen rejects history and, therefore, cannot read. Of course, he also cannot write. "History," Stephen says, "is a nightmare from which I am trying to awake" (1986, 28). In history, Stephen sees nets that would entrap his soul, be that history paternity, native roots, or environment.[4] However, Stephen can never learn to read without the acceptance of history, of metaphor. Given the allusive quality of *Ulysses* and the elusive reality Stephen seeks, as well as the obvious metaphorical nature of the word, it is clear that when Stephen says "Signature of all things I am here to read," Joyce means this to be ironic, not only because Stephen's eyesight is so poor, but because such reading is impossible without metaphor, metaphor is impossible without history, and Stephen wishes to reject history. Even as late as the "Circe" chapter, Stephen still admits his failure to read the signatures he so desperately desires: "I never could read His handwriting except His criminal thumbprint on the haddock"(1986, 458). Stephen can only come to some facilitation with reading when he sees himself in relation to Bloom: Then Stephen has at the same time become his own father and invented the paternity he needs. In gazing at Bloom, Stephen sees himself. Reading the text permits this play: Bloom does not question Stephen's creative act. In that gaze, however, Stephen constructs his identity. This pedagogy of reading produces the self and the text.

Jacob Horner

What Stephen Dedalus learns—what Stephen Dedalus becomes—Jacob Horner, the protagonist in John Barth's novel *The End of the Road* (1967/1977), never achieves. Stephen learns to read and becomes an agent; Jacob Horner fails to learn and never comes to agency. His destination and his condition, expressed in the book's final line is "Terminal." There is no hope for Jacob Horner: There is no Jacob Horner. Though he knows all of the letters and many of the words, Horner is incapable of reading. This is to say that, by the definitions we have adopted, Horner can construct no meaning in the world. Without meaning, there is no consciousness, no self. Horner's presenting problem in the book is a psychological paralysis that manifests itself in a physical immobility. But as the Doctor attests, "There is no such thing as *paralysis* . . . there is only paralyzed Jacob Horner" (81). And paralyzed Jacob Horner is only in a sense Jacob Horner.

Horner does not search, as does Stephen Dedalus, for an ideal and permanent reality, for a substance behind the signatures, and then fail to read because the forms in their change deny that reality. Rather, Horner cannot bring anything to form at all, is incapable of producing meaning at all, incapable of even perceiving signatures. Horner does not know what he sees; for him, everything is equal, is indistinguishable. He cannot bring meaning to anything. If, as Frank Smith said above, prediction is necessary because the world is so potentially multiform that we must limit our possibilities if we are to decide what we see at all, then Horner is incapable of such vision. Horner states that ". . . when one is faced with such a multitude of desirable choices, no one choice seems satisfactory for very long by comparison with the aggregate desirability of all the rest, though compared to any *one* of the others it would not be found inferior" (3). Horner cannot choose because he cannot distinguish one thing from another; without choice there can be no construction. Unable to qualitatively characterize one choice from the next, Horner reveals his incapacity to make meaning. He is incapable or unwilling to make predictions and literally cannot then move through the world. He cannot act upon the knowledge he has already to make choices about future behavior, in essence, because he has no knowledge he can make of use. Without the capacity to predict, Horner is immobilized; he is immobilized because he cannot construct meaning: He cannot discern true ideas from false ones because he cannot act. Psychologist William James had said (1907, 133) that *"True ideas are those that we can assimilate, validate, corroborate and verify. False ideas are those that we cannot."* Because Horner cannot predict, he will not act and he will never have a true or a false idea: He will not have an idea. Thus it is that Horner cannot read.

Phrased even more extremely, Horner's failure to read is a failure to be. Incapable of reading, Horner ceases to exist. There occurs no event of consciousness because no meaning is constructed from the available data. Without meaning, there can be no meaner. Indeed, the doctor who will eventually treat Jacob Horner discovers him on a train station bench at the Pennsylvania Station where he has been sitting for a full evening because he could not choose a destination for which to purchase a ticket. In that paralysis there is no consciousness. Returning to the bench in the ticket room having failed to choose a destination and obtain a ticket, Horner sits incapable of choice: "I sat immobile on the bench. After a while Cincinnati, Crestline,

Dayton, and Lima dropped from my mind, and their place was taken by that test pattern of my consciousness, *Pepsi-Cola hits the spot*, intoned with silent oracularity. But it, too, petered away into the void, and nothing appeared in its stead" (Barth, 1967/1977, 74). By his own admission, Horner could have remained there indefinitely: immobile and unconscious, incapable of reading.

In that failure, Horner resigns himself to an existence over which he has no control. "In a sense, I am Jacob Horner," the narrator states at the opening sentence of the novel. Which is to say, I think, that Horner understands that his being is contingent upon an actual definition of being. And if being is the exercise of consciousness and the construction of reality, then Horner *in that sense* does not exist. Thus it is that Horner is only so constituted by an extremely limited capacity for participation. Describing himself Horner states, "I was neither bored nor fatigued nor sad, nor excited nor fresh nor happy: merely a placid animal" (99). For Horner, being is not willed but is, rather, dependent upon external factors over which he has almost no control and over which resistance is not likely. To the extent that he is simply subject to the vagaries of the environment in which he finds himself, Horner only in that sense exists. Like a leaf blown about by the wind, Horner has no willed or consistent control over his behavior. Everything depends upon the environment in which he finds himself. "I had, abstractly at least," Horner admits, "a tremendous sympathy for that sort of weakness—a person's inability either to control his behavior by his own standards or to discipline his standards, down to the last shred of conscience, to fit his behavior . . ." (30). To the extent that Jacob Horner cannot will his behavior, he has no agency, he has no character: He does not exist. That there are consequences to his nonexistence is the subject of the novel.

Horner's behavior is dependent on the constraints placed upon him by others. For without constraints, Horner is rendered immobile. He is consistently incapable of making choices. He was incapable of choosing a major in college, taking classes, he says, in "arts and sciences" (4). And though he passes the oral examinations for his master's degree, having been asked specific questions that he must answer, he cannot then choose a thesis topic and does not ever complete his degree. His doctor orders him to teach prescriptive grammar for which there are inviolable rules that cannot be breached. "You will teach prescriptive grammar. . . . No description at all. No optional situations. Teach the rules. Teach the truth about grammar" (5). Whenever a choice is required, Horner cannot act except on impulse derived from physical desire. Without that stimulus, he is paralyzed. Horner recounts his dream about a weatherman who announces to him in the dream that the forecast for the next day is that there will be no weather. Horner details the dream to depict this defining feature or aspect of his personality.

> That was the end of the dream, and I woke up very much upset. I tell it now to illustrate a difference between moods and the weather, their usual analogy: a day without weather is unthinkable, but for me at least there were frequently days without any mood at all. On these days Jacob Horner, except in a meaningless metabolistic sense, ceased to exist, for I was without personality. Like those microscopic specimens that biologists must dye in order to make them visible at all, I had to be colored with some mood or other if there was to be a recognizable self to me. The fact that my successive and discontinuous selves were linked to one another by the two unstable threads of body and memory; the fact that in the nature of Western languages the word *change* presupposes something upon which the changes operate; the fact that although the specimen is invisible without the dye, the dye is not the specimen—these are considerations of which I was aware, but in which I had no interest. (36)

Horner has no personality except that which he is given or assigned. The notion of choice is impossible for Horner: He can only act when his choices are severely constrained by others. Rennie Morgan, the married woman whom Horner makes pregnant, says of Horner: "I think you don't exist at all. There's too many of you. It's more than just masks that you put on and take off—we all have masks. But you're different all the way through, every time. You cancel yourself out. You're more like somebody in a dream. You're not strong and you're not weak. You're nothing" (67). When he sleeps with Rennie despite his doctor's orders to abstain from any relations, Horner cannot organize a response to the situation because he cannot explain in any sense why he engaged in sexual relations with her at all. "I didn't *want* to do it . . . I don't know why I did it . . . I don't know what unconscious motives I might have had . . . but whatever they were, they were unconscious, so I can't know anything about them" (110). Like the Laocoön[5] he carries with him everywhere, he is immobilized; or is rather, as Horner himself admits, annihilated, by the two serpents, imagination and knowledge, wrapped about his torso. Incapable of explanation, he is tormented by the Morgans, Rennie and Joe, for whom explanation is absolutely required, and he is condemned by the necessity of action and the responsibility that attaches to it.

Joe Morgan, Jacob's colleague at the college, insists on explanation and responsibility, even if it is not completely accurate. "A man can act coherently; he can act in ways that he can explain, if he wants to,"(47) Joe declares to Horner for whom, of course, coherence is unthinkable. Consistency is all Joe asks, but which is, of course, impossible for Horner. Joe Morgan pretends not to wear masks, and it is this inconsistency that perhaps ultimately makes Rennie's faith in him falter, as he demands explanation for every act, denying contingency, spontaneity, or contradiction, all characteristics of much human behavior. Rennie Morgan is aware that there were motives for her adultery, though what they are are as yet unknown to her. Indeed, it is Joe's insistence that reasons be found—or at least invented— for Rennie's adultery, and that they reveal consistency that drives the novel and leads ultimately to Rennie's death.[6] It is Rennie who must account for the adultery; for finally, Horner, incapable of impelling action but merely responding to it, could not account for action. But as Horner states, "To feel no regret for anything one has done in the past requires at least a strong sense of one's personal unity, and such a sense is one of the things I've always lacked" (142). Horner never knows who he is until he has been told what he is.

The cure Horner's doctor prescribes for his condition is Mythotherapy, a narrative strategy in which one merely assigns oneself a role in the story of one's life and then behaves consistently with that role. In this manner, one's life may be described by many stories. As long as the story has at its center the teller, it does not matter if the story changes; what is crucial is that a role is assigned within a defined story. For as result of the narrated story, action is predetermined. In such a way, Horner can exist. The doctor explains:

> Here's the point: an immobility such as you experienced that time in Penn Station is possible only to a person who for some reason or other has ceased to participate in Mythotherapy. At that time on the bench you were neither a major or minor character: you were no character at all. . . . It's extremely important that you learn to assume those masks wholeheartedly. Don't think there's anything behind them: *ego* means *I*, and *I* means *ego*, and the ego is by definition a mask. Where there's no ego—this is you on the bench—there's no *I*. (89–90)

Whatever judgment we would make of the doctor's metanarrative, it is my argument in this book that consciousness is the making of narrative, the creation of story and storyteller in a single act. Without narrative there is no storyteller.

Horner suffers from absolute immobility. He is incapable of making choices, and, therefore, does not exist. "It is the malady *cosmopsis*, the cosmic view, that afflicted me. When one has it, one is frozen like the bullfrog when the hunter's light strikes him full in the eyes, only with cosmopsis there is no hunger, and no quick hand to terminate the moment—there's only the light" (74). Horner's condition renders him immobile, incapable of action. Unable to make choices, he can create no narrative and he ceases to exist. Thus, we might say that Horner cannot read because he cannot sample the environment for cues. Not that he does not function in the environment, but that he can construct nothing from or of it. There is neither a knower to know nor a world to know. The environment is without meaning. Faced with choice, he is incapable of choosing unless directed and, incapable of choosing, is rendered paralyzed. This paralysis derives not from the situation, however, but from the absence of character within that situation. All situations demand choice of one form or another: In a sense, Horner exists in that his physical body and his name are engaged. But Horner does not exist because he is incapable of willed action. He can act when there is no choice afforded him, but to choose on his own

is impossible. On his own, he does not exist. His doctor lectures
him:

> You claim to be unable to choose in many situations. Well
> I claim that that inability is only theoretically inherent in
> situations, when there's no chooser. Given a particular
> choice, it's unthinkable. So, since the inability *was*
> displayed in your case, the fault lies not in the situation
> but in the fact that there was no chooser. Choosing is
> existence: to the extent that you don't choose, you don't
> exist. (83)

His therapy is an attempt to give him the possibility of motion
and, hence, character.

> Above all, act impulsively; don't let yourself get stuck
> between alternatives, or you're lost. You're not that strong.
> If the alternatives are side by side, choose the one on the
> left; if they're consecutive in time, choose the earlier. If
> neither of these applies, choose the alternative whose
> name begins with the earlier letter of the alphabet. These
> are the principles of Sinistrality, Antecedence, and
> Alphabetical Priority—there are others, and they're
> arbitrary, but useful. (85)

Of course, not to choose is a choice, and one consequence
of not choosing is to be subject to the directions of others. It is to
be assigned a role and the illusion of agency, but is actually its
opposite. Horner's therapist places him in such a situation in
which choice is unnecessary: "Your position then (which has the
appearance of choice, because you are not ordered to sit thus, but
which is chosen only in a very limited sense, since there are no
alternatives), is as follows: you sit rather rigidly in your white
chair, your back and thighs describing the same right angle
described by the structure of the chair, and keep your legs
together, your thighs and lower legs describing another right
angle" (2). He directs him to teach prescriptive grammar: "No
description at all. No optional situations. Teach the rules. Teach
the truth about grammar" (5).

Jacob Horner finds prescription immensely attractive and
can even rationalize his position, invent the narrative. He tells an
argumentative student, "If you *do* want intelligibility, then the
only way to get 'free' of the rules is to master them so

thoroughly that they're second nature to you . . . in any kind of complicated society a man is usually free only to the extent that he embraces all the rules of that society" (136). Of course, in this situation a person is not required to create any narratives but merely to act in that of others. *In a sense,* (recall the opening sentence of the novel) the individual exists but is not required to make meaning. I have explored in some depth how this form of pedagogy has come to dominate American reading, its pedagogy to determine reading, and reading instruction throughout American history. And I have shown how this particular pedagogy denies agency and creativity and breeds self-hate and distrust. Jacob Horner's terminal condition epitomizes the product of such pedagogy. Incapable of reading, Horner is incapable of existence.

Daniel Isaacson

Reading as we have conceptualized it here may also be understood as a material process. Reading is a process that creates material form—the text and identity or consciousness—by establishing the material roots that comprise those forms. Reading is an activity in which the physical text is produced by its interrogation by a consciousness that comes into being in that interrogation. As Daniel Dennett (1991, 166) asks: "Couldn't consciousness be a matter not of arrival at a point but rather a matter of a representation exceeding some threshold of activation over the whole cortex or large parts thereof? On this model, an element of content becomes conscious at some time t, not by entering some functionally defined and anatomically located system, but by changing state right where it is: by acquiring some property or by having the intensity of one of its properties boosted above some threshold." Consciousness creates form even as form creates consciousness: Consciousness and form are identical.

This interrogation asks the text what knowledge it produces and upon what bases that knowledge is constructed. In that sense, the text appears as a product of reading and as both producer and product of knowledge, both object and subject of knowledge. Reading in this manner also produces the self: The interrogation of the text makes possible the appearance of the subject, the reader. This synchronous process asks the self who am *I*, the reader, that I may see *it*, the text, and how is it that I know what the text knows. This form of reading historicizes the text and self because this interrogation, in situating the text and the self in material conditions, assumes the production of the phenomena of text and self (as neither Stephen Dedalus nor Jacob Horner can do) by "imperious agents of causality (cultural traditions, institutions, race, ethnicity, relations of gender, economic and physical environment, dispositions of power)" (Lentricchia, 1989, 231). This reading, which posits forms of knowledge both in the text and of it, also produces consciousness of the self as both subject and object, both producer and product of knowledge. For every text addresses an object, and only subjects may produce knowledge.

Thus, reading depends upon the reader's ability to situate both her/himself and the text in a particular situation from which the appearance of both text and self may be explained. That appearance is constitutive of identity. To read, then, may be understood as the establishment of relationships between the text as phenomenon and its material roots—to discover the means by which its knowledge is produced in the presentation of a specifically peopled world; and the establishment of relationships between the phenomenal text and the reader's perception of her/himself as one who constructs that text—the subject of history's construction. Which is to say that the reader reads, as George Lukács states, "for the material roots of each phenomenon, regards them in their historical connections and movement, ascertains the laws of such movement and demonstrates their development from root to flower, and in so doing lifts every phenomenon out of a merely emotional, irrational mystic fog and brings it to the light of understanding"(Lukács, 1964, 1). These material roots made conscious are the production of self and text; they are what Stephen Dedalus cannot do, searching as he does for an ahistorical ideality, and what Jacob Horner is incapable of achieving because he refuses to engage in the search at all.

In this sense, we might also consider reading as the
making of connections. In that activity, world and self are
discovered even as they are produced. Daniel Isaacson, in E.L.
Doctorow's novel, *The Book of Daniel* (1972, 155), says:

> I have an idea for an article. If I write it maybe I can sell it
> and see my name in print. The idea is the dynamics of
> radical thinking. With each new cycle of radical thought
> there is a stage of genuine creative excitement during
> which the connections are made. The radical discovers
> connections between available data and the root
> responsibility. Finally he connects everything. . . .

Of course, to make connections is what Daniel must do to exist if
he is ever to understand his troubling and troubled vision. "Of
one thing we are sure," Daniel writes, "Justice is elusive.
Revolutionary morality is elusive. Human character. Quarters
for the cigarette machine. You've got these two people in the
poster, Daniel, now how are you going to get them out? And
you've got a grandma you mention once or twice, but we don't
know anything about her. And some colored man in the
basement—what is that all about? What has that got to do with
anything"? (54). Of course, it is not the images that Daniel must
interpret: not the words he must identify. Rather, it is the
connections between them that he must make. For it is the
images themselves that have become the problem, as they have
come to represent reality by denying the complex historical
forces of which they are only the reified phenomenon. Like
Disneyland, to which Daniel must go in his search for
connections, images "construct a reality based on a radical
process of reduction, where the complexities and darknesses of
myth, legend, literature or history are denied," and where the
"value of the experience is not the ride itself but its vicarious-
ness" (304). It is his own efforts to make connections that
becomes Daniel in his reading: in an engagement with the
world's knowledge and his personal access to it. When he has
finished reading—making connections—Daniel has effectively
produced a life, his own, "Submitted," he tells us, "in Partial
Fulfillment of the Requirements for the Doctoral Degree in Social
Biology, Gross Entomology, Women's Anatomy, Children's

Cacophony, Arch Demonology, Eschatology, and Thermal Pollution" (118).

Prior to learning to read—to make connections—these various visions represented in the language of his final degree troubled Daniel. As with his Biblical counterpart, Daniel could make no sense of any of them. Indeed, as a graduate student Daniel "reads" all of the time, but he understands very little: "IS IT SO TERRIBLE NOT TO KEEP THE MATTER IN MY HEART, TO GET THE MATTER OUT OF MY HEART, TO EMPTY MY HEART OF THIS MATTER? WHAT IS THE MATTER WITH MY HEART" (27)? Daniel can read others' texts, as a student of history he can read curriculum as document, but he is incapable of producing himself. It is no accident that, as a student, Daniel's means of discovery lie in his growing understanding of the nature of the written word, itself an image and a pretender to reality. Susan, Daniel's sister, had in her contempt for him written, "Someday, Daniel, following your own pathetic demons, you are going to disappear up your own asshole. To cover the time until then, I'm writing you out of my mind. You no longer exist" (89–90). But Daniel recognizes in Susan's phrases the means of his redemption: The image is not reality. Hence, the curse is a written image intended to exile him from the human community until his eventual physical disappearance. The image is a substitution for the reality and is, hence, an ideological construction. He may be "not yet beyond redemption . . . someday is not today. Nevertheless he must be purged" (95). Daniel must come to know that the images by which he has constructed reality are only images; the forces that construct the images and then manipulate them are the real sources of power, which must be understood if they are to be met and resisted. To do this, Daniel must understand how he, too, has been constructed as an image, as an object of history. This is only possible by reading—and its counterpart, writing.

> I sit at a table with a floor lamp at my shoulder. Outside this paneled room with its book-lined wallcovers is the Periodical Room. The Periodical Room is filled with newspapers on sticks, magazines from round the world, and the droppings of the learned societies. Down the hall is the main Reading Room and the entrance to the stacks.

On the floors are the special collections of the various
school libraries including the Library School Library.
Downstairs there is even a branch of the Public School
library.

The inability to make connections precludes reading for
images appear to be arbitrary and without context, as they must
for children taught to name call and to simply decode. Certainly,
for Daniel, his visions mystify and even threaten him. He is
unable to comprehend. But in the act of reading, Daniel is
empowered by the production of his subjectivity. Reading is the
making of connections: "It is clear," Marx said in *The German
Ideology* (1988, 55), "that the real intellectual wealth of the
individual depends entirely on the wealth of his real
connections. Only then will the separate individual be liberated
from the various national and local barriers, be brought into
practical connection with the material and intellectual
production of the whole world and be put in a position to
acquire the capacity to enjoy this all-sided production the whole
earth (the creations of man)."

Daniel Isaacson discovers in the explorations of the
troubled visions in his head how he has become objectified by
the images by which he has come to know reality. The son of
executed Communist spies, Paul and Rochelle, Daniel discovers
how his entire existence has been produced out of the
construction of his parents as condemned state enemies, itself a
creation of the dominant powers who control the creation of
images. Daniel discovers how he has constructed himself only
from the images made available to him. As a result, he has been
rendered impotent and silent. "We have none of us," Daniel says
about himself and his family, "ever had enough [air] to breathe"
(131). Premising his entire existence upon this image, Daniel
denies himself subjectivity. He exists only as image: ". . . nothing
about his appearance was accidental. If he'd lived in the
nineteen-thirties and came on this way he would be a young
commie. A Cafeteria commie" (13). And as image, he accepts the
powerlessness to which he is condemned. Susan pointedly
accuses him of a "phony cynicism bag that conveniently saves
you from doing anything" (93) when he refuses participation in
the establishment of a revolutionary fund to be named in honor

of his executed parents. Daniel himself, excusing his unwilling-ness to engage in any form of activism, blames his complacency on this powerlessness which results from his objectification: "They have no discoveries to make about me," says Daniel about the government.

> No matter what political or symbolic act I perform in protest and disobedience, no harm will befall me. I have worked this out. It's true. I am totally deprived of the right to be dangerous. If I were to assassinate the President, the criminality of my family, its genetic criminality, would be established. There is nothing I can do, mild or extreme, that they cannot have planned for. . . . If on the other hand I were to become publically militant Daniel Isaacson all their precaution would have been justified. (84–5)

Remaining aloof, ensconced in the library, Daniel's entire reality is structured on the images promulgated by the ruling powers to represent the world and which serve to deny him voice. Abstaining from production, Daniel's world—his visions—is incomprehensible to him.

Daniel must make connections—learn to read—and discover how the development of a particular set of images determines a specific reality, and how individuals are then constrained to create themselves and their world out of those images made available to them. It is what we have described earlier as the process of teaching people what to read by teaching them how to read, by controlling production of meaning by a pedagogy of reading. During the course of the novel, Daniel learns to read—discovers the semiotic power of images to create and to control reality. Daniel learns how to make connections; narrating the accounts of Bukharin's ordeal in Stalinist Russia Daniel notes, "Actually there are separate mysteries to be examined here. Why do the facts of Russian national torment make Americans feel smug? Why do two state cops, finding a young girl bleeding to death in the ladies' room of a Howard Johnson's, take her not to the nearest hospital but the nearest public insane asylum. On second thought these mysteries may not be unrelated" (249). Daniel's efforts to make connections permit his discovery of the forces operating in his world and afford his troubled heart relief in the achievement of subjectivity, situating his construction as a product of the material conditions of the world. Refusal to accept—to purchase—those images has serious consequences which are experienced as madness, persecution, and objectivity, each resulting in voicelessness and silence. Certainly we may understand here the experience of many in schooling. In this way, the power of the ruling classes—those who establish the images by which reality may be known—is maintained even as the rebellious subject is objectified in the act of revolt.

Having constructed himself based on the image of his parents as convicted and condemned spies, Daniel has accepted himself as object. Speaking in the third person, the narrator Daniel announces that "This orphan state . . . obliterated everything else and separated them [he and Susan] from everyone else, and always would no matter what he did to deny it" (19). In this acceptance and willed isolation, Daniel denies the complex historical conditions by which his parents were themselves originally constructed and condemned, and accepts himself as the product of the image. Daniel denies himself agency. Daniel, unlike Jacob Horner, suffers not from paralysis, but from confusion. He can make no sense of his world.

In that construction of reality by the dominant powers, the ideological image is made to appear substantive and the subject is made object. Actions in which people engage are organized by the dominant powers as a product of the images they have constructed to be reality and are often contradictory to the actual experience.

> But—the kids who go to school for careers and the blue-collar sell-outs and all the suburban hustlers in the land who make the hustle system work, who carry it on their backs and think they're its beneficiaries—I mean, it's a double-think system, it is not ordinary repression, right? My country knees you in the neck and you think you're standing upright. It presses your face in the muck and you think you're looking at the sky. I mean you cannot make connections between what you do and why they hate you in Chile. You are hung up on identity crises. (153)

In Daniel's investigations, he learns how the images promulgated by the ruling classes of America have determined the behaviors of all involved in the arrest, trial, and execution of his parents. To attempt to argue with the images is, ultimately, to accept their reality. Sternlicht, the radical, tells Daniel: "Your folks didn't know shit. The way they handled themselves at their trial was pathetic. I mean they played it by *their* rules . . . they made motions, they pleaded innocent, they spoke only when spoken to, they played the game . . . the whole frame of reference brought them down because they acted like defendants at a trial" (167). In the terms with which we have spoken about reading, the Isaacsons accepted the reality given them by others and denied themselves and their world in the process. Their execution was merely the physical annihilation of what they had already experienced by their failure to read. But Daniel, as he makes connections and learns to read, begins to understand. He says, "I am beginning to be intolerant of reformers. . . . Ascher depending on the appellate courts . . . I am beginning to be nauseated by men of good will. We are dealing here with a failure to make connections. The failure to make connections is complicity. Reform is complicity. It is complicity in the system to be appalled with the moral structure of the system" (243). For if the system is constructed upon images, then the moral structure, too, is a product of those images and, hence, derives from the motives of the ruling power which, as Daniel discovers, in the post–World War II world have little to do with morality and a great deal to do with economics and politics. It is a connection Daniel makes and one which helps him understand his visions. It is in making connections that Daniel learns to read.

Indeed, it is the revelation of the image as image that governs the movement of the book; Daniel makes connections between the various visions in his head until he has recovered the real historical forces that have determined his objectivity. Of course, all the forces in society have been directed to obscure these connections. But in this discovery—in his learning to read—Daniel achieves subjectivity—agency and identity. The obfuscation of reality by the image is a process that Daniel comes to understand about the nature and function of the quint-essential image park, Disneyland, and what he must accept about his own construction of the world: The images are presented as isolable structures devoid of historical connection and serve as a substitute for the complexities offered in literature, myth, or history. The images of which Disneyland is comprised pretend to a complete knowledge while at the same time obscuring the roots of that knowledge.

There is, of course, no way that I can ever declare that my readings of these novels are, indeed, authentic readings, or that my idea of reading is portrayed with certainty in these books. But, it is clear to me that I can make sense of the novels when I understand that reading or its failure is at the center of each, and that the characters proceed through the novels based upon their facility to read. I have argued throughout this book that reading is a creative process, and what I have portrayed in this chapter is the idea that what is created in reading is the reader and the text s/he reads. A pedagogy of reading can do nothing less than permit the reader to come to being not by teaching reading but by permitting its being learned.

NOTES

1. Recall Whitman's "Out of the Cradle, Endlessly Rocking":

> A word the, (for I will conquer it,)
> The word final, superior to all . . .
> My own songs awaked from that hour,
> And with them the key, the word up from the waves,
> The word of the sweetest song and all songs
> That strong and delicious word which, creeping to my
>   feet . . .
> The sea whisper'd me.

For Whitman, the word known to all men is Death, and when he understands the word, then he can read himself in the world.

2. I do not mean to valorize the profession of artist; Winnicott has taught that creativity is the process of a healthy existence, and no one is more creative than the ordinary, but Jewish, Leopold Bloom, whose very survival in hostile Dublin bespeaks his creativity.

3. It is, of course, ironic that plagiarism constitutes the unforgivable sin in the cultural field, and yet it is this very act that we demand of our students in reading when we ask them to discover the meanings that have always been found.

4. Stephen boldly announces that "When the soul of man is born in this country there are nets flung at it to hold it back from flight. You talk to me of nationality, language, religion. I shall try to fly by those nets" (1966, 203).

5. Laocoön was the Trojan priest killed with his sons by two sea serpents after warning the Trojans against the wooden horse.

6. It might be said that Joe Morgan too cannot read, for in his insistence on defining what meaning must be acceptable to him, he does not pick up the data available and construct reality. Rennie's death must rest partly with Joe's failure to read.

Bibliography

Adams, J. 1986. *The Conspiracy of the Text*. New York: Routledge & Kegan Paul.

Adams, M.J. 1990. *Beginning to Read*. Cambridge, Mass.: The MIT Press.

Anderson, R.C. 1985. *Becoming a Nation of Readers*. Washington, D. C.: National Institute of Education.

Ariès, P. 1962. *Centuries of Childhood*. Trans. R. Baldick. New York: Vintage Books.

Athey, I. 1970. "Affective Factors in Reading." In *Theoretical Models and Processes of Reading*, ed. H. Singer and R.B Ruddell. Newark, Del.: International Reading Association.

Avrich, P. 1980. *The Modern School Movement: Anarchism and Education in the United States*. Princeton: Princeton University Press.

Balota, D., A. Pollatsek, and K. Rayner. 1985. "The Intervention of Context and Parafoveal Visual Information in Reading." *Cognitive Psychology* 17: 364–390.

Barth, J. 1967/1977. *The End of the Road*. New York: Bantam Books.

Bateson, G. 1972. *Steps to an Ecology of Mind*. New York: Ballantine Books.

Benjamin, W. 1969. *Illuminations*. Trans. and ed. H. Arendt. New York: Schocken Books.

Bintz, W.P. 1993. "Resistant Readers in Secondary Education: Some Insights and Implications." *Journal of Reading* 36(8): 604–615.

Blake, C. 1990. *Beloved Community*. Chapel Hill: University of North Carolina Press.

Block, A. 1992. *Anonymous Toil: A Re-evaluation of the American Radical Novel in the Twentieth Century*. Lanham, Md.: University Press of America.

———. 1989. "The Answer Is Blowin' in the Wind: A Deconstructive Reading of the School Text." *The Journal of Curriculum Theorizing*, 8(4): 23–52.

———. Forthcoming. "'It's Alright Ma (I'm Only Bleeding)': Education as the Practice of Social Violence Against the Child." *Taboo*, 1(1).

Blumenthal, A. 1980. "Wundt and Early American Psychology." In *Wilhelm Wundt and the Making of a Scientific Psychology*, ed. R.W. Rieber. New York: Plenum Books.

Bolt, R. 1962. *A Man for All Seasons*. New York: Vintage Books.

Brentano, F. 1930/1966. *The True and the Evident*. Ed. R.M. Chisholm. Trans. R.M. Chisholm, I. Politzer, and K.R. Fischer. New York: The Humanities Press.

Britton, J. 1972. *Language and Learning*. Baltimore: Penguin Books.

Bruner, J. 1990. *Acts of Meaning*. Cambridge: Harvard University Press.

———. 1983. *In Search of Mind*. New York: Harper & Row.

Calvino, I. 1981. *If on a winter's night a traveler*. Trans. W. Weaver. New York: Harcourt Brace Jovanovich.

———. 1972. *Invisible Cities*. San Diego & New York: Harcourt Brace Jovanovich.

Carroll, J. 1970. "The Nature of the Reading Process." In *Theoretical Processes and Models of Reading*, ed. H. Singer, and R.B. Ruddell. Newark, Del.: International Reading Association.

Carver, R.P. 1992. "Reading Rate: Theory, Research, and Practical Implications." *Journal of Reading* October: 84–95.

Cattell, J. M. 1886. "The Time It Takes to See and Name Objects." *Mind* November: 63–65.

Chall, J. 1967. *Learning to Read: The Great Debate*. Cambridge: Harvard University Press.

————. 1983. *Stages of Reading Development*. New York: McGraw-Hill.

Chall, J., and S.S. Conard. 1991. *Should Textbooks Challenge Students? The Case for Easier or Harder Textbooks*. New York: Teacher's College Press.

Cherryholmes, C. 1993. "Reading Research." *Journal of Curriculum Studies*, 25(1): 1–33.

Chomsky, N. 1975. *Reflections on Language*. New York: Pantheon Books.

Clay, M. 1991. *Becoming Literate: The Construction of Inner Control*. Portsmouth, N.H.: Heinemann Educational Books.

————. 1972. *Sand: The Concepts About Prints Tests*. Portsmouth, N.H.: Heinemann.

Cooke, F.J. 1900. "Reading in the Primary Grades." *The Course of Study*, 1(2): 111–115.

Courtis, S. 1926. "Contributions in General to Education." *Teachers College Record*, 27(6): 557–564.

Crowder, R.G., and R.K. Wagner. 1992. *The Psychology of Reading: An Introduction*. New York: Oxford University Press.

Danziger, K. 1980a. "Wundt's Theory of Behavior and Volition." In *Wilhelm Wundt and the Making of a Scientific Psychology*, ed. R. Rieber. New York: Plenum Books.

————. 1980b. "Wundt and the Two Traditions of Psychology." In *Wilhelm Wundt and the Making of a Scientific Psychology*, ed. R. Rieber. New York: Plenum Books.

Davidson, J.L., ed. 1988. *Counterpoint and Beyond: A Response to Becoming a Nation of Readers*. Urbana, Ill.: NCTE.

Dechant, E. 1991. *Understanding and Teaching Reading*. Hillsdale, N.J.: Lawrence Erlbaum Associates.

Dennett, D.C. 1991. *Consciousness Explained*. Boston: Little, Brown.

Dennison, G. 1969. *The Lives of Children: Story of the First Street School*. New York: Vintage Books.

Derrida, J. 1976. *Of Grammatology*. Trans. G.C. Spivak. Baltimore: Johns Hopkins University Press.

Dewey, J. 1902/1956. *The Child and the Curriculum/The School and Society*. Chicago: University of Chicago Press.

———. 1916/1966. *Democracy and Education*. New York: The Free Press.

———. 1929/1971. *Experience and Nature*. La Salle, Illinois: Open Court Publishing.

———. 1910/1991. *How We Think*. Buffalo, N.Y.: Prometheus Books.

———. 1898a. "Language Study in Primary Education." *New York Teachers' Monographs* November: 39–44.

———. 1898b. "The Primary Education Fetich." *Forum*, 25: 315–328.

———. 1929. *The Quest for Certainty*. New York: Minton, Balch & Company.

Doctorow, E.L. 1972. *The Book of Daniel*. New York: New American Library.

Donogue, D. 1993. "Bewitched, Bothered, & Bewildered." *New York Review of Books*, 40(6): 46–53.

Dreyfus, H.L., and S.E. Dreyfus. 1992. *What Computers Still Can't Do*. Cambridge, Mass.: The MIT Press.

Dreyfus, H.L., and S.E. Dreyfus. 1986. *Mind Over Machine*. New York: The Free Press.

Eagleton, T. 1991. *Ideology: An Introduction*. London: Verso Books.

———. 1983. *Literary Theory: An Introduction*. Minneapolis: University of Minnesota Press.

Earle, W. 1972. *The Autobiographical Consciousness: A Philosophical Inquiry into Existence*. Chicago: Quadrangle Books.

Ehri, L.C. 1992. "Learning to Read and Spell Words." In *Learning to Read*, ed. L. Rieben, and C.A. Perfetti. Hillsdale, N.J.: Lawrence Erlbaum Associates.

Emerson, R.W. 1982. *Emerson in His Journal*. Ed. J. Porte. Cambridge: Harvard University Press.

Erlisch, S.F., and K. Rayner. 1981. "Contextual Effects of Word Perception and Eye Movements during Reading." *Journal of Verbal Learning and Verbal Behavior* 20: 641–655.

Farnham, G.L. 1891/1895. *The Sentence Method of Teaching Reading,Writing, and Spelling*. New York: C.W. Bardeen, Publisher.

Febvre, L., and H.-J. Martin. 1990. *The Coming of the Book: The Impact of Printing, 1450–1800*. Trans. D. Gerard. New York: Verso.

Feffer, A. 1993. *The Chicago Pragmatists and American Progressivism*. Ithaca, N.Y.: Cornell University Press.

Felman, S. 1982. "Psychoanalysis and Education: Teaching Terminable and Interminable." *Yale French Studies* 63: 22–44.

Ferreiro, E., and A. Teberosky. 1982. *Literacy Before Schooling*. Portsmouth, N.H.: Heinemann Educational Books.

Fleming M. 1904. "Must It Be a Lost Art." *Elementary School Teacher* 4: 541–553.

Foucault, M. 1978. *Discipline and Punish*. New York: Vintage Books.

Freeman, W. 1991. "The Physiology of Perception." *Scientific American* February: 78–85.

Freire, P. 1991. "The Importance of Reading." In *Rewriting Literacy*, ed. C. Mitchell and P.K. Weiler. Boston: Bergin & Garvey.

Freire, P., and D. Macedo. 1986. *Literacy: Reading the Word and the World*. South Hadley, Mass.: Bergin & Garvey.

Freud, S. 1963. "Analysis Terminable and Interminable." In *Therapy and Technique*, ed. P. Rieff. New York: Collier Books.

Fries, C.C. 1963. *Linguistics and Reading*. New York: Holt, Rinehart and Winston.

Fromm, E. 1966. *The Economic and Philosophic Manuscripts*. Trans. T. Bottomore. New York: Ungar Publishing.

Gabriel, S.L., and I. Smithson, eds. 1990. *Gender in the Classroom*. Urbana: University of Illinois Press.

Gardner, H. 1983. *The Mind's New Science*. New York: Basic Books.

Gates, A.I. 1926. "Contributions to the Psychology of the Elementary School Subjects." *Teachers College Record* 27(6): 548–558.

———. 1935. *The Improvement of Reading*. New York: Macmillan.

———. 1926. "A Modern Systematic Approach Versus an Opportunistic Method of Teaching." *Teachers College Record*, 27(8): 679–700.

Gates, A.I., A.T. Jerslid, T. McConnell, and R.C. Challman. 1949. *Educational Psychology*. New York: Macmillan.

Gee, J. 1991. "Discourse System and Aspirin Bottles." In *Rewriting Literacy*, ed. C. Mitchell, and K. Weiler. New York: Bergin & Garvey.

———. 1990. *Social Linguistics and Literacies*. New York: Falmer Press.

Gibson, E.J., and H. Levin. 1975. *The Psychology of Reading*. Cambridge, Mass.: The MIT Press.

Gibson, J.J. 1979. *The Ecological Approach to Visual Perception*. Boston: Houghton Mifflin.

Goelman, H., A. Oberg, and F. Smith. 1984. *Awakening to Literacy*. Portsmouth, N.H.: Heinemann Educational Books.

Goodman, K.S. 1971. "Decoding—From What to What?" *Journal of Reading* April: 455–498.

———. 1982. *Language and Literacy*. Vol. 2. New York: Routledge & Kegan Paul.

———. 1988. "Look What They've Done to Judy Blume! The 'Basalization' of Children's Literature." *The New Advocate* 1(1): 29–41.

———. 1970. "Reading: A Psycholinguistic Guessing Game." In *Theoretical Models and Processes of Reading*, ed. H. Singer, and R.B. Ruddell. Newark, Del.: International Reading Association.

———. 1986. *What's Whole in Whole Language*. Portsmouth, N.H.: Heinemann Educational Books.

———. 1989. "Whole-Language Research: Foundations and Development." *Elementary School Journal* 90(2): 205–221.

————. 1992. "Why Whole Language Is Today's Agenda in Education." *Language Arts* 69(5):354–365.

Goodman, K.S., E.B. Smith, R. Meredith, and Y.M. Goodman. 1987. *Language and Thinking in Schools*. Katonah, N.Y.: Richard C. Owen Publishers.

Goodman, K.S., and J.T. Fleming, eds. 1968/1972. *Psycholinguistics and the Teaching of Reading*. Newark, Del.: International Reading Association.

Goodman, K.S., P. Shannon, Y.S. Freeman, and S. Murphy. 1987. In *Report Card on Basal Readers*. Katonah, N.Y.: Richard C. Owen Publishers.

Goodman, K.S., and Y.M. Goodman. 1982. "Learning to Read Is Natural." In *Language and Literacy*, Vol. 2, ed. F.V. Gollasch. London: Routledge & Kegan Paul.

Goodman, Y.M. 1989. "Roots of the Whole-Language Movement." *Elementary School Journal* 90(2): 113–127.

Goodman, Y.M., and C. Burke. 1980. *Reading Strategies: Focus on Comprehension*. Katonah, N.Y.: Richard C. Owen Publishers.

Goodwyn, L. 1978. *The Populist Moment*. New York: Oxford University Press.

Gough, P.B., and C. Juel. 1992. "The First Stages of Word Recognition." In *Learning to Read*, ed. L. Rieben, and C. A. Perfetti. Hillsdale, N.J. : Lawrence Erlbaum Associates.

Gough, P.B., C. Juel, and P.L. Griffith. 1991. "Reading, Spelling, and the Orthographic Cipher." In *Reading Acquisition*, ed. P.B. Gough, L.C. Ehri, and R. Trieman. Hillsdale, N.J.: Lawrence Erlbaum Associates.

Gray, W.S. 1937. "The Nature and Types of Reading." In *The Teaching of Reading: A Second Report, The Thirty-Sixth Yearbook of the National Society for the Study of Education*. ed. G.M. Whipple. Bloomington, Ill.: Public School Publishing Company.

————. 1919. "Principles of Method in Teaching Reading, As Derived from Scientific Investigation." In *The Eighteenth Yearbook of the National Society for the Study of Education*, Part 2.

Greene, J. 1974. *Psycholinguistics*. Baltimore: Penguin Books.

Grumet, M.R. 1988. *Bitter Milk*. Amherst: The University of Massachusetts Press.

Halliday, M. 1975. *Learning How to Mean: Explorations in the Development of Language*. New York: Elsevier North-Holland.

Harste, J.C., V.A. Woodward, and C.L. Burke. 1984. *Language Stories & Literacy Lessons*. Portsmouth, N.H.: Heinemann Educational Books.

Heath, S.B. 1982. *Ways with Words*. New York: Cambridge University Press.

Hemingway, E. 1921/1954. *In Our Time*. New York: Scribner.

Henry, N.B., ed. 1961. *Development in and Through Reading: The Sixtieth Yearbook of the National Society for the Study of Education*. Chicago: University of Chicago Press.

————, ed. 1949. *Reading in the Elementary School: The Forty-Eighth Yearbook of the National Society for the Study of Education*. Chicago: University of Chicago Press.

Herber, H. 1984. "Subject Matter Texts-Reading to Learn: Response to Paper by Thomas H. Anderson and Bonnie Armbruster." In *Learning to Read in American Schools*, ed. R.C. Anderson, J. Osborn, and R.J. Tierney. Hillsdale, N.J.: Lawrence Erlbaum Associates.

Hilgard, E.R. 1987. *Psychology in America: A Historical Survey*. New York: Harcourt Brace Jovanovich.

Hochberg, J., and V. Brooks. 1970. "Reading as an Intentional Behavior." In *Theoretical Models and Processes of Reading*, ed. H. Singer, and R.B. Ruddell. Newark, Del.: International Reading Association.

Hollinger, D. 1980. "The Problem of Pragmatism in American History." *Journal of American History* 67: 88–107.

Holmes, J.A. 1970. "The Substrata-Factor Theory of Reading: Some Experimental Evidence." In *Theoretical Models and Processes of Reading*, ed. H. Singer, and R.B. Ruddell. Newark, Del.: International Reading Association.

Hook, S. 1974. *Pragmatism and the Tragic Sense of Life*. New York: Basic Books.

Horton, M. 1990. *The Long Haul*. New York: Doubleday.

Howe, I. 1954. "The Age of Conformity." *Partisan Review* 23: 8–34.

Huey, E.B. 1908/1968. *The Psychology and Pedagogy of Reading*. Cambridge, Mass.: The MIT Press.

Iser, W. 1980. *The Act of Reading: A Theory of Aesthetic Response*. Baltimore: Johns Hopkins University Press.

James, W. 1907/1970. *Pragmatism and Four Essays from the Meaning of Truth*. New York: Meridian Books.

————. 1907/1978. *Pragmatism and the Meaning of Truth*. Cambridge: Harvard University Press.

Jameson, F. 1981. *The Political Unconscious*. Ithaca, N.Y.: Cornell University Press.

Jonçich, G. 1968. *The Sane Positivist*. Middletown, Conn.: Wesleyan University Press.

Jowett, M. 1937. *The Dialogues of Plato*. Trans. H. Gabler. New York: Vintage Books.

Joyce, J. 1966. *A Portrait of the Artist as a Young Man*. New York: Viking.

————. 1986. *Ulysses*. Ed. H. Gabler. New York: Vintage Books.

Just, M.A., and P. Carpenter. 1987. *The Psychology of Reading and Language Comprehension*. Newton, Mass.: Allyn & Bacon.

Kaestle, C., H. Damon-Moore, L.C. Stedman, K. Tinsley, and W.V.J. Trollinger. 1991. *Literacy in the United States*. New Haven: Yale University Press.

Kleibard, H. 1987. *The Struggle for the American Curriculum*. New York: Routledge & Kegan Paul.

Kolers, P. 1968. "Reading Is Only Incidentally Visual." In *Psycholinguistics and Reading*, ed. K.S. Goodman, and J.T. Fleming. Newark, Del.: International Reading Association.

————. 1970. "Three Stages of Reading." In *Basic Studies in Reading*, ed. H. Levin, and J.P. Williams. New York: Basic Books.

Kozol, J. 1985. *Illiterate America*. New York: New American Library.

Kristeva, J. 1989. *Language: The Unknown*. Trans. A.M. Menke. New York: Columbia University Press.

Lasch, C. 1991. *The True and Only Heaven*. New York: Norton.

Lemaire, A. 1986. *Jacques Lacan*. Trans. C. Macey. New York: Routledge & Kegan Paul.

Lentricchia, F. 1989. "Foucault's Legacy—A New Historicism?" In *The New Historicism*, ed. H.A. Veeser. New York: Routledge, Chapman Hall.

Levin, H., and A. Buckley. 1979. *The Eye-Voice Span*. Cambridge, Mass.: The MIT Press.

Levin, H., and J.P. Williams, eds. 1970. *Basic Studies in Reading*. New York: Basic Books.

Lewis, C. 1993. "Give People a Chance: Acknowledging Social Differences in Reading." *Language Arts* 70(6): 454–461.

Lukács, G. 1964. *Studies in European Realism*. New York: Grosset & Dunlap.

Machan, T.R. 1985. *Introduction to Philosophical Inquiries*. Lanham, Md.: University Press of America.

Marx, K., and F. Engels. 1988. *The German Ideology*. Ed. C. Arthur. New York: International Publishers.

Mathews, M.M. 1966. *Teaching to Read*. Chicago: University of Chicago Press.

Matlin, M. 1983. *Cognition*. New York: Holt, Rinehart and Winston.

Mayher, J. 1990. *Uncommon Sense*. Portsmouth, N.H.: Boynton/Cook.

Meier, D.W. 1992. "Myths, Lies and Public Schools." *The Nation* September 21: 271–272.

Mendelson, M., and M.M. Haith. 1976. "The Relation Between Audition and Vision in the Human Newborn." *Monographs of the Society and Research in Child Development* 41(4).

Miller, G. 1956. "The Magical Number 7, Plus or Minus Two: Some Limits on Our Capacity for Processing Information." *The Psychological Review* 63(2): 81–97.

Miller, J.H. 1987. *The Ethics of Reading.* New York: Columbia University Press.

Mills, C.W. 1963. *Power, Politics, and People: The Collected Essays of C. Wright Mills.* Ed. I.L. Horowitz. New York: Oxford University Press.

Mills, H., and J.A. Clyde, eds. (1990). *Portraits of Whole Language Classrooms.* Portsmouth, N.H.: Heinemann Educational Books.

Mills, H., T. O'Keefe, and D. Stephens. 1992. *Looking Closely.* Urbana, Ill.: National Council of Teachers of English.

Milner, M. 1950/1990. *On Not Being Able to Paint.* Madison, Conn.: International Universities Press.

———. 1987. *The Suppressed Madness of Sane Men.* London: Tavistock Publications.

Muskopf, H. 1970. "Reactions to Affective Factors in Reading." In *Theoretical Models and Processes in Reading,* ed. H. Singer, and R.B. Ruddell. Newark, Del.: International Reading Association.

Neisser, U., ed. 1989. *Concepts and Conceptual Development: Ecological and Intellectual Factors in Categorization.* New York: Cambridge University Press.

Ollman, B. 1988. *Alienation.* 2nd ed. Cambridge: Cambridge University Press.

Olney, J., ed. 1980. *Autobiography: Essays Theoretical and Critical.* Princeton: Princeton University Press.

Olson, D.R., and N. Torrance, eds. 1991. *Literacy and Orality.* New York: Cambridge University Press.

Ong, W.J. 1982. *Orality and Literacy.* New York: Methuen.

O'Regan, J.K., and A. Lévy-Schoen. 1987. "Eye-Movement Strategy and Tactics in Word Recognition and Reading." In *Attention and Performance XII: The Psychology of Reading,* ed. M. Coltheart. Hillsdale, N.J.: Lawrence Erlbaum Associates.

Pagano, J.A. 1990. *Exiles and Communities: Teaching in the Patriarchal Wilderness*. Albany: State University of New York Press.

Parker, F.W. 1894/1969. *Talks on Pedagogics*. New York: Arno Press and The New York Times.

Patterson, K., and V. Coltheart. 1987. "Phonological Processes in Reading." In *Attention and Performance XII: The Psychology of Reading*, ed. M. Coltheart. Hillsdale, N.J.: Lawrence Erlbaum Associates.

Peirce, C.S. 1991. *Peirce on Signs*. Ed. J. Hoopes. Chapel Hill: University of North Carolina Press.

Perfetti, C. 1992. "Representation Problem in Reading Acquisition." In *Reading Acquisition*, ed. P.B. Gough, L. Ehri, and R. Treiman. Hillsdale, N.J.: Lawrence Erlbaum, Associates.

Pettit, P. 1975. *The Concept of Structuralism: A Critical Analysis*. Berkeley: University of California Press.

Phillips, A. 1993. *On Kissing, Tickling, and Being Bored*. Cambridge: Harvard University Press.

Piaget, J. 1968. *Six Psychological Studies*. Trans. and ed. D. Elkind. New York: Vintage Books.

Pinar, W.F., W. Reynolds, P. Slattery, and P. Taubman. In press. *Understanding Curriculum*. New York: Peter Lang Publishers.

Pinar, W.F., and M.R. Grumet. 1976. *Toward a Poor Curriculum*. Dubuque, Iowa: Kendall/Hunt Publishing Company.

Plato. 1986. *Phaedrus and the Seventh and Eighth Letters*. Trans. W. Hamilton. New York: Penguin Books.

Porte, J. 1982. *Emerson in His Journals*. Cambridge: The Belknap Press of Harvard University Press.

Rayner, K., and A. Pollatsek. 1987. "Eye Movement in Reading." In *Attention and Performance XII: The Psychology of Reading*, ed. M. Coltheart. Hillsdale, N.J.: Lawrence Erlbaum Associates.

Read, C. 1971. "Pre-school Children's Knowledge of English Phonology." *Harvard Educational Review* 41(1): 1–34.

Robinson, D.N. 1982. *Toward a Science of Human Nature*. New York: Columbia University Press.

Rorty, R. 1991. *Consequences of Pragmatism*. Minneapolis: University of Minnesota Press.

Rosenblatt, L. 1938. *Literature as Exploration*. New York: Modern Language Association.

———. 1978. *The Reader, the Text, the Poem*. Carbondale: Southern Illinois University Press.

Rothman, R. 1990. "From a 'Great Debate' to a Full-Scale War: Dispute over Teaching Reading Heats Up." *Education Week* March 21: 9–12.

Rumelhart, D., G. Hinton, and J. McClelland. 1986. "A General Framework for Parallel Distributed Processing." In *Parallel Distributed Processing: Explorations in the Microstructure of Cognition*, ed. D. Rumelhart, J. McClelland, and PDP Research Group. Cambridge, Mass.: Bradford Books.

Sacks, O. 1993. "Making Up the Mind." *New York Review of Books* 40(7) April 8: 42–49.

Scholes, R. 1982. *Semiotics and Interpretation*. New Haven: Yale University Press.

Schubert, W. 1986. *Curriculum: Perspective, Paradigm, Possibility*. New York: Macmillan.

Schwarz, D. 1987. *Reading Joyce's Ulysses*. New York: St. Martin's Press.

Searle, J. 1992. *The Rediscovery of the Mind*. Cambridge, Mass.: The MIT Press.

Shaffer, P. 1979. *Equus*. New York: Penguin Books.

Shannon, P. 1989. *Broken Promises*. Granby, Mass.: Bergin & Garbay Publishers.

———. 1990. *The Struggle to Continue: Progressive Reading Instruction in the United States*. Portsmouth, N.H.: Heinemann Educational Books.

Simpson, D. 1985. *The Politics of American English*. New York: Oxford University Press.

Smith, F. 1984. "The Creative Achievement of Literacy." In *Awakening to Literacy*, ed. H. Goelman, A. Oberg, and F. Smith. Portsmouth, N.H.: Heinemann Educational Books.

———. 1989. *Insult to Intelligence*. Portsmouth, N.H.: Heinemann Educational Books.

———. 1988a. *Joining the Literacy Club*. Portsmouth, N.H.: Heinemann Educational Books.

———. 1973. *Psycholinguistics and Reading*. New York: Holt, Rinehart and Winston.

———. 1985. *Reading Without Nonsense*. New York: Teacher's College Press.

———. 1990. *To Think*. New York: Teacher's College Press.

———. 1978. *Understanding Reading*, 2d ed. New York: Holt, Rinehart and Winston.

———. 1988b. *Understanding Reading*, 4th ed. Hillsdale, N.J.: Lawrence Erlbaum Associates.

Smith, N.B. 1934/1986. *American Reading Instruction*. Newark, Del. : International Reading Association.

Stanovich, K.E. 1991. "Changing Models of Reading and Reading Acquisitions." In *Learning to Read: Basic Research and Its Implications*. Hillsdale, N.J.: Lawrence Erlbaum Associates.

Stern, D. 1985. *The Interpersonal World of the Child*. New York: Basic Books.

Sternberg, R.J. 1991. "Intelligence." In *The Psychology of Human Thought*, ed. R.J. Sternberg and E.M. Smith. New York: Cambridge University Press.

Stoppard, T. 1968. *Rosencrantz and Guildenstern are Dead*. New York: Grove Press.

Thorndike, E.L. 1921. *The Teacher's Word Book*. New York: Teacher's College Press.

Tompkins, J. 1980. "The Reader in History." In *Reader Response Criticism*, ed. J. Tompkins. Baltimore: Johns Hopkins University Press.

Vellutino, F.R., and D.M. Scanlon. 1991. "The Effects of Instructional Bias on Word Identification." In *Learning to*

Read: Basic Research and Its Implications. Hillsdale, N.J.: Lawrence Erlbaum Associates.

Vygotsky, L. 1981. *Mind in Society*. Cambridge: Harvard University Press.

————. 1978. *Mind and Society*, ed. M. Cole, V. Steiner-John, S. Scribner, and E. Souberman. Cambridge: Harvard University Press.

————. 1988. *Thought and Language*. Trans. and ed. A. Kozulin. Cambridge, Mass.: The MIT Press.

Walkerdine, V. 1988. *The Mastery of Reason Cognitive Development and the Production of Rationality*. New York: Routledge.

Weaver, C. 1985. "Parallels Between New Paradigms in Science and in Reading and Literary Theories." *Research in the Teaching of English* 19(3): 298–316.

————. 1988. *Reading Process and Practice: From Socio-Psycholinguistics to Whole Language*. Portsmouth, N.H.: Heinemann Educational Books.

Wells, G. 1986. *The Meaning Makers: Children Learning Language and Using Language to Learn*. Portsmouth, N.H.: Heinemann Educational Books.

West, C. 1989. *The American Evasion of Philosophy: A Genealogy of Pragmatism*. Madison: University of Wisconsin Press.

Westbrook, R. 1991. *John Dewey and American Democracy*. New York.

Winnicott, D.W. 1986. *Home Is Where We Start From*. New York: Norton.

————. 1971. *Playing and Reality*. New York: Basic Books.

Wolf, S.A., and S.B. Heath. 1992. *The Brain of Literature*. Cambridge: Harvard University Press.

Wolfe, B. 1964. *Three Who Made a Revolution*. New York: Dell.

Wundt, W. 1912/1973. *An Introduction to Psychology*. Trans. R. Pintner. New York: Arno Press.

————. 1897/1969. *Outlines of Psychology*. Trans. C. Judd. St. Clare Shores, Mich.: Scholarly Press.

Yarington, D.J. 1978. *The Great American Reading Machine*. Rochelle Park, N.J.: Hayden Book Company.

Index